From Finance
to Function

M L Ruscsak

Trient Press

Except for the original story material written by the author, all songs, song titles, and lyrics mentioned in the novel From Finance to Function are the exclusive property of the respective artists, songwriters, and copyright holder.

Trient Press
3375 S Rainbow Blvd
#81710, SMB 13135
Las Vegas,NV 89180

Ordering Information:
Quantity sales. Special discounts are available on quantity purchases by corporations, associations, and others. For details, contact the publisher at the address above.
Orders by U.S. trade bookstores and wholesalers. Please contact Trient Press: Tel: (775) 996-3844; or visit www.trientpress.com.

Printed in the United States of America

Publisher's Cataloging-in-Publication data
Ruscsak, M.L.
A title of a book :From Finance to Function
ISBN
Hard Cover   979-8-88990-095-5

Paper Back   979-8-88990-096-2

Ebook   979-8-88990-097-9

Exploring the Intersection of Business Functions for Financial Success

Exploring the Intersection of Business Functions for Financial Success

PART 1:
INTRODUCTION

In today's fast-paced and ever-changing business landscape, it is essential for non-financial professionals to possess a basic understanding of financial intelligence. Financial intelligence is the ability to understand financial data, analyze financial statements, and make informed decisions based on financial information. In this chapter, we will explore why financial intelligence is important for non-financial professionals, and how it can help individuals and organizations make better business decisions.

Why Financial Intelligence is Important for Non-Financial Professionals
Financial intelligence is not just the domain of finance professionals. Every business decision has a financial impact, and non-financial professionals who lack financial intelligence may make decisions that are not in the best interest of their organization. For example, a marketing manager who lacks financial intelligence may make pricing decisions that are not profitable for the company, or an HR manager who lacks financial intelligence may not understand the cost of employee turnover.

Furthermore, having financial intelligence can help non-financial professionals to communicate more effectively with their finance colleagues. By speaking the same financial language, they can work together to make informed decisions that benefit the organization.

Introduction to Financial Statements
To understand financial intelligence, it is important to have a basic understanding of financial statements. Financial statements are documents that provide an overview of a company's financial performance. The three main financial statements are the balance sheet, the income statement, and the cash flow statement. In this chapter, we will introduce these financial statements and explain their importance in financial intelligence.

Analyzing Financial Statements
Analyzing financial statements is a crucial skill for non-financial professionals. In this chapter, we will cover the key financial metrics and ratios that are used to analyze financial statements, such as revenue growth, profit margin, and return on

investment. We will explain how these metrics can be used to evaluate a company's financial performance and make informed business decisions.

Chapter 2: Introduction to the Intersection of Finance with Marketing, Customer Service, Human Resources, and CRM

Introduction
In this chapter, we will explore how finance intersects with other business functions, such as marketing, customer service, human resources, and customer relationship management (CRM). We will explain the importance of understanding these intersections for non-financial professionals, and how they can use this knowledge to make better business decisions.

Finance and Marketing
Marketing and finance are two key functions in any business. In this section, we will explore how marketing decisions can impact financial performance, and how financial considerations can influence marketing strategies. We will cover topics such as budgeting for marketing activities, pricing strategies, and return on marketing investment.

Finance and Customer Service
Customer service is an essential part of any business, and it has a direct impact on financial performance. In this section, we will explore how financial considerations can influence customer service strategies, and how customer service can impact financial performance. We will cover topics such as understanding the financial impact of customer service, measuring customer satisfaction, and customer profitability analysis.

Finance and Human Resources
Human resources is another key function in any business, and it also has a direct impact on financial performance. In this section, we will explore how financial considerations can influence human resources strategies, and how human resources can impact financial performance. We will cover topics such as understanding the cost of employee turnover, the impact of employee engagement on financial performance, and the financial impact of HR policies and practices.

Finance and Customer Relationship Management (CRM)
CRM is a strategy for managing interactions with customers and potential customers. In this section, we will explore how financial considerations can influence CRM strategies, and how CRM can impact financial performance. We will cover topics such as the importance of CRM in financial performance, techniques for

measuring the financial impact of CRM, and the role of CRM in customer retention and loyalty.

In conclusion, financial intelligence is a crucial aspect of business management and decision-making, and it is essential for non-financial professionals to have a basic understanding of finance. In this section, we have explored the intersection of finance with marketing, customer service, human resources, and CRM, and how financial considerations can impact these areas.

We have covered topics such as the importance of financial statements and key financial metrics for non-financial professionals, budgeting for marketing activities, pricing strategies and their impact on financial performance, measuring return on marketing investment (ROMI), and customer profitability analysis. Additionally, we explored the financial impact of customer service, measuring customer satisfaction and its impact on financial performance, and the role of customer service in customer retention and lifetime value.

Furthermore, we discussed the financial impact of human resources, the cost of employee turnover, and the impact of employee engagement and satisfaction on financial performance. Finally, we examined CRM as a strategy for managing interactions with customers and potential customers, and its impact on financial performance.

As non-financial professionals, having financial intelligence will allow individuals to make better-informed decisions, improve communication and collaboration with finance teams, and ultimately drive better financial performance. By understanding the financial implications of business decisions, non-financial professionals can play a more active role in driving the success of their organization.

In the next section, we will dive deeper into financial analysis, exploring financial statements and key financial metrics in more detail, and learning techniques for financial analysis that can be applied across all areas of business.

CHAPTER 1: THE IMPORTANCE OF FINANCIAL INTELLIGENCE FOR NON-FINANCIAL PROFESSIONALS

In today's highly competitive business environment, it is essential for non-financial professionals to have a solid understanding of financial concepts and principles. This knowledge enables individuals to make informed decisions that impact the financial performance of their organizations. In this chapter, we will explore the importance of financial intelligence for non-financial professionals, and how this knowledge can be leveraged to drive business success.

Why is financial intelligence important for non-financial professionals?

Financial intelligence refers to the ability to understand and analyze financial information, such as financial statements, budgets, and performance metrics. This knowledge enables individuals to make informed decisions that impact the financial performance of their organizations. Financial intelligence is important for non-financial professionals for several reasons:

Understanding Financial Statements
Financial statements provide a snapshot of a company's financial health, including revenue, expenses, assets, and liabilities. Non-financial professionals who have a basic understanding of financial statements can use this information to assess the financial performance of their organization and make informed decisions about resource allocation and investment.

Budgeting and Forecasting
Effective budgeting and forecasting are essential for financial success. Non-financial professionals who understand the budgeting process can contribute to the development of accurate and realistic budgets that align with the organization's strategic goals. Additionally, the ability to analyze financial data and make informed forecasts enables individuals to identify potential financial risks and opportunities.

Evaluating Investment Opportunities
Non-financial professionals who understand financial principles can evaluate investment opportunities and assess their potential impact on the organization's financial performance. This knowledge enables individuals to make informed decisions about investments and to prioritize opportunities that align with the organization's strategic goals.

Effective Communication with Financial Professionals
The ability to communicate effectively with financial professionals, such as accountants and financial analysts, is essential for non-financial professionals. By having a basic understanding of financial concepts, non-financial professionals can effectively communicate with financial professionals and ensure that financial information is accurate and relevant to their decision-making process.

Examples of Financial Intelligence in Action

Financial intelligence is essential for non-financial professionals in a variety of industries and roles. Here are a few examples of financial intelligence in action:

Marketing Professionals
Marketing professionals who understand financial principles can use this knowledge to develop effective marketing strategies that align with the organization's financial goals. For example, by analyzing financial data, marketers can identify target markets and develop campaigns that maximize the return on investment.

Human Resources Professionals
Human resources professionals who understand financial principles can contribute to the development of effective compensation and benefits packages that align with the organization's financial goals. Additionally, by understanding the financial impact of employee turnover, HR professionals can develop retention strategies that reduce costs and improve organizational performance.

Customer Service Professionals
Customer service professionals who understand financial principles can identify opportunities to improve customer satisfaction and retention, which can have a positive impact on the organization's financial performance. For example, by analyzing customer data, customer service professionals can identify trends and develop strategies to address customer needs and preferences.

Exercises

Review your organization's financial statements and identify key performance metrics. How do these metrics align with the organization's strategic goals?

Develop a budget for a hypothetical project. Identify potential financial risks and opportunities.

Analyze a potential investment opportunity and assess its potential impact on the organization's financial performance.

Financial intelligence is essential for non-financial professionals in today's competitive business environment. By understanding financial concepts and principles, individuals can make informed decisions that impact the financial performance of their organizations. In the following chapters, we will explore the intersection of finance with marketing, customer service, human resources, and CRM, and how financial intelligence can be leveraged to drive business success.

Understanding the importance of financial literacy for non-financial professionals

In today's business world, it is essential for professionals to possess a basic level of financial literacy. This is not limited to just finance and accounting professionals, but also to non-financial professionals such as marketing, human resources, legal, and operations personnel. Financial intelligence is the ability to understand and effectively use financial information to make informed business decisions. It is a critical skill that enables professionals to contribute to the success of their organization.

The Importance of Financial Intelligence for Non-Financial Professionals

In the past, financial management was considered the sole responsibility of the finance department. However, with the increasing complexity of the business environment, it has become imperative for non-financial professionals to understand and apply financial concepts in their day-to-day operations. This is because the success of any organization depends on its ability to generate profits, manage costs, and make sound financial decisions.

Financial intelligence allows non-financial professionals to analyze financial statements, interpret financial ratios, understand the cost structure of their organization, and assess the financial impact of their decisions. This enables them to contribute to the financial health of their organization by identifying and implementing cost-saving measures, improving profitability, and making informed decisions that align with the organization's financial objectives.

Examples of the Importance of Financial Intelligence

Consider a marketing professional who is responsible for developing a new advertising campaign. Without financial intelligence, this individual may not be able to assess the cost of the campaign or the expected return on investment (ROI). This could lead to a situation where the campaign exceeds the marketing budget, resulting in a financial loss for the organization.

Similarly, a human resources professional who is responsible for managing the organization's workforce may not be able to analyze the cost of employee benefits or understand the impact of turnover on the organization's financial performance. This could result in the organization experiencing a higher turnover rate and incurring additional costs associated with recruitment and training.

Benefits of Financial Intelligence

Financial intelligence provides several benefits to non-financial professionals. These benefits include:

Improved Decision-Making: Financial intelligence enables professionals to make informed decisions based on financial data and analysis. This results in decisions that are aligned with the organization's financial objectives and contribute to its overall success.

Enhanced Communication: Financial intelligence allows non-financial professionals to communicate more effectively with their finance counterparts. This results in better collaboration and alignment of financial and non-financial functions.

Increased Career Opportunities: Professionals with financial intelligence have a competitive advantage in the job market. They are better equipped to assume leadership roles and make strategic business decisions.

Improved Financial Performance: Financial intelligence enables non-financial professionals to contribute to the financial health of their organization. This results in improved profitability, reduced costs, and increased shareholder value.

Conclusion

In conclusion, financial intelligence is a critical skill for non-financial professionals. It enables professionals to contribute to the success of their organization by making informed decisions, improving communication, increasing career opportunities, and enhancing financial performance. In the following chapters, we will explore the intersection of finance with other functions such as marketing, human resources, legal, and customer relationship management (CRM).

The benefits of financial intelligence for career advancement and decision-making

Financial intelligence is becoming increasingly important for professionals across all industries. No longer is it enough to leave financial matters to the finance department or the CFO; instead, a basic understanding of finance is essential for anyone in a position of responsibility. In this section, we will explore the benefits of financial intelligence for career advancement and decision-making. We will cover topics such as how financial intelligence can impact career prospects, the role of financial intelligence in effective decision-making, and how to develop and improve your own financial intelligence.

The Benefits of Financial Intelligence for Career Advancement:

In today's competitive job market, having financial intelligence can give you a significant advantage when seeking career advancement. Understanding financial statements, budgets, and financial projections can help you make informed decisions that align with the company's financial goals. This, in turn, can lead to greater job security, promotion opportunities, and even higher salaries.

For example, consider two candidates applying for a management position in a company. One candidate has a strong financial background and can easily understand the company's financial statements. The other candidate has limited financial knowledge and may struggle to understand the financial implications of their decisions. The first candidate would likely be seen as a stronger candidate, as they are better equipped to make informed decisions that align with the company's financial objectives.

Furthermore, having financial intelligence can help you stand out from your colleagues and demonstrate your value to the company. For instance, if you are able to identify inefficiencies in the company's financial processes and suggest improvements, you will be seen as a valuable asset to the company.

The Role of Financial Intelligence in Decision-Making:

Financial intelligence is also essential for effective decision-making. In many instances, financial considerations are at the heart of the decision-making process, and an understanding of financial concepts is necessary to make informed decisions.

For example, consider a company that is deciding whether to invest in a new product line. By analyzing financial projections, the company can estimate the potential return on investment and determine whether the investment is financially viable. Without financial intelligence, the company may make a decision based on emotion or intuition, rather than objective data.

Moreover, financial intelligence is crucial when making personal financial decisions. Whether you are considering purchasing a new home, investing in the stock market, or planning for retirement, an understanding of financial concepts can help you make informed decisions that align with your personal financial goals.

Developing and Improving Your Financial Intelligence:

Fortunately, financial intelligence is a skill that can be developed and improved over time. One of the best ways to improve your financial intelligence is to educate yourself about financial concepts and principles. This can be done through a variety of means, such as reading books and articles, attending seminars and workshops, or taking online courses.

In addition, gaining hands-on experience with financial analysis and reporting can be an excellent way to improve your financial intelligence. This may involve volunteering to work on financial projects at work or taking on a part-time job in a finance-related field.

Furthermore, seeking out mentors and networking with individuals who have strong financial backgrounds can be invaluable for improving your financial intelligence. These individuals can offer guidance and advice, as well as provide opportunities for professional development.

Conclusion:

In conclusion, financial intelligence is essential for non-financial professionals in today's business world. The benefits of financial intelligence extend beyond personal financial management and can significantly impact career advancement and decision-making. Developing and improving your financial intelligence is an ongoing process, but the benefits are well worth the effort. By investing in your financial intelligence, you can position yourself for success in both your personal and professional life.

Practical examples of the consequences of financial illiteracy in the workplace

Financial literacy is a crucial skill for non-financial professionals, as it allows them to understand and analyze financial information, make informed decisions, and effectively communicate with financial experts. However, the consequences of financial illiteracy in the workplace can be significant, ranging from poor decision-making to financial fraud and legal liabilities. This section will provide practical examples of the consequences of financial illiteracy in the workplace, and how they can be avoided through the development of financial intelligence.

Case Studies

Enron Corporation
The Enron Corporation was an American energy company that filed for bankruptcy in 2001, in one of the largest corporate scandals in history. Enron's executives engaged in widespread financial fraud and accounting manipulations, hiding billions of dollars in debt and losses from investors and regulators. The consequences of Enron's financial illiteracy were catastrophic, as thousands of employees lost their jobs and savings, and investors lost billions of dollars in value. Moreover, the scandal led to the passage of the Sarbanes-Oxley Act of 2002, which increased corporate transparency and accountability, and created new legal liabilities for corporate executives.

Lehman Brothers
Lehman Brothers was a global investment bank that filed for bankruptcy in 2008, during the financial crisis. Lehman Brothers had invested heavily in subprime mortgages, which turned out to be toxic assets, as homeowners defaulted on their loans. The consequences of Lehman Brothers' financial illiteracy were far-reaching, as it triggered a global financial meltdown, and led to the collapse of other financial institutions, such as Bear Stearns and AIG. The crisis caused massive job losses, a sharp decline in economic growth, and a loss of confidence in the financial system.

Olympus Corporation
The Olympus Corporation is a Japanese manufacturer of medical and optical equipment, that was involved in a financial scandal in 2011. The company's executives had concealed losses of over $1.7 billion through fraudulent accounting practices, such as using acquisition fees to cover up investment losses. The consequences of Olympus' financial illiteracy included a sharp decline in the company's stock price, a loss of trust from investors and customers, and legal liabilities for the executives involved. Moreover, the scandal highlighted the need for stronger corporate governance and internal controls, to prevent similar incidents from occurring.

Lessons Learned

These case studies illustrate the importance of financial intelligence in the workplace, and the consequences of financial illiteracy. Non-financial professionals need to be able to understand and interpret financial information, identify potential risks and opportunities, and make informed decisions based on sound financial analysis. Moreover, they need to be aware of the legal and ethical implications of financial decisions, and the potential consequences for themselves and their organizations.

Practical Exercises

To develop financial intelligence, non-financial professionals can engage in the following exercises:

Analyze financial statements of a publicly traded company, and identify key financial ratios, such as liquidity, profitability, and solvency.

Evaluate the financial risks and opportunities of a potential investment, such as a real estate property or a stock portfolio.

Develop a budget and financial forecast for a department or project, and track actual results against projections.

Participate in financial training programs and seminars, and seek feedback and guidance from financial experts.

Conclusion

Financial intelligence is a critical skill for non-financial professionals, as it allows them to make informed decisions, mitigate risks, and advance their careers. The consequences of financial illiteracy in the workplace can be severe, including financial fraud, legal liabilities, and reputational damage. However, by developing financial intelligence through practical exercises and training, non-financial professionals can avoid these pitfalls and become more valuable assets to their organizations.

Case study: The Enron scandal and the importance of financial ethics

Financial ethics plays a significant role in the functioning of the modern business world. Businesses, especially those in the financial sector, are expected to operate ethically and transparently, with a focus on maximizing shareholder value while also acting in the best interests of their stakeholders. Failure to do so can result in serious consequences, as was seen in the case of Enron. This case study explores the Enron scandal and highlights the importance of financial ethics in preventing such incidents.

Background:

Enron was a Houston-based energy company that was once one of the largest and most successful companies in the United States. The company's rapid growth was largely fueled by a complex web of off-balance sheet partnerships that allowed Enron to conceal massive debts and inflate profits. The company's executives, including CEO Jeffrey Skilling and CFO Andrew Fastow, engaged in a variety of fraudulent activities to hide the company's financial situation from investors, analysts, and the public. These activities included manipulating financial statements, hiding losses, and inflating earnings.

The Enron scandal came to light in October 2001 when the company announced that it had overstated its earnings by $586 million over the previous four years. The announcement led to a sharp decline in Enron's stock price and triggered a chain of events that eventually led to the company's bankruptcy. The scandal had far-reaching consequences, including the loss of jobs, pensions, and life savings for thousands of employees and investors.

Lessons Learned:

The Enron scandal serves as a cautionary tale about the dangers of financial misconduct and the importance of financial ethics. The case highlights the need for businesses to be transparent in their financial reporting and to act in the best interests of their stakeholders. It also demonstrates the importance of effective oversight by boards of directors, auditors, and regulators.

One of the key lessons from the Enron scandal is the need for a culture of ethical behavior within organizations. Enron's executives created a culture of greed and arrogance that allowed them to engage in unethical behavior without fear of consequences. A strong ethical culture is essential for preventing financial misconduct and promoting responsible behavior among employees at all levels of the organization.

Another lesson from the Enron scandal is the importance of effective internal controls and risk management. Enron's executives were able to engage in fraudulent activities in large part because of weaknesses in the company's internal controls and risk management systems. Effective internal controls and risk management are critical for preventing financial misconduct and ensuring the accuracy and reliability of financial reporting.

Conclusion:

The Enron scandal serves as a reminder of the importance of financial ethics in the modern business world. The case highlights the need for transparency, ethical behavior, and effective oversight to prevent financial misconduct and promote responsible behavior among businesses and their employees. Businesses must be proactive in creating a culture of ethical behavior, implementing effective internal controls and risk management systems, and providing ongoing training and education for their employees. By doing so, they can help prevent incidents like the Enron scandal and maintain the trust and confidence of their stakeholders.

Exercise: Assessing your own financial literacy and identifying areas for improvement

Assessing your own financial literacy is an important step towards making informed financial decisions. Understanding your current level of financial knowledge and identifying areas for improvement can help you achieve your financial goals and avoid costly mistakes. In this section, we will provide you with a step-by-step guide on how to assess your own financial literacy and identify areas for improvement.

Step 1: Evaluate Your Current Financial Knowledge

The first step in assessing your financial literacy is to evaluate your current financial knowledge. Take some time to think about your financial knowledge and answer the following questions:

Do you understand the basics of personal finance, such as budgeting, saving, and investing?
Do you know how to read financial statements, such as balance sheets and income statements?
Do you understand the different types of financial products, such as stocks, bonds, and mutual funds?
Do you know how to manage your debt and credit score?
Do you understand the tax implications of different financial decisions?
These questions will give you a general idea of your current level of financial knowledge. If you are unsure about any of these topics, you may need to improve your financial literacy.

Step 2: Identify Areas for Improvement

Once you have evaluated your current financial knowledge, the next step is to identify areas for improvement. Think about the areas where you feel least confident or knowledgeable. These may be areas where you need to improve your financial literacy.

One way to identify areas for improvement is to take a financial literacy quiz or assessment. There are many online resources available that offer financial literacy assessments. These assessments can help you identify areas where you need to improve your financial knowledge.

Another way to identify areas for improvement is to talk to a financial advisor. A financial advisor can help you evaluate your financial knowledge and identify areas where you may need to improve.

Step 3: Develop a Plan to Improve Your Financial Literacy

Once you have identified areas for improvement, the next step is to develop a plan to improve your financial literacy. There are many ways to improve your financial knowledge, including:

Reading financial books and articles
Attending financial seminars or workshops
Taking online courses or classes
Talking to a financial advisor
You may need to use a combination of these methods to improve your financial literacy. Make a list of the resources that are available to you and create a plan that works best for your needs and schedule.

Step 4: Evaluate Your Progress

The final step in assessing your own financial literacy is to evaluate your progress. After you have implemented your plan to improve your financial knowledge, take some time to evaluate your progress. Ask yourself the following questions:

Have you gained a better understanding of the areas where you were previously less knowledgeable?
Have you made better financial decisions as a result of your increased financial knowledge?
Do you feel more confident about your ability to manage your finances?

If you have made progress, congratulate yourself and continue to work towards improving your financial literacy. If you still feel like there is room for improvement, continue to seek out resources and support to help you achieve your financial goals.

Assessing your own financial literacy is an important step towards achieving your financial goals. By evaluating your current financial knowledge, identifying areas for improvement, and developing a plan to improve your financial literacy, you can make informed financial decisions and avoid costly mistakes. Remember, improving your financial literacy is a lifelong process, so continue to seek out resources and support to help you achieve financial success.

CHAPTER 2: THE INTERSECTION OF FINANCE WITH MARKETING, CUSTOMER SERVICE, HUMAN RESOURCES, AND CRM

In today's rapidly changing business world, companies need to embrace a customer-centric approach to remain competitive. The intersection of finance with marketing, customer service, human resources, and customer relationship management (CRM) is essential to achieving this goal. Finance professionals can no longer operate in isolation from these functions. Instead, they must work in tandem to create a cohesive and unified customer experience.

The chapter will explore the different ways finance interacts with marketing, customer service, human resources, and CRM. It will explain how these functions overlap and affect each other. The chapter will also discuss the benefits of integrating these functions, including improved customer satisfaction, increased profitability, and streamlined operations.

Finance and Marketing:

Marketing and finance are two of the most crucial functions in any organization. Marketing is responsible for creating and executing campaigns that drive sales, while finance is responsible for managing the company's finances and ensuring that the company is profitable. The intersection of finance and marketing is essential for companies to create an effective marketing strategy.

Finance plays a vital role in the marketing process by providing the necessary funds for marketing campaigns. Without adequate funding, marketing campaigns may not reach their full potential, and the company may miss out on potential customers. Finance also helps to evaluate the return on investment (ROI) of marketing campaigns, ensuring that the company is getting the best value for its money.

Marketing, on the other hand, helps finance by providing insight into customer behavior and preferences. By understanding customer needs and desires, finance can allocate resources more effectively, resulting in increased profitability. Marketing also plays a vital role in shaping the company's brand image, which can affect the company's financial performance.

Finance and Customer Service:

Customer service is another critical function that intersects with finance. The quality of customer service can significantly impact a company's reputation and financial performance. Finance plays a critical role in ensuring that the company can provide quality customer service.

Finance provides the necessary funds to hire and train customer service representatives, as well as to implement customer service technologies. Finance also helps to evaluate the ROI of customer service investments, ensuring that the company is getting the best value for its money.

Customer service, on the other hand, provides finance with valuable customer feedback. By understanding customer needs and preferences, finance can allocate resources more effectively, resulting in increased profitability. Customer service can also help finance to identify potential areas for cost savings, which can improve the company's financial performance.

Finance and Human Resources:

Human resources (HR) is responsible for recruiting, hiring, and managing employees. HR also plays a crucial role in ensuring that the company's employees are productive and engaged. Finance and HR intersect in several ways, including compensation and benefits, employee training and development, and employee retention.

Finance plays a critical role in providing the necessary funds for employee compensation and benefits. Finance also helps HR to evaluate the ROI of employee training and development programs, ensuring that the company is getting the best value for its money. Additionally, finance helps HR to identify potential areas for cost savings related to employee compensation and benefits.

HR provides finance with valuable insight into employee productivity and engagement. By understanding the needs and preferences of employees, finance can allocate resources more effectively, resulting in increased profitability. HR can also help finance to identify potential areas for cost savings related to employee productivity and engagement.

Finance and CRM:

CRM is a critical function that helps companies manage their relationships with customers. CRM systems are designed to collect, store, and analyze customer data, providing companies with valuable insights into customer behavior and preferences. Finance and CRM intersect in several ways, including sales forecasting, customer segmentation, and pricing strategies.

Finance plays a critical role in sales forecasting by providing the necessary funds for sales and marketing campaigns. By understanding sales trends and forecasting future sales,

Understanding the role of finance in different business functions

Finance is a critical function in any organization, providing the necessary capital and resources to support operations, growth, and innovation. However, the role of finance extends beyond simply providing funding. Finance also intersects with other business functions, such as marketing, customer service, human resources, and CRM, to ensure that the organization's goals and objectives are aligned and that resources are allocated effectively. In this section, we will explore the role of finance in these different business functions and examine how they intersect.

Finance and Marketing

Marketing is the process of creating, communicating, and delivering value to customers. Finance and marketing intersect in several ways, including sales forecasting, pricing strategies, and budgeting.

Sales Forecasting: Finance plays a critical role in sales forecasting by providing the necessary funds for sales and marketing campaigns. By understanding sales trends and forecasting future sales, finance can ensure that marketing campaigns are appropriately funded and that resources are allocated effectively.

Pricing Strategies: Pricing strategies are a critical component of marketing, and finance plays a key role in determining pricing levels. Finance can analyze the cost of production, overhead expenses, and other factors to determine the appropriate price for a product or service. Additionally, finance can work with marketing to determine pricing strategies for new products or services.

Budgeting: Finance and marketing also intersect in the budgeting process. Finance can provide guidance on how much money should be allocated to marketing campaigns, and marketing can provide input on the types of campaigns that are most effective. By working together, finance and marketing can ensure that resources are allocated effectively and that marketing campaigns are aligned with the organization's goals and objectives.

Finance and Customer Service

Customer service is a critical component of any business, and finance plays an important role in ensuring that customer service is effective and efficient. Finance and customer service intersect in several ways, including budgeting, resource allocation, and performance metrics.

Budgeting: Finance can provide guidance on how much money should be allocated to customer service, including training, staffing, and technology. By working together, finance and customer service can ensure that resources are allocated effectively and that customer service is adequately funded.

Resource Allocation: Finance can also play a role in determining how resources are allocated within customer service. For example, finance can analyze customer data to determine which channels are most effective for customer service, such as phone, email, or chat. By understanding customer preferences and behavior, finance can ensure that resources are allocated to the channels that are most effective.

Performance Metrics: Finance can also work with customer service to develop performance metrics that are aligned with the organization's goals and objectives. For example, finance can help develop metrics that measure customer satisfaction, response times, and first-call resolution rates. By measuring performance and tracking progress over time, finance and customer service can identify areas for improvement and ensure that customer service is meeting the needs of the organization and its customers.

Finance and Human Resources

Human resources is responsible for managing the organization's workforce, including recruitment, hiring, training, and development. Finance and human resources intersect in several ways, including budgeting, compensation, and performance management.

Budgeting: Finance can provide guidance on how much money should be allocated to human resources, including recruitment, training, and development. By understanding the organization's staffing needs and goals, finance can ensure that human resources is adequately funded and that resources are allocated effectively.

Compensation: Finance also plays a key role in determining compensation levels for employees. Finance can analyze market data and internal benchmarks to determine appropriate compensation levels for different positions and roles within the organization. Additionally, finance can work with human resources to develop compensation strategies that are aligned with the organization's goals and objectives.

Performance Management: Finance and human resources also intersect in performance management. Finance can work with human resources to develop performance metrics that are aligned with the organization's goals and objectives. Additionally, finance can analyze the financial impact of different performance management strategies and provide recommendations to improve overall performance.

For example, finance can use data analysis to identify the most effective employee performance metrics and compare them to industry benchmarks. This can help companies understand which metrics are most valuable for their specific business goals and make informed decisions about compensation and promotions.

Furthermore, finance can help companies evaluate the financial impact of different performance management strategies. For instance, implementing a performance-based compensation plan may result in increased productivity, but it could also lead to increased expenses for the company. Finance can evaluate the costs and benefits of such a plan and make recommendations to ensure that it aligns with the organization's financial goals.

Recruiting and Retention: Finance also plays an important role in recruiting and retaining top talent. Finance can work with human resources to develop competitive compensation packages and benefits that attract and retain high-performing employees. This can include evaluating the financial impact of different benefits, such as healthcare, retirement plans, and other perks.

Moreover, finance can analyze data related to employee turnover rates and make recommendations to improve retention. For example, if a company has a high turnover rate, finance can analyze the cost of turnover and make recommendations to improve employee engagement and reduce turnover.

In conclusion, finance plays a critical role in various business functions, including human resources, marketing, customer service, and operations. By working together, finance and other departments can develop effective strategies that align with the organization's overall goals and objectives. Understanding the role of finance in different business functions is essential for business students who seek to understand the broader impact of financial decisions on organizational performance.

The impact of marketing on financial performance

Marketing and finance are two interdependent functions in an organization. While marketing focuses on identifying and meeting customer needs, finance is responsible for ensuring the financial stability and success of the organization. Despite being distinct functions, marketing and finance share a common goal: to generate revenue and maximize profits for the organization.

Marketing has a significant impact on the financial performance of an organization. Effective marketing strategies can help increase sales, improve customer retention, and enhance brand awareness. Conversely, poor marketing strategies can lead to decreased sales, negative brand perception, and lower profits.

One way that marketing impacts financial performance is through the creation of a strong brand. A brand is a company's identity in the market and is created through various marketing efforts, including advertising, public relations, and social media. A strong brand can lead to increased customer loyalty, improved reputation, and higher profits.

Marketing also plays a critical role in identifying customer needs and preferences, which can help inform pricing strategies. By understanding the value that customers place on products or services, marketing can help finance determine the appropriate pricing levels that will maximize profits.

Moreover, marketing can also impact the financial performance of an organization through effective product development and launch strategies. By conducting market research, marketing can identify gaps in the market and develop new products or services that meet customer needs. Effective product launch strategies can generate buzz and excitement, leading to increased sales and revenue.

However, marketing efforts can also lead to unnecessary costs, negatively impacting financial performance. For instance, marketing campaigns that are not well-planned or executed can result in wasted resources and low returns on investment. Therefore, it is crucial to have a balance between marketing expenditures and expected returns.

In conclusion, marketing and finance are two interdependent functions that play a crucial role in the financial performance of an organization. Effective marketing strategies can lead to increased sales, improved customer retention, and a stronger brand identity, all of which can positively impact the organization's financial success. However, it is essential to maintain a balance between marketing expenditures and expected returns to avoid unnecessary costs that can negatively impact financial performance.

The financial impact of customer service and its role in customer retention and loyalty

Customer service is a critical function for any business that wants to succeed. It involves creating a positive experience for customers by addressing their needs, concerns, and complaints. In today's competitive business environment, companies are realizing the importance of customer service in driving customer retention and loyalty, which, in turn, leads to increased financial performance. This section will explore the financial impact of customer service and its role in customer retention and loyalty.

The Financial Impact of Customer Service:

Customer service has a direct impact on a company's financial performance. Companies that provide exceptional customer service are more likely to retain customers, which translates into increased revenue and profitability. According to a study by Bain & Company, increasing customer retention rates by just 5% can lead to an increase in profits of up to 95%. Additionally, it is much more cost-effective to retain existing customers than to acquire new ones. In fact, it costs five times as much to acquire a new customer as it does to retain an existing one.

Furthermore, customer service can also impact a company's brand reputation and market share. Customers who have a positive experience with a company's customer service are more likely to become loyal customers and recommend the company to others. This can lead to increased market share and a competitive advantage.

Customer Retention and Loyalty:

Customer retention and loyalty are closely linked to customer service. Retaining customers is critical for a company's long-term success because it provides a stable revenue stream and reduces the need for costly marketing campaigns to attract new customers. Additionally, loyal customers are more likely to make repeat purchases and recommend the company to others.

To achieve high levels of customer retention and loyalty, companies need to focus on providing exceptional customer service. This involves understanding customers' needs and preferences, responding promptly to their inquiries and complaints, and going above and beyond to create a positive experience for them. Companies that prioritize customer service are more likely to retain customers and build long-term loyalty.

The Role of Customer Service in Customer Retention and Loyalty:

Customer service plays a crucial role in customer retention and loyalty. Customers who have a positive experience with a company's customer service are more likely to continue doing business with that company. Additionally, customers who feel valued and appreciated are more likely to become loyal customers and recommend the company to others.

To achieve high levels of customer retention and loyalty, companies need to make customer service a top priority. This involves investing in training and development programs for customer service representatives, providing them with the necessary resources and tools to do their job effectively, and creating a culture that prioritizes customer service. Companies that prioritize customer service are more likely to retain customers and build long-term loyalty.

Examples of Companies That Prioritize Customer Service:

Several companies have achieved success by prioritizing customer service. One example is Zappos, an online retailer that is known for its exceptional customer service. Zappos offers free shipping and returns, a 365-day return policy, and 24/7 customer service. The company's focus on customer service has helped it build a loyal customer base and achieve a high level of customer retention.

Another example is Ritz-Carlton, a luxury hotel chain that is known for its exceptional customer service. The company has a motto of "We are Ladies and Gentlemen serving Ladies and Gentlemen" and empowers its employees to go above and beyond to create a positive experience for guests. Ritz-Carlton's focus on customer service has helped it build a strong brand reputation and achieve a high level of customer loyalty.

Customer service plays a critical role in driving customer retention and loyalty, which, in turn, leads to increased financial performance. Companies that prioritize customer service are more likely to retain customers and build long-term loyalty. To achieve high levels of customer retention and loyalty, companies need to make customer service a top priority and invest in the necessary resources to support it.

The financial impact of customer service cannot be underestimated. Research has shown that it is much more expensive to acquire a new customer than to retain an existing one. According to the Harvard Business Review, acquiring a new customer can cost anywhere from five to 25 times more than retaining an existing one. Additionally, existing customers are more likely to make repeat purchases and spend more money over time, further increasing the financial benefits of customer retention.

Moreover, happy customers are more likely to recommend a company to others, which can lead to new customers and increased revenue. According to a study by the Temkin Group, customers who have had a positive experience with a company are 11 times more likely to recommend that company to others.

To ensure that customer service is a top priority, companies should invest in training and development programs for their customer service employees. This includes providing ongoing training to ensure that employees are up-to-date with the latest customer service trends and techniques. Companies should also ensure that their customer service employees have the necessary resources and tools to provide exceptional customer service, such as access to customer data and customer feedback.

In addition, companies should use customer feedback to continuously improve their customer service. This includes collecting feedback through surveys and social media, as well as monitoring online reviews and other forms of customer feedback. Companies should use this feedback to identify areas where they can improve their customer service and make necessary changes.

In conclusion, customer service plays a critical role in driving customer retention and loyalty, which ultimately leads to increased financial performance. Companies that prioritize customer service and invest in the necessary resources to support it are more likely to retain customers, build long-term loyalty, and increase revenue. By providing exceptional customer service, companies can differentiate themselves from their competitors and create a strong brand reputation that leads to continued success.

The cost of employee turnover and the importance of employee engagement and satisfaction on financial performance

Employee turnover is a significant concern for businesses across all industries. It refers to the number of employees who leave a company over a given period of time, often due to reasons such as low job satisfaction, inadequate compensation, lack of career growth opportunities, and poor working conditions. High levels of employee turnover can have a negative impact on a company's financial performance, as it can lead to increased recruitment and training costs, decreased productivity, and decreased customer satisfaction.

Employee engagement and satisfaction, on the other hand, are critical factors that can contribute to a company's financial performance. Engaged and satisfied employees are more likely to remain with a company for longer periods, which can reduce employee turnover costs and increase productivity. Additionally, employees who are engaged and satisfied are more likely to provide better customer service and contribute to a positive company culture, which can lead to increased customer satisfaction and retention.

In this section, we will explore the cost of employee turnover and the importance of employee engagement and satisfaction on financial performance. We will examine the impact of high employee turnover rates on a company's bottom line, as well as strategies that can be implemented to improve employee engagement and satisfaction.

The Cost of Employee Turnover:

Employee turnover can be costly for businesses in a number of ways. One of the most significant costs associated with employee turnover is the cost of recruitment and training. When an employee leaves a company, the company must invest time and resources into finding a replacement and training them to perform the job duties. This process can be expensive, particularly if the company must hire a specialized candidate or provide extensive training.

Additionally, high levels of employee turnover can lead to decreased productivity. When employees leave, it can take time for their replacements to get up to speed, which can result in a temporary decrease in productivity. This can be particularly damaging if the employee who left was a high-performing member of the team.

High levels of employee turnover can also have a negative impact on customer satisfaction. When employees leave, it can disrupt the customer experience, particularly if the departing employee had a strong relationship with the customer.

This can lead to decreased customer satisfaction and retention, which can ultimately harm a company's financial performance.

Importance of Employee Engagement and Satisfaction:

Employee engagement and satisfaction are critical factors that can impact a company's financial performance. Engaged and satisfied employees are more likely to remain with a company for longer periods, reducing employee turnover costs and improving productivity. They are also more likely to provide better customer service and contribute to a positive company culture, which can lead to increased customer satisfaction and retention.

There are several strategies that companies can use to improve employee engagement and satisfaction. One approach is to provide employees with opportunities for career growth and development. When employees feel that they have opportunities to advance within a company, they are more likely to feel engaged and motivated to perform at their best.

Another approach is to provide employees with a positive work environment. This can include factors such as flexible work schedules, opportunities for social interaction with colleagues, and recognition for a job well done. When employees feel that they are valued and supported in their work, they are more likely to be engaged and satisfied.

Finally, companies can improve employee engagement and satisfaction by offering competitive compensation and benefits packages. When employees feel that they are being compensated fairly for their work, they are more likely to be satisfied with their job and remain with the company for longer periods.

Employee turnover can be costly for businesses in a number of ways, including recruitment and training costs, decreased productivity, and decreased customer satisfaction. However, companies can mitigate these costs by improving employee engagement and satisfaction. Engaged and satisfied employees are more likely to remain with a company for longer periods, improving productivity and customer satisfaction. To improve employee engagement and satisfaction, companies can provide opportunities for career growth and development, create a positive work culture, provide competitive compensation and benefits packages, and listen to and act upon employee feedback.

One way companies can provide opportunities for career growth and development is through training and development programs. These programs can help employees acquire new skills and knowledge that can improve their job performance and lead to career advancement. Providing opportunities for employee career growth and development can increase employee engagement and satisfaction, as employees feel valued and invested in by their employer.

Creating a positive work culture is also important for improving employee engagement and satisfaction. A positive work culture can foster a sense of community and purpose among employees, leading to higher levels of job satisfaction and engagement. This can be achieved through initiatives such as team-building activities, employee recognition programs, and open communication channels between management and employees.

Offering competitive compensation and benefits packages is another important factor in improving employee engagement and satisfaction. Employees who feel that they are being fairly compensated for their work are more likely to be engaged and satisfied with their jobs. In addition to competitive pay, companies can also offer benefits such as healthcare, retirement plans, and paid time off to help attract and retain top talent.

Finally, listening to and acting upon employee feedback is critical for improving employee engagement and satisfaction. Employees who feel that their opinions and concerns are valued by their employer are more likely to be engaged and satisfied with their jobs. Companies can solicit feedback through employee surveys, suggestion boxes, and regular one-on-one meetings with managers.

In conclusion, employee turnover can have a significant impact on a company's financial performance, but companies can mitigate these costs by improving employee engagement and satisfaction. By providing opportunities for career growth and development, creating a positive work culture, offering competitive compensation and benefits packages, and listening to and acting upon employee feedback, companies can improve employee engagement and satisfaction, leading to increased productivity, customer satisfaction, and ultimately, financial performance.

The role of CRM in customer retention and financial performance

Customer Relationship Management (CRM) is an essential aspect of modern business operations. It refers to a comprehensive set of strategies, technologies, and processes that businesses use to manage and analyze customer interactions and data throughout the customer lifecycle. In today's highly competitive business landscape, businesses are increasingly focusing on building long-term relationships with customers to drive customer retention and increase financial performance. This section will provide an in-depth analysis of the role of CRM in customer retention and financial performance.

The Role of CRM in Customer Retention:
One of the primary goals of CRM is to improve customer retention by creating personalized experiences for customers. CRM enables businesses to collect and analyze customer data, such as demographics, purchasing behavior, and preferences, to better understand their customers' needs and preferences. This understanding helps businesses to tailor their products and services to meet the unique needs of individual customers.

Moreover, CRM provides businesses with the tools and capabilities to provide personalized customer experiences. With CRM, businesses can automate and personalize marketing campaigns, sales processes, and customer service interactions. This personalization helps to build stronger relationships with customers, leading to increased customer retention.

CRM also enables businesses to provide better customer service, another critical factor in customer retention. With CRM, businesses can track customer interactions and inquiries, providing a comprehensive view of each customer's needs and concerns. This information enables businesses to address customer issues quickly and efficiently, leading to higher levels of customer satisfaction and increased customer retention.

The Role of CRM in Financial Performance:
CRM also plays a critical role in driving financial performance. By improving customer retention, businesses can increase their revenue and profitability. Retained customers are more likely to purchase additional products and services, providing a steady stream of revenue. Moreover, retained customers are more likely to refer new customers, leading to further revenue growth.

CRM also enables businesses to identify high-value customers, allowing them to focus their marketing efforts on those customers most likely to generate revenue. With CRM, businesses can segment their customer base based on demographics, purchasing behavior, and other criteria, allowing them to develop targeted marketing campaigns that appeal to specific customer groups.

CRM also helps businesses to optimize their sales processes, increasing the efficiency and effectiveness of their sales teams. With CRM, businesses can track sales performance, identify areas for improvement, and provide sales teams with the tools and resources they need to close more deals.

Challenges and Limitations of CRM:
While CRM offers significant benefits, there are also challenges and limitations to its implementation. One of the biggest challenges is the complexity of CRM systems. Implementing a comprehensive CRM system requires significant resources, including financial and human capital. Moreover, the implementation process can be lengthy and disruptive, requiring significant changes to existing business processes and systems.

Another challenge of CRM is the need for accurate and timely data. CRM relies on accurate customer data to provide personalized experiences and drive effective marketing campaigns. However, data quality issues, such as incomplete or outdated data, can undermine the effectiveness of CRM initiatives.

Moreover, CRM is not a one-size-fits-all solution. The effectiveness of CRM initiatives can vary based on the type of business, industry, and customer base. Additionally, while CRM can provide valuable insights into customer behavior and preferences, it cannot predict future behavior with certainty.

Conclusion:
CRM is an essential aspect of modern business operations, playing a critical role in driving customer retention and financial performance. By providing personalized customer experiences, improving customer service, and optimizing sales processes, CRM can help businesses to retain customers, increase revenue, and improve profitability. However, the implementation of CRM initiatives can be challenging, requiring significant resources and careful planning. As such, businesses must carefully evaluate their needs and objectives before implementing CRM systems and initiatives.

Case study: The financial impact of a customer loyalty program

Customer loyalty programs are a popular marketing tool used by businesses to increase customer retention and loyalty. These programs offer customers rewards or benefits for their repeat business, with the aim of encouraging them to continue doing business with the company. In this case study, we will examine the financial impact of a customer loyalty program on a hypothetical business, and analyze the potential benefits and drawbacks of such a program.

Case Study

Company X is a retail business that sells a variety of consumer products. The company has been experiencing a decline in customer retention and has identified this as a major concern. To address this issue, the company decides to launch a customer loyalty program. The program offers customers discounts on future purchases, free products or services, and other incentives for their repeat business.

To determine the financial impact of the loyalty program, Company X analyzes the cost of implementing and managing the program, as well as the potential revenue generated from increased customer retention and loyalty. The company estimates that the cost of implementing the program will be $50,000 per year, which includes the cost of software, staff training, and marketing materials.

Benefits of the Customer Loyalty Program

Increased Revenue

The customer loyalty program is expected to lead to increased revenue for the company. The program encourages customers to make repeat purchases and to spend more money each time they visit the store. This increased spending can be attributed to the rewards and incentives offered by the program. As customers accumulate rewards points or receive discounts, they may be more likely to purchase additional items, or to purchase items at a higher price point.

Customer Retention

The loyalty program is also expected to increase customer retention for Company X. By offering incentives for repeat business, the program provides an additional reason for customers to choose Company X over competitors. This increased loyalty can translate into a higher lifetime customer value for the company, as customers are more likely to continue doing business with Company X over the long term.

Data Collection

To track the effectiveness of the program, Company X collects data on customer behavior and spending patterns before and after the launch of the loyalty program. This data can be used to determine the program's impact on customer retention and spending, and to make adjustments to the program over time.

Drawbacks of the Customer Loyalty Program

Costs

One major drawback of the customer loyalty program is the cost of implementation and management. As previously mentioned, Company X estimates the cost of implementing and managing the program to be $50,000 per year. This cost may be prohibitive for smaller businesses, or for businesses operating on a tight budget.

Discounting

Another potential drawback of the program is the impact of discounts on profit margins. By offering discounts to customers, Company X may be reducing its profit margin on each sale. While this may be offset by increased revenue from increased customer retention, it is important for the company to carefully analyze the impact of discounts on profit margins.

Conclusion

Overall, the financial impact of a customer loyalty program can be positive for businesses looking to increase customer retention and loyalty. By offering incentives for repeat business, the program can lead to increased revenue and higher lifetime customer value. However, businesses must carefully weigh the costs of implementing and managing the program against the potential benefits. Additionally, companies must be mindful of the impact of discounts on profit margins, and must monitor the program's effectiveness over time to ensure that it continues to generate positive results.

Exercise: Analyzing the financial impact of a marketing campaign or customer service initiative

Marketing campaigns and customer service initiatives can have a significant impact on a company's financial performance. Analyzing the financial impact of these initiatives is essential for companies to make informed decisions about their marketing and customer service strategies. In this exercise, we will analyze the financial impact of a marketing campaign or customer service initiative for a hypothetical company. We will use financial metrics such as return on investment (ROI) and customer lifetime value (CLV) to assess the success of the initiative.

Step 1: Define the Initiative

The first step in analyzing the financial impact of a marketing campaign or customer service initiative is to define the initiative. For this exercise, let's assume that the initiative is a marketing campaign aimed at increasing sales of a new product line. The campaign will include social media advertising, email marketing, and influencer partnerships. The goal of the campaign is to increase sales of the new product line by 20% over the next six months.

Step 2: Determine the Cost of the Initiative

The next step is to determine the cost of the initiative. The cost will include the cost of creating and running the campaign, as well as any costs associated with creating new products or services. For this exercise, let's assume that the total cost of the initiative is $50,000.

Step 3: Calculate the Return on Investment (ROI)

The ROI is a financial metric used to measure the success of an initiative. It is calculated by dividing the net profit by the total cost of the initiative. For this exercise, let's assume that the net profit from the initiative is $100,000. Using the formula, the ROI is calculated as follows:

ROI = (Net Profit / Total Cost) x 100%
ROI = ($100,000 / $50,000) x 100%
ROI = 200%

A positive ROI of 200% indicates that the initiative is profitable and has generated significant returns for the company.

Step 4: Calculate the Customer Lifetime Value (CLV)

The customer lifetime value (CLV) is another important financial metric used to assess the success of a marketing campaign or customer service initiative. The CLV is calculated by multiplying the average customer value by the average customer lifespan. For this exercise, let's assume that the average customer value for the new product line is $500, and the average customer lifespan is 2 years. Using these assumptions, the CLV can be calculated as follows:

CLV = Average Customer Value x Average Customer Lifespan
CLV = $500 x 2
CLV = $1,000

This means that on average, each customer for the new product line is worth $1,000 in lifetime value to the company.

Step 5: Analyze the Results

Based on the financial metrics calculated above, it is clear that the marketing campaign has been successful. The ROI of 200% indicates that the campaign has generated significant returns for the company, while the CLV of $1,000 suggests that each customer for the new product line is valuable to the company over the long term. The company should continue to monitor the success of the campaign over time and adjust its marketing strategy accordingly.

Analyzing the financial impact of a marketing campaign or customer service initiative is crucial for companies to make informed decisions about their marketing and customer service strategies. By calculating financial metrics such as ROI and CLV, companies can assess the success of their initiatives and make necessary adjustments to improve their financial performance. This exercise has demonstrated the importance of analyzing the financial impact of initiatives and has provided a framework for how to do so.

PART 2: FINANCIAL ANALYSIS FOR NON-FINANCIAL PROFESSIONALS

Part 2 of this textbook focuses on financial analysis, which is the process of evaluating the financial health and performance of a business. Financial analysis is a critical skill for non-financial professionals to develop because it enables them to make informed decisions about the allocation of resources, investment opportunities, and overall business strategy.

Financial analysis involves the examination of a company's financial statements, including the income statement, balance sheet, and cash flow statement, to determine its profitability, liquidity, and solvency. This information is used to assess a company's ability to generate income, manage its debts and expenses, and invest in future growth.

The financial analysis process is complex and requires an understanding of accounting principles, financial ratios, and financial forecasting. Non-financial professionals may find the terminology and concepts associated with financial analysis daunting, but with practice, it is possible to master these skills and use them to make better business decisions.

In this part of the textbook, we will explore the basics of financial analysis, including financial statement analysis, ratio analysis, and financial forecasting. We will also cover key financial metrics and terminology, including revenue, profit, cash flow, assets, liabilities, and equity.

Additionally, we will discuss the importance of financial analysis for different types of businesses, including startups, small businesses, and publicly-traded companies. We will examine case studies and provide exercises to help students apply financial analysis concepts in real-world scenarios.

By the end of this part, students will have a comprehensive understanding of financial analysis and its importance for making informed business decisions. They will also have practical skills that they can apply in their future careers as non-financial professionals.

CHAPTER 3: INTRODUCTION TO FINANCIAL STATEMENTS AND THEIR IMPORTANCE

Chapter 3 focuses on introducing financial statements and their importance to business professionals. Financial statements are key documents that provide information about a company's financial position and performance. They are critical to the decision-making process of investors, creditors, and other stakeholders, as they provide information about the company's profitability, liquidity, solvency, and overall financial health.

In this chapter, we will explore the three main financial statements: the balance sheet, the income statement, and the cash flow statement. We will discuss their purpose, the information they provide, and how to interpret the data presented. We will also delve into the importance of financial statements in making business decisions, including investment and financing decisions.

In addition, this chapter will introduce several key financial ratios, which are important tools for analyzing financial statements. Ratios help to identify trends and patterns in financial data and can provide insight into a company's financial health. We will discuss how to calculate and interpret ratios such as liquidity ratios, profitability ratios, and debt ratios.

By the end of this chapter, readers will have a solid understanding of the key financial statements and ratios used in business and finance, as well as their importance in decision-making. This knowledge is essential for any business professional, regardless of their role or industry, as financial statements and ratios are integral to understanding a company's financial performance and potential.

Examples, Problems, and Exercises

Review the balance sheet, income statement, and cash flow statement for a publicly traded company. Analyze the information presented and identify key trends and patterns in the data. What insights can you draw from the financial statements about the company's financial health and performance?

Calculate and analyze liquidity ratios, such as the current ratio and quick ratio, for a company of your choice. How do these ratios compare to industry averages? What insights can you draw from the ratios about the company's liquidity?

Using financial statements from two companies in the same industry, calculate and compare profitability ratios, such as return on assets and return on equity. What insights can you draw from the ratios about the relative profitability of the two companies?

In a group project, analyze the financial statements and ratios for a small business. Identify potential strengths and weaknesses in the company's financial performance, and make recommendations for improvement. Present your findings and recommendations to the class.

Research a recent financial scandal involving a public company. What financial statements and ratios could have been used to identify warning signs of the scandal? How could the scandal have been prevented or mitigated if these warning signs had been recognized and addressed in a timely manner?

Understanding the purpose and components of financial statements (balance sheet, income statement, cash flow statement)

Financial statements are a crucial aspect of any business's financial management. They are used to present financial information about a company to both internal and external stakeholders. Understanding financial statements and the information they provide is essential for making informed business decisions. In this chapter, we will discuss the purpose and components of financial statements, including the balance sheet, income statement, and cash flow statement.

Purpose of Financial Statements

The primary purpose of financial statements is to provide information to stakeholders about a company's financial performance and position. This information can be used to make informed decisions about investing, lending, and managing a business. Financial statements are also used by internal stakeholders, such as management, to evaluate a company's financial performance and make strategic decisions.

Components of Financial Statements

There are three primary financial statements: the balance sheet, the income statement, and the cash flow statement. Each statement provides different information about a company's financial position and performance.

Balance Sheet

The balance sheet is a snapshot of a company's financial position at a specific point in time. It provides information about a company's assets, liabilities, and equity. The balance sheet equation is Assets = Liabilities + Equity. This equation must always balance, which means that the total assets must equal the total liabilities and equity.

The balance sheet is divided into two sections: the assets section and the liabilities and equity section. The assets section includes current assets, such as cash and accounts receivable, and long-term assets, such as property, plant, and equipment. The liabilities and equity section includes current liabilities, such as accounts payable, and long-term liabilities, such as loans and bonds, as well as equity.

The balance sheet provides information about a company's liquidity, or its ability to meet short-term obligations, as well as its solvency, or its ability to meet long-term obligations.

Income Statement

The income statement, also known as the profit and loss statement, provides information about a company's revenue and expenses over a specific period, typically a year or a quarter. The income statement equation is Revenue - Expenses = Net Income.

The income statement is divided into two sections: the revenue section and the expenses section. The revenue section includes sales revenue and other income, while the expenses section includes cost of goods sold, operating expenses, interest expense, and taxes.

The income statement provides information about a company's profitability, or its ability to generate income, as well as its operating efficiency.

Cash Flow Statement

The cash flow statement provides information about a company's cash inflows and outflows over a specific period, typically a year or a quarter. The cash flow statement equation is Cash Inflows - Cash Outflows = Net Cash Flow.

The cash flow statement is divided into three sections: operating activities, investing activities, and financing activities. Operating activities include cash inflows and outflows from the company's core business operations, such as sales and purchases. Investing activities include cash inflows and outflows from the company's investments, such as buying or selling property or equipment. Financing activities include cash inflows and outflows from the company's financing activities, such as issuing or repaying debt or issuing or buying back equity.

The cash flow statement provides information about a company's liquidity, or its ability to generate cash to meet its obligations, as well as its investment and financing activities.

Conclusion

Financial statements are essential for understanding a company's financial position and performance. The balance sheet provides information about a company's assets, liabilities, and equity, the income statement provides information about a company's revenue and expenses, and the cash flow statement provides information about a company's cash inflows and outflows. By understanding financial statements and the information they provide, stakeholders can make informed decisions about investing, lending, and managing a business.

The importance of financial statements for decision-making and performance evaluation

In today's fast-paced business environment, financial statements are a critical tool for decision-making and performance evaluation. Financial statements provide valuable insights into a company's financial health, including its profitability, liquidity, and solvency. Business owners, managers, investors, and other stakeholders use financial statements to make informed decisions about the allocation of resources, financing, and strategic planning.

This section will explore the importance of financial statements for decision-making and performance evaluation. We will discuss how financial statements are used to analyze a company's financial performance, including its profitability, liquidity, and solvency. We will also discuss the various components of financial statements and how they provide valuable information to stakeholders.

The Importance of Financial Statements for Decision-Making:

Financial statements are critical tools for decision-making, as they provide important information about a company's financial position, performance, and cash flow. Financial statements are used by business owners, managers, investors, creditors, and other stakeholders to make informed decisions about the allocation of resources, financing, and strategic planning.

For example, a business owner may use financial statements to evaluate the profitability of the company's operations and to identify areas where costs can be reduced. A manager may use financial statements to analyze the performance of individual business units and to identify areas where improvements can be made. An investor may use financial statements to evaluate the financial health of a company before making an investment decision.

Financial statements can also be used to evaluate a company's cash flow. Cash flow is a critical component of a company's financial health, as it indicates whether the company has enough cash on hand to meet its obligations. By analyzing a company's cash flow statement, stakeholders can identify areas where the company may be experiencing cash flow problems and take steps to address these issues.

The Importance of Financial Statements for Performance Evaluation:

Financial statements are also important tools for performance evaluation. By analyzing a company's financial statements, stakeholders can evaluate the company's financial performance over time and compare it to other companies in the same industry.

For example, a financial analyst may use financial statements to evaluate the profitability of a company over the past several years and to compare it to other companies in the same industry. This analysis can help the analyst identify trends and patterns in the company's financial performance and make recommendations for improvement.

Financial statements can also be used to evaluate a company's liquidity and solvency. Liquidity refers to a company's ability to meet its short-term obligations, while solvency refers to its ability to meet its long-term obligations. By analyzing a company's balance sheet, stakeholders can evaluate the company's liquidity and solvency and identify areas where improvements can be made.

Components of Financial Statements:

Financial statements are comprised of three main components: the balance sheet, income statement, and cash flow statement. Each component provides different information about a company's financial health and is used for different purposes.

The balance sheet provides information about a company's assets, liabilities, and equity at a specific point in time. It is used to evaluate a company's liquidity and solvency and to calculate various financial ratios, such as the debt-to-equity ratio and the current ratio.

The income statement provides information about a company's revenues, expenses, and net income over a specific period of time. It is used to evaluate a company's profitability and to calculate various financial ratios, such as the gross profit margin and the net profit margin.

The cash flow statement provides information about a company's cash inflows and outflows over a specific period of time. It is used to evaluate a company's cash flow and to identify areas where cash flow problems may be occurring.

Conclusion:

In conclusion, financial statements are critical tools for decision-making and performance evaluation. They provide important information about a company's financial position, performance, and cash flow. Business owners, managers, investors , creditors, and other stakeholders rely on financial statements to make informed decisions about a company.

Understanding financial statements is essential for non-financial professionals, as they are often involved in decision-making processes that can have significant financial implications. By gaining a solid understanding of financial statements, non-financial professionals can effectively evaluate the financial health of a company and make informed decisions.

It is important to note that financial statements should not be analyzed in isolation. They should be considered in conjunction with other factors, such as industry trends, economic conditions, and the competitive landscape, to gain a comprehensive understanding of a company's financial position and performance.

Moreover, financial statements can be used to identify areas for improvement and growth, which can lead to more effective decision-making and improved performance. For example, by analyzing financial statements, a company may identify areas where it can reduce costs, increase revenue, or improve operational efficiency.

Finally, it is important to keep in mind that financial statements are not infallible. There may be limitations to the accuracy and completeness of the information presented in financial statements. As such, it is important to exercise caution when relying solely on financial statements to make important decisions.

In summary, financial statements are essential tools for decision-making and performance evaluation. They provide important information about a company's financial position, performance, and cash flow. Non-financial professionals should strive to gain a solid understanding of financial statements to effectively evaluate the financial health of a company and make informed decisions. However, financial statements should be analyzed in conjunction with other factors and used cautiously, as there may be limitations to their accuracy and completeness.

Practical examples of financial statements for different types of businesses

In the previous sections, we have discussed the importance of financial statements and their components. Now, we will provide practical examples of financial statements for different types of businesses. These examples will illustrate how financial statements can be used to assess a company's financial health and make informed business decisions.

Financial statements for small businesses:
Small businesses are typically privately owned and have fewer than 500 employees. As such, their financial statements are typically simpler than those of larger companies. Small businesses typically produce three financial statements: a balance sheet, an income statement, and a cash flow statement.

a) Balance sheet:

A balance sheet is a financial statement that reports a company's assets, liabilities, and equity at a specific point in time. It shows what a company owns, what it owes, and what is left over for the owners. Here's an example of a balance sheet for a small retail store:

Balance Sheet
As of December 31, 2021
Assets

Current assets
Cash $10,000
Inventory $25,000
Total current assets $35,000

Fixed assets
Equipment $15,000
Less accumulated depreciation ($2,000) $13,000
Total fixed assets $13,000

Total assets $48,000

Liabilities and Equity
Current liabilities
Accounts payable $5,000
Short-term loan $10,000
Total current liabilities $15,000

Long-term liabilities
Mortgage loan $18,000
Total long-term liabilities $18,000

Owners' equity
Retained earnings $15,000
Total owners' equity $15,000

Total liabilities and equity $48,000

In this example, the balance sheet shows that the retail store has assets totaling $48,000, which are financed by $33,000 in liabilities and $15,000 in owners' equity.

b) Income statement:

An income statement is a financial statement that reports a company's revenues, expenses, and net income over a period of time. It shows how much money a company made or lost during the period. Here's an example of an income statement for the same small retail store:

Income Statement
For the year ended December 31, 2021
Revenues
Sales revenue $100,000

Cost of goods sold
Beginning inventory $0
Purchases $50,000
Ending inventory ($25,000)
Total cost of goods sold $25,000

Gross profit $75,000

Expenses
Rent $10,000
Utilities $5,000
Salaries and wages $30,000
Depreciation $2,000
Total expenses $47,000

Net income $28,000

In this example, the income statement shows that the retail store generated $100,000 in sales revenue and had expenses of $47,000, resulting in a net income of $28,000.

c) Cash flow statement:

A cash flow statement is a financial statement that reports a company's cash inflows and outflows over a period of time. It shows how much cash a company generated or used during the period. Here's an example of a cash flow statement for the same small retail store:

Cash Flow Statement
For the year ended December 31, 2021
Cash flows from operating activities
Net income $28,000
Depreciation $2,000
Increase in accounts payable $5,000
Increase in short-term loan $10,000
Net cash provided by operating activities $45,000

Cash flows from investing activities
Purchase of equipment ($15,000)
Net cash used by investing activities ($15,000)

Cash flows from financing activities
Proceeds from long-term loan $20,000
Repayment of long-term loan ($5,000)
Payment of dividends ($10,000)
Net cash provided by financing activities $5,000

Net increase in cash and cash equivalents $35,000
Cash and cash equivalents, beginning of year $15,000
Cash and cash equivalents, end of year $50,000

In this example, we see a company's cash flows for the year ended December 31, 2021. The statement is divided into three sections: cash flows from operating activities, cash flows from investing activities, and cash flows from financing activities.

The cash flows from operating activities section shows the cash generated from the company's primary operations, which is the sale of goods or services. In this example, the company generated $45,000 in cash from operating activities. This includes the net income of $28,000 and the depreciation of $2,000, which is a non-cash expense. Additionally, there was an increase in accounts payable of $5,000, which means the company had to pay more to suppliers during the year. The company also took out a short-term loan of $10,000, which is a source of cash.

The cash flows from investing activities section shows the cash used for investing in long-term assets, such as equipment, buildings, or investments. In this example, the company spent $15,000 on equipment, which is a use of cash.

The cash flows from financing activities section shows the cash used to finance the company's operations, such as obtaining loans or issuing stock, as well as the cash returned to shareholders. In this example, the company received $20,000 from a long-term loan and repaid $5,000 of that loan. The company also paid $10,000 in dividends to its shareholders. This section shows the cash inflows and outflows related to financing activities.

The statement ends with the net increase in cash and cash equivalents, which is the difference between the beginning and ending balances of cash and cash equivalents. In this example, the company had a net increase in cash of $35,000, which increased the cash balance from $15,000 to $50,000.

It is important to note that the cash flow statement provides information about a company's cash inflows and outflows but does not provide information about its profitability or financial position. Investors and analysts may use the statement to assess a company's ability to generate cash from its operations and to determine how the company is financing its operations.

Case study: Analyzing the financial statements of a publicly traded company

Analyzing financial statements is an important skill for investors and financial analysts. By reviewing financial statements, one can gain insight into a company's financial health and make informed decisions about whether to invest in the company or not. In this case study, we will analyze the financial statements of a publicly traded company, XYZ Corporation, to gain an understanding of its financial position and performance.

Background Information

XYZ Corporation is a multinational technology company that specializes in software development, computer hardware, and other technology products. The company is publicly traded on the New York Stock Exchange (NYSE) and has a market capitalization of $200 billion. The company has a strong reputation in the technology industry and is known for its innovative products and services.

Financial Statements

To analyze XYZ Corporation's financial position and performance, we will review the company's financial statements for the year ended December 31, 2021. The financial statements include the following:

Balance Sheet
Income Statement
Cash Flow Statement
Balance Sheet

The balance sheet provides a snapshot of a company's financial position at a specific point in time. It lists the company's assets, liabilities, and shareholders' equity. Below is XYZ Corporation's balance sheet as of December 31, 2021:

XYZ Corporation
Balance Sheet (in millions)

Assets
Current assets:
Cash and cash equivalents $10,000

Accounts receivable $20,000
Inventory $15,000
Total current assets $45,000

Long-term investments $20,000
Property, plant and equipment $80,000
Total assets $145,000

Liabilities and Shareholders' Equity
Current liabilities:
Accounts payable $10,000
Short-term debt $5,000
Total current liabilities $15,000

Long-term debt $40,000
Shareholders' equity $90,000
Total liabilities and shareholders' equity $145,000

The balance sheet shows that XYZ Corporation has $145 billion in total assets, with $45 billion in current assets, $20 billion in long-term investments, and $80 billion in property, plant and equipment. The company's liabilities include $15 billion in current liabilities and $40 billion in long-term debt. Shareholders' equity is listed at $90 billion, indicating that the company has a strong financial foundation.

Income Statement

The income statement, also known as the profit and loss statement, provides information on a company's revenue and expenses over a specific period. Below is XYZ Corporation's income statement for the year ended December 31, 2021:

XYZ Corporation
Income Statement (in millions)

Revenue $100,000
Cost of goods sold $40,000
Gross profit $60,000

Operating expenses $30,000
Operating income $30,000

Interest expense $5,000
Income before taxes $25,000

Income tax expense $7,000
Net income $18,000

The income statement shows that XYZ Corporation generated $100 billion in revenue and had a gross profit of $60 billion after deducting $40 billion for the cost of goods sold. The company's operating expenses are listed at $30 billion, resulting in an operating income of $30 billion. The company paid $5 billion in interest expense and $7 billion in income tax, resulting in a net income of $18 billion.

Cash Flow Statement

The cash flow statement provides information on a company's cash inflows and outflows over a specific period. It includes cash flows from operating, investing, and financing activities. Below is XYZ Corporation's cash flow statement for the year ended December 31, 2021:

XYZ Corporation
Cash Flow Statement (in millions)

Cash flows from operating activities:
Net income $250
Adjustments to reconcile net income to net cash provided by operating activities:
Depreciation and amortization $50
Stock-based compensation expense $10
Increase in accounts receivable ($20)
Increase in inventory ($30)
Decrease in accounts payable ($5)
Net cash provided by operating activities $255

Cash flows from investing activities:
Purchases of property and equipment ($100)
Proceeds from sale of investments $20
Net cash used in investing activities ($80)

Cash flows from financing activities:
Proceeds from long-term debt $150
Repayment of long-term debt ($50)
Dividends paid to shareholders ($20)
Net cash provided by financing activities $80

Net increase in cash and cash equivalents $255

Analysis:

The cash flow statement provides valuable information about a company's ability to generate cash from its operations and investments, as well as its financing activities. In this case, XYZ Corporation generated a net cash inflow of $255 million from operating activities, which indicates that the company was able to generate sufficient cash from its operations to cover its expenses and fund its investments.

However, the company also had a net cash outflow of $80 million from investing activities, which suggests that it invested heavily in property and equipment during the year. This could be a positive sign, indicating that the company is investing in its future growth and development. However, it could also be a concern if the investments are not generating the expected returns.

In terms of financing activities, the company generated a net cash inflow of $80 million, primarily from the issuance of long-term debt. This could be a concern if the company is relying heavily on debt to finance its operations, as it could lead to increased financial risk if the debt cannot be repaid.

Overall, the cash flow statement provides valuable insights into XYZ Corporation's financial health and performance, highlighting its ability to generate cash from operations, its investment activities, and its financing activities. By analyzing the cash flow statement, investors and other stakeholders can gain a better understanding of the company's financial position and make informed decisions about their investments.

Exercise: Creating a simple set of financial statements for a hypothetical business

In this exercise, we will walk through the process of creating a simple set of financial statements for a hypothetical business. The business we will be working with is a small retail store that sells clothing and accessories. The store has been in operation for one year and is owned by a single individual.

Balance Sheet

The balance sheet is a snapshot of a company's financial position at a specific point in time. It shows the company's assets, liabilities, and equity.

To create the balance sheet for our hypothetical retail store, we will need to gather information about the company's assets and liabilities as of December 31, 2021. We will assume that the company has the following information:

Cash: $10,000
Inventory: $20,000
Furniture and Fixtures: $5,000
Accounts Payable: $5,000
Owner's Equity: $30,000
Using this information, we can create the following balance sheet:

Hypothetical Retail Store
Balance Sheet (as of December 31, 2021)

Assets:
Cash: $10,000
Inventory: $20,000
Furniture and Fixtures: $5,000
Total Assets: $35,000

Liabilities:
Accounts Payable: $5,000
Total Liabilities: $5,000

Owner's Equity:
Owner's Equity: $30,000
Total Liabilities and Owner's Equity: $35,000

Income Statement

The income statement shows a company's revenues, expenses, and net income or loss over a specific period. To create the income statement for our hypothetical retail store, we will need to gather information about the company's revenues and expenses for the year ended December 31, 2021. We will assume that the company has the following information:

Sales Revenue: $100,000
Cost of Goods Sold: $50,000
Rent Expense: $10,000
Wages Expense: $20,000
Supplies Expense: $5,000
Utilities Expense: $2,000

Insurance Expense: $1,000
Depreciation Expense: $500
Using this information, we can create the following income statement:

Hypothetical Retail Store
Income Statement (for the year ended December 31, 2021)

Revenue:
Sales Revenue: $100,000

Expenses:
Cost of Goods Sold: $50,000
Rent Expense: $10,000
Wages Expense: $20,000
Supplies Expense: $5,000
Utilities Expense: $2,000
Insurance Expense: $1,000
Depreciation Expense: $500
Total Expenses: $88,500

Net Income: $11,500

Cash Flow Statement

The cash flow statement shows a company's cash inflows and outflows over a specific period. To create the cash flow statement for our hypothetical retail store, we will need to gather information about the company's cash inflows and outflows for the year ended December 31, 2021. We will assume that the company has the following information:

Net Income: $11,500
Depreciation Expense: $500
Increase in Accounts Payable: $2,000
Increase in Inventory: $5,000
Using this information, we can create the following cash flow statement:

Hypothetical Retail Store
Cash Flow Statement (for the year ended December 31, 2021)

Cash Flows from Operating Activities:
Net Income: $11,500
Depreciation Expense: $500

Increase in Accounts Payable: $2,000
Cash Flow Statement (for the year ended December 31, 2021)

Cash Flows from Operating Activities:
Net Income: $11,500
Depreciation Expense: $500
Increase in Accounts Payable: $2,000
Cash Flows from Operating Activities: $14,000

Cash Flows from Investing Activities:
Purchase of Equipment: ($5,000)
Cash Flows from Investing Activities: ($5,000)

Cash Flows from Financing Activities:
Increase in Long-term Debt: $4,000
Payment of Dividends: ($2,000)
Cash Flows from Financing Activities: $2,000

Net Increase in Cash: $11,000

The cash flow statement shows the inflows and outflows of cash for the retail store for the year ended December 31, 2021. The statement is divided into three categories: operating activities, investing activities, and financing activities.

In the operating activities section, the retail store had a net income of $11,500. The store also had $500 in depreciation expenses and an increase in accounts payable of $2,000. These activities generated cash flows of $14,000 from operating activities.

In the investing activities section, the retail store had a cash outflow of $5,000 due to the purchase of equipment.

In the financing activities section, the retail store had an increase in long-term debt of $4,000 and paid out $2,000 in dividends. These activities resulted in a net cash inflow of $2,000 from financing activities.

Finally, the net increase in cash for the retail store was $11,000, indicating that the store had more cash at the end of the year than at the beginning of the year.

It is important for business owners to regularly create and analyze their financial statements in order to make informed decisions about their business. By creating a set of financial statements, a business owner can gain a better understanding of their financial position and make strategic decisions about how to grow their business.

CHAPTER 4: UNDERSTANDING KEY FINANCIAL METRICS AND RATIOS

In the world of finance, there are a variety of financial metrics and ratios that are used to assess the health and performance of a company. These metrics and ratios provide insights into a company's financial position, profitability, liquidity, solvency, and efficiency. They are used by investors, lenders, creditors, and other stakeholders to make informed decisions regarding a company's prospects and potential risks.

This chapter will provide an overview of the key financial metrics and ratios that are commonly used in financial analysis. We will explore the purpose and significance of these metrics and ratios, how they are calculated, and how they can be used to evaluate a company's financial performance.

The first section of this chapter will cover financial metrics, which are quantitative measures of a company's financial performance. We will discuss metrics such as revenue, net income, gross margin, and operating margin. These metrics provide a broad overview of a company's financial performance and are often used to compare the performance of companies within the same industry.

The second section of this chapter will focus on financial ratios, which are calculated by dividing one financial metric by another. Ratios are used to provide a more detailed and nuanced view of a company's financial performance. We will explore ratios such as the current ratio, debt-to-equity ratio, return on equity, and return on assets.

The third section of this chapter will cover some of the limitations of financial metrics and ratios. While these tools are valuable for assessing a company's financial performance, they are not without their limitations. We will discuss factors such as industry-specific metrics, changes in accounting standards, and the limitations of financial statements.

Finally, we will provide an exercise for students to practice calculating and interpreting financial metrics and ratios. This exercise will involve creating financial statements for a hypothetical business and using financial metrics and ratios to analyze its financial performance.

Overall, this chapter will provide a comprehensive introduction to financial metrics and ratios. By the end of the chapter, students should have a solid understanding of the key financial tools used in financial analysis and be able to apply them to real-world scenarios.

The importance of financial metrics and ratios for performance evaluation and decision-making

In the world of finance and business, financial metrics and ratios are used to evaluate the performance of a company and make important decisions. These metrics and ratios provide valuable insights into a company's financial health and can be used by a wide range of stakeholders, including investors, lenders, managers, and analysts.

Financial metrics and ratios are essential tools for understanding a company's financial statements, including the income statement, balance sheet, and cash flow statement. By analyzing these statements, investors and other stakeholders can gain a deeper understanding of a company's financial performance, profitability, and liquidity.

In this chapter, we will explore the importance of financial metrics and ratios for performance evaluation and decision-making. We will discuss some of the most commonly used financial metrics and ratios, and explain how they can be used to analyze a company's financial performance. We will also provide examples of how financial metrics and ratios can be used to make informed decisions about investing, lending, and managing a company.

Why Financial Metrics and Ratios are Important

Financial metrics and ratios are important for a variety of reasons. First, they provide a snapshot of a company's financial performance at a given point in time. This allows investors and other stakeholders to assess the financial health of a company and make informed decisions about investing, lending, and managing.

Second, financial metrics and ratios can be used to compare a company's financial performance to industry benchmarks and competitors. This can help investors and other stakeholders identify trends, spot potential problems, and make informed decisions about investing, lending, and managing.

Third, financial metrics and ratios can be used to evaluate a company's financial health over time. By tracking key financial metrics and ratios over a period of time, investors and other stakeholders can identify trends, spot potential problems, and make informed decisions about investing, lending, and managing.

Finally, financial metrics and ratios can be used to evaluate a company's financial performance in relation to its strategic goals and objectives. By analyzing financial metrics and ratios in the context of a company's strategic goals and objectives, investors and other stakeholders can determine whether the company is on track to achieve its goals, and make informed decisions about investing, lending, and managing.

Commonly Used Financial Metrics and Ratios

There are a wide variety of financial metrics and ratios that can be used to analyze a company's financial performance. Some of the most commonly used metrics and ratios include:

Profitability ratios: These ratios are used to measure a company's ability to generate profits. Common profitability ratios include gross profit margin, operating profit margin, and net profit margin.

Liquidity ratios: These ratios are used to measure a company's ability to meet its short-term obligations. Common liquidity ratios include the current ratio, quick ratio, and cash ratio.

Debt ratios: These ratios are used to measure a company's ability to manage its debt. Common debt ratios include the debt-to-equity ratio, the debt-to-assets ratio, and the interest coverage ratio.

Efficiency ratios: These ratios are used to measure a company's ability to manage its resources efficiently. Common efficiency ratios include inventory turnover, accounts receivable turnover, and accounts payable turnover.

Valuation ratios: These ratios are used to measure a company's valuation relative to its earnings or assets. Common valuation ratios include the price-to-earnings ratio, the price-to-book ratio, and the enterprise value-to-EBITDA ratio.

Using Financial Metrics and Ratios for Performance Evaluation and Decision-Making

Financial metrics and ratios can be used for a wide range of performance evaluation and decision-making purposes. Some of the most common uses of financial metrics and ratios include:

Investment decisions: Investors can use financial metrics and ratios to assess the potential risks and rewards of investing in a particular company or industry. For example, a high price-to-earnings (P/E) ratio may indicate that a company's stock is overvalued, while a low P/E ratio may indicate that the stock is undervalued. Similarly, investors can use return on investment (ROI) and return on equity (ROE) metrics to evaluate the profitability and efficiency of a company, and make informed investment decisions.

Credit decisions: Lenders and creditors use financial metrics and ratios to assess the creditworthiness of a company before extending credit. For instance, they may use the debt-to-equity (D/E) ratio to determine the amount of leverage a company has, or the interest coverage ratio to assess a company's ability to service its debt. A low D/E ratio may suggest that a company has a low level of debt and is therefore less risky to lend to, while a high interest coverage ratio may indicate that a company has sufficient cash flow to cover its debt obligations.

Operational decisions: Financial metrics and ratios can also be used to assess the operational efficiency of a company. For example, inventory turnover ratio can be used to determine how quickly a company's inventory is sold, while the asset turnover ratio can help to evaluate how effectively a company is using its assets to generate revenue. Additionally, financial metrics and ratios can be used to identify areas where a company may need to make improvements in order to increase its profitability or efficiency.

Comparative analysis: Financial metrics and ratios can be used to compare the performance of different companies or industries. For example, investors may compare the financial metrics of companies in the same industry to identify trends or outliers. Similarly, companies may use financial metrics and ratios to benchmark their performance against industry averages or the performance of their competitors.

Forecasting: Financial metrics and ratios can also be used to make forecasts and projections about a company's future performance. For instance, a company may use past revenue growth rates to predict future revenue growth, or use past net income margins to forecast future profitability.

Overall, financial metrics and ratios provide a valuable tool for performance evaluation and decision-making. They allow investors, creditors, and managers to make informed decisions based on objective and quantitative data, rather than relying solely on subjective opinions or intuition. However, it's important to note that financial metrics and ratios should not be used in isolation, and should always be considered in conjunction with other relevant factors such as industry trends, economic conditions, and company-specific factors.

Key financial metrics and ratios (liquidity ratios, profitability ratios, efficiency ratios, leverage ratios)

Financial metrics and ratios are used by businesses to analyze their financial health, evaluate their performance, and make informed decisions. There are many financial metrics and ratios available, but the most commonly used ones fall into four categories: liquidity ratios, profitability ratios, efficiency ratios, and leverage ratios.

Liquidity Ratios

Liquidity ratios measure a company's ability to meet its short-term obligations. These ratios provide insight into the company's ability to pay its bills and meet its financial obligations on time. The most common liquidity ratios are:

Current Ratio: The current ratio measures a company's ability to pay its current liabilities with its current assets. The formula for calculating the current ratio is:
Current Ratio = Current Assets / Current Liabilities

A current ratio of 1.5 or higher is generally considered to be healthy, indicating that the company has enough current assets to pay its current liabilities.

Quick Ratio: The quick ratio, also known as the acid-test ratio, measures a company's ability to meet its short-term obligations with its most liquid assets. The formula for calculating the quick ratio is:
Quick Ratio = (Current Assets - Inventory) / Current Liabilities

A quick ratio of 1 or higher is generally considered to be healthy, indicating that the company has enough liquid assets to pay its current liabilities.

Profitability Ratios

Profitability ratios measure a company's ability to generate profits. These ratios provide insight into the company's ability to generate profits from its operations. The most common profitability ratios are:

Gross Profit Margin: The gross profit margin measures the percentage of sales that is left after deducting the cost of goods sold. The formula for calculating the gross profit margin is:

Gross Profit Margin = (Gross Profit / Sales) x 100

A higher gross profit margin indicates that the company is generating more profit per dollar of sales.

Net Profit Margin: The net profit margin measures the percentage of sales that is left after deducting all expenses, including interest and taxes. The formula for calculating the net profit margin is:

Net Profit Margin = (Net Profit / Sales) x 100

A higher net profit margin indicates that the company is generating more profit per dollar of sales.

Efficiency Ratios

Efficiency ratios measure a company's ability to manage its assets and liabilities to generate revenue. These ratios provide insight into the company's operational efficiency. The most common efficiency ratios are:

Inventory Turnover Ratio: The inventory turnover ratio measures how quickly a company sells its inventory. The formula for calculating the inventory turnover ratio is:

Inventory Turnover Ratio = Cost of Goods Sold / Average Inventory

A higher inventory turnover ratio indicates that the company is selling its inventory more quickly.

Accounts Receivable Turnover Ratio: The accounts receivable turnover ratio measures how quickly a company collects its accounts receivable. The formula for calculating the accounts receivable turnover ratio is:

Accounts Receivable Turnover Ratio = Sales / Average Accounts Receivable

A higher accounts receivable turnover ratio indicates that the company is collecting its accounts receivable more quickly.

Leverage Ratios

Leverage ratios measure a company's level of debt and its ability to repay its debt. These ratios provide insight into the company's financial risk. The most common leverage ratios are:

Debt-to-Equity Ratio: The debt-to-equity ratio measures the amount of debt a company has relative to its equity. The formula for calculating the debt-to-equity ratio is:
Debt-to-Equity Ratio = Total Liabilities / Total Equity

A lower debt-to-equity ratio indicates that the company has less debt relative to its equity.

Interest Coverage Ratio: The interest coverage ratio measures a company's ability to pay its interest expense. The formula for calculating the interest coverage ratio is:

Interest Coverage Ratio = Earnings Before Interest and Taxes (EBIT) / Interest Expense

This ratio indicates the number of times a company can cover its interest expense with its earnings before interest and taxes. A higher interest coverage ratio indicates that the company is more capable of paying its interest expense.

Debt-to-Asset Ratio: The debt-to-asset ratio measures the percentage of a company's assets that are financed by debt. The formula for calculating the debt-to-asset ratio is:

Debt-to-Asset Ratio = Total Liabilities / Total Assets

This ratio indicates the extent to which a company is using debt to finance its assets. A higher debt-to-asset ratio indicates that the company has a higher level of debt relative to its assets.

Leverage ratios are important for lenders and investors as they provide information about a company's financial risk. A company with a high level of debt may be more vulnerable to changes in interest rates or economic conditions. Lenders and investors will want to see that a company is capable of repaying its debt and has a plan for managing its debt levels.

For example, a bank considering a loan to a company with a high debt-to-equity ratio may be hesitant to provide financing without additional collateral or a higher interest rate. Similarly, investors may be less likely to invest in a company with a high debt-to-asset ratio, as it may indicate a higher level of financial risk.

It is important to note that leverage ratios should be considered in conjunction with other financial metrics and ratios, as well as qualitative factors such as management experience and industry trends. A company may have a high debt-to-equity ratio, for example, but if it has a strong cash flow and solid growth prospects, it may still be an attractive investment opportunity. Conversely, a company with a low debt-to-equity ratio may not be a good investment if it is not generating sufficient earnings or experiencing operational difficulties.

How financial metrics and ratios can vary by industry and company size

Financial metrics and ratios play a critical role in evaluating a company's financial health and making informed decisions about investments, financing, and operations. However, it's important to note that financial metrics and ratios can vary significantly by industry and company size. This section will explore how financial metrics and ratios can vary in different industries and company sizes and the factors that can influence their variation.

Variation in Financial Metrics and Ratios by Industry

Different industries have unique characteristics that can affect their financial metrics and ratios. For example, some industries may require high levels of capital investment, while others may require minimal capital investment but have higher operating expenses. Therefore, a financial metric that is considered healthy in one industry may not be appropriate for another industry.

To illustrate this point, consider the debt-to-equity ratio, which measures a company's debt relative to its equity. A higher debt-to-equity ratio may be acceptable in industries such as telecommunications or utilities, which require significant capital investments, but may not be acceptable in industries such as retail or hospitality, where capital investments are lower. Similarly, the profit margins of technology companies tend to be higher than those of retail companies due to their economies of scale and lower operating expenses.

Efficiency ratios such as inventory turnover and days sales outstanding can also vary significantly across industries. For example, retailers may have high inventory turnover ratios, while manufacturers may have lower inventory turnover ratios due to their longer production cycles. Similarly, the days sales outstanding metric, which measures the number of days it takes a company to collect its outstanding accounts receivable, may be longer in industries such as construction or consulting, where payment terms are typically longer.

Profitability ratios such as return on equity (ROE) and return on assets (ROA) can also vary by industry. For example, high ROE ratios are common in industries such as finance and technology, while low ROE ratios are common in industries such as retail and hospitality due to their lower profit margins.

Variation in Financial Metrics and Ratios by Company Size
In addition to industry differences, financial metrics and ratios can also vary by company size. Smaller companies may have different financial metrics and ratios than larger companies due to their different capital structures and growth prospects.

For example, small companies may have higher debt-to-equity ratios than larger companies due to their limited access to capital markets. Additionally, smaller companies may have higher operating expenses and lower profit margins than larger companies due to their limited economies of scale.

Efficiency ratios such as inventory turnover and days sales outstanding can also vary by company size. For example, smaller companies may have lower inventory turnover ratios than larger companies due to their limited bargaining power with suppliers. Similarly, smaller companies may have longer days sales outstanding metrics than larger companies due to their limited access to credit and slower payment cycles.

Profitability ratios such as ROE and ROA can also vary by company size. Smaller companies may have higher ROE ratios than larger companies due to their higher risk profiles and potential for growth. However, larger companies may have higher ROA ratios than smaller companies due to their greater economies of scale and access to capital markets.

Factors Influencing Variation in Financial Metrics and Ratios
The variation in financial metrics and ratios across industries and company sizes can be influenced by several factors, including:

Capital structure: The capital structure of a company can affect its financial metrics and ratios. For example, companies with higher levels of debt may have higher interest expenses, leading to lower profitability ratios.

Growth prospects: The growth prospects of a company can affect its financial metrics and ratios. Companies with high growth prospects may have higher valuations and higher price-to-earnings (P/E) ratios.

Competitive landscape: The competitive landscape of an industry can affect its financial metrics and ratios. Industries with high competition may have lower profit margins, leading to lower profitability ratios.

Regulatory environment: The regulatory environment can affect financial metrics and ratios in industries that are heavily regulated. For example, healthcare companies may have higher levels of debt due to regulations that require them to maintain large reserves.

Business model: The business model of a company can also affect its financial metrics and ratios. For example, a company with a subscription-based model may have a higher customer lifetime value, leading to higher profitability ratios.

Company size: Company size can also play a role in the variation of financial metrics and ratios. Smaller companies may have lower profit margins due to higher operating costs, leading to lower profitability ratios.

In addition to these factors, financial metrics and ratios can also vary based on the specific accounting practices of a company. For example, companies that use aggressive accounting practices may have higher earnings per share (EPS) and higher P/E ratios, but may also have higher levels of financial risk.

It's important for investors and financial analysts to be aware of these factors when evaluating financial metrics and ratios, as they can impact the comparability of financial statements across industries and company sizes. In order to make meaningful comparisons, adjustments may need to be made to account for these differences.

For example, when comparing profitability ratios across industries with different levels of competition, it may be more meaningful to compare the ratios of companies within the same industry, rather than across industries. Similarly, when evaluating leverage ratios, it may be necessary to adjust for differences in the regulatory environment.

In conclusion, financial metrics and ratios are important tools for evaluating a company's financial performance and making informed investment decisions. However, they can vary significantly across industries and company sizes, and are influenced by a wide range of factors. It's important to be aware of these factors and make appropriate adjustments to ensure that comparisons are meaningful and accurate.

Practical examples of financial metrics and ratios for different types of businesses

Financial metrics and ratios can be applied to businesses of all sizes and industries to evaluate their financial health, performance, and potential risks. However, the types of financial metrics and ratios that are most relevant and useful may vary depending on the nature of the business. In this section, we will discuss practical examples of financial metrics and ratios for different types of businesses, including small businesses, publicly traded companies, and nonprofit organizations.

Small Businesses

Small businesses, which typically have limited financial resources and operate in a highly competitive market, need to carefully manage their finances to ensure their survival and growth. Some of the financial metrics and ratios that are particularly important for small businesses include:

Gross Profit Margin: The gross profit margin is the percentage of revenue that is left after deducting the cost of goods sold. It is a key indicator of a small business's ability to generate profits and cover its operating expenses.

Current Ratio: The current ratio measures a small business's ability to pay its short-term liabilities with its short-term assets. A current ratio of 1 or higher is generally considered to be a good indicator of a small business's liquidity.

Debt-to-Equity Ratio: The debt-to-equity ratio measures a small business's level of debt relative to its equity. A high debt-to-equity ratio can indicate that the business is relying too much on debt financing, which can increase its financial risk.

Customer Acquisition Cost: The customer acquisition cost measures the amount of money a small business spends to acquire a new customer. This metric is important for small businesses that rely on a limited customer base and need to maximize their marketing and sales efforts.

Publicly Traded Companies

Publicly traded companies, which are subject to strict financial reporting requirements and investor scrutiny, need to maintain a strong financial position to attract and retain investors. Some of the financial metrics and ratios that are particularly important for publicly traded companies include:

Price-to-Earnings Ratio: The price-to-earnings (P/E) ratio measures a company's stock price relative to its earnings per share. A high P/E ratio can indicate that investors are willing to pay a premium for the company's growth prospects.

Return on Equity: The return on equity (ROE) measures the amount of profit a company generates relative to its equity. A high ROE can indicate that a company is effectively using its resources to generate profits and create value for its shareholders.

Debt-to-Asset Ratio: The debt-to-asset ratio measures a company's level of debt relative to its total assets. A high debt-to-asset ratio can indicate that a company is relying too much on debt financing, which can increase its financial risk.

Dividend Yield: The dividend yield measures the annual dividend payout of a company relative to its stock price. This metric is important for investors who are looking for a steady income stream from their investments.

Nonprofit Organizations

Nonprofit organizations, which operate in a different financial context than for-profit businesses, need to manage their finances effectively to achieve their mission and goals. Some of the financial metrics and ratios that are particularly relevant for nonprofit organizations include:

Program Expense Ratio: The program expense ratio measures the percentage of a nonprofit organization's expenses that are directly related to its mission and programs. A high program expense ratio indicates that the organization is effectively using its resources to achieve its goals.

Fundraising Efficiency Ratio: The fundraising efficiency ratio measures the amount of money a nonprofit organization spends on fundraising relative to the amount of money it raises. A high fundraising efficiency ratio indicates that the organization is using its resources effectively to raise funds for its programs.

Cash Reserve Ratio: The cash reserve ratio measures the amount of cash and cash equivalents that a nonprofit organization has on hand relative to its annual expenses. This ratio is important because nonprofit organizations often face unpredictable revenue streams and may need to rely on reserves to meet their obligations. A high cash reserve ratio indicates that the organization is financially stable and prepared for unexpected expenses.

In addition to these ratios, there are other financial metrics that are important for nonprofits, such as:

Donor Retention Rate: The donor retention rate measures the percentage of donors who continue to give to the organization year after year. A high donor retention rate is a sign that the organization is effective at building and maintaining relationships with its supporters.

Volunteer Retention Rate: The volunteer retention rate measures the percentage of volunteers who continue to work with the organization year after year. A high volunteer retention rate is a sign that the organization is effective at engaging and motivating its volunteers.

Grant Funding Ratio: The grant funding ratio measures the percentage of a nonprofit organization's revenue that comes from grants. A high grant funding ratio indicates that the organization is successful at securing grant funding to support its programs.

Nonprofit organizations can also use financial metrics and ratios to evaluate their fundraising campaigns, such as:

Cost per Dollar Raised: The cost per dollar raised measures the amount of money a nonprofit organization spends on fundraising for every dollar it raises. A low cost per dollar raised is a sign that the organization is using its resources effectively to raise funds.

Return on Investment (ROI): The return on investment measures the amount of money a nonprofit organization raises for every dollar it spends on fundraising. A high ROI indicates that the organization is successful at raising funds and using its resources effectively.

Overall, financial metrics and ratios can help nonprofit organizations to make informed financial decisions and assess their financial performance. By tracking and analyzing these metrics, nonprofit organizations can ensure that they are effectively managing their finances and using their resources to achieve their mission and goals.

Case study: Analyzing financial ratios of two competing companies

Analyzing financial ratios is an essential part of financial analysis, as it provides insights into the financial health of a company. In this case study, we will analyze the financial ratios of two competing companies in the same industry to determine which one is in a better financial position. The two companies we will be analyzing are Company A and Company B, both of which are in the retail industry.

Company A

Company A is a well-established retail chain with over 500 stores across the country. The company has been in business for over 50 years and has a loyal customer base. Company A's financial statements for the year 2022 are as follows:

Income Statement:

Revenue	$5,000,000
COGS	$3,000,000
Gross Profit	$2,000,000
Operating Expenses	$1,200,000
Operating Income	$800,000
Interest Expense	$100,000
Net Income	$700,000

Balance Sheet:

Assets		Liabilities and Equity	
Current Assets		Current Liabilities	
Cash	$100,000	Accounts Payable	$300,000
Accounts Receivable	$200,000	Accrued Expenses	$50,000
Inventory	$500,000	Total Current Liabilities	$350,000
Total Current Assets	$800,000	Long-term Debt	$500,000
Property, Plant, and Equipment	$1,500,000	Total Liabilities	$850,000
Total Assets	$2,300,000	Shareholders' Equity	$1,450,000
		Total Liabilities and Equity	$2,300,000

Financial Ratios:

Ratio	Company A
Current Ratio	2.29
Quick Ratio	1.43
Debt-to-Equity Ratio	0.34
Gross Margin	40.0%

Operating Margin	16.0%
Return on Assets (ROA)	30.4%
Return on Equity (ROE)	48.3%

Company B

Company B is a new entrant in the retail industry, having opened its first store just two years ago. The company has been growing rapidly, but has yet to establish a strong customer base. Company B's financial statements for the year 2022 are as follows:

Income Statement:

Revenue	**$2,500,000**
COGS	$1,500,000
Gross Profit	$1,000,000
Operating Expenses	$800,000
Operating Income	$200,000
Interest Expense	$50,000
Net Income	$150,000

Balance Sheet:

Assets		**Liabilities and Equity**	
Current Assets		Current Liabilities	
Cash	$50,000	Accounts Payable	$150,000
Accounts Receivable	$100,000	Accrued Expenses	$30,000
Inventory	$300,000	Total Current Liabilities	$180,000
Total Current Assets	$450,000	Long-term Debt	$250,000
Property, Plant, and Equipment	$750,000	Total Liabilities	$430,000
Total Assets	$1,200,000	Shareholders' Equity	$

Based on the analysis of the financial ratios for both companies, it appears that Company A has performed better in terms of profitability and liquidity ratios, while

Company B has performed better in terms of efficiency and solvency ratios. However, it is important to note that financial ratios should not be analyzed in isolation, as they provide only a snapshot of a company's financial performance at a given point in time.

It is also important to consider the context in which the companies are operating. For example, Company A may have higher profitability ratios because it operates in a niche market with limited competition, while Company B operates in a highly competitive market with lower profit margins. Similarly, Company B may have higher efficiency ratios because it has implemented more efficient operational processes, while Company A may have lower efficiency ratios due to its focus on producing high-quality, artisanal products.

Overall, the analysis of financial ratios for these two companies highlights the importance of considering both quantitative and qualitative factors when evaluating a company's financial performance. By analyzing financial ratios in the context of the industry and the company's strategic goals, investors and analysts can gain a more comprehensive understanding of a company's financial health and make more informed investment decisions.

To further develop skills in analyzing financial ratios, students may consider additional case studies that explore the financial performance of companies in different industries and geographic regions. In-class exercises may involve analyzing financial statements and calculating various financial ratios for a range of companies, and then discussing the implications of the results. Such exercises can help students develop a deeper understanding of the factors that influence financial ratios and their significance in evaluating a company's financial health.

Exercise: Calculating and analyzing financial ratios for a hypothetical business

In this exercise, we will use financial statements to calculate and analyze key financial ratios for a hypothetical business. We will then use our analysis to identify areas where the business is doing well and where it could improve.

Hypothetical business information:

Company Name: XYZ Corporation
Industry: Retail
Revenue: $10,000,000
Cost of Goods Sold: $6,000,000
Gross Profit: $4,000,000
Operating Expenses: $2,500,000

Net Income: $1,500,000
Total Assets: $8,000,000
Total Liabilities: $3,000,000
Shareholders' Equity: $5,000,000
Step 1: Calculate profitability ratios

a. Gross Profit Margin

The gross profit margin measures the percentage of sales that remain after deducting the cost of goods sold. It is calculated as follows:

Gross Profit Margin = (Gross Profit / Revenue) x 100

In the case of XYZ Corporation, the gross profit margin is:

Gross Profit Margin = ($4,000,000 / $10,000,000) x 100 = 40%

This means that for every dollar in sales, the company generates 40 cents in gross profit.

b. Net Profit Margin

The net profit margin measures the percentage of sales that remain after deducting all expenses, including taxes. It is calculated as follows:

Net Profit Margin = (Net Income / Revenue) x 100

In the case of XYZ Corporation, the net profit margin is:

Net Profit Margin = ($1,500,000 / $10,000,000) x 100 = 15%

This means that for every dollar in sales, the company generates 15 cents in net income.

c. Return on Equity (ROE)

The return on equity measures the percentage of return on investment that the shareholders receive. It is calculated as follows:

ROE = (Net Income / Shareholders' Equity) x 100

In the case of XYZ Corporation, the return on equity is:

ROE = ($1,500,000 / $5,000,000) x 100 = 30%

This means that the shareholders of XYZ Corporation receive a return on their investment of 30%.

Step 2: Calculate liquidity ratios

a. Current Ratio

The current ratio measures the ability of the company to pay its short-term debts with its current assets. It is calculated as follows:

Current Ratio = Current Assets / Current Liabilities

In the case of XYZ Corporation, the current ratio is:

Current Ratio = $4,000,000 / $1,500,000 = 2.67

This means that XYZ Corporation has 2.67 times more current assets than current liabilities.

b. Quick Ratio

The quick ratio measures the ability of the company to pay its short-term debts with its quick assets, which are assets that can be easily converted to cash. It is calculated as follows:

Quick Ratio = (Current Assets - Inventory) / Current Liabilities

In the case of XYZ Corporation, the quick ratio is:

Quick Ratio = ($4,000,000 - $1,000,000) / $1,500,000 = 2

This means that XYZ Corporation has 2 times more quick assets than current liabilities.

Step 3: Calculate efficiency ratios

a. Inventory Turnover

The inventory turnover measures how many times the company sells and replaces its inventory during a given period. It is calculated as follows:

Inventory Turnover = Cost of Goods Sold / Average Inventory

In the case of XYZ Corporation, the inventory turnover is:

Inventory Turnover = $6million / (($900,000 + $700,000)/2) = 8 times

This means that the company is selling and replacing its inventory 8 times during the given period. A high inventory turnover is generally desirable, as it indicates that the company is effectively managing its inventory and not overstocking.

b. Accounts Receivable Turnover

The accounts receivable turnover measures how quickly the company collects payment for its sales. It is calculated as follows:

Accounts Receivable Turnover = Net Sales / Average Accounts Receivable

In the case of XYZ Corporation, the accounts receivable turnover is:

Accounts Receivable Turnover = $12 million / (($1,200,000 + $800,000)/2) = 10 times

This means that the company collects payment for its sales 10 times during the given period. A high accounts receivable turnover is generally desirable, as it indicates that the company is collecting payments quickly and efficiently.

c. Debt-to-Equity Ratio

The debt-to-equity ratio measures the amount of debt financing relative to equity financing used by the company. It is calculated as follows:

Debt-to-Equity Ratio = Total Liabilities / Total Equity

In the case of XYZ Corporation, the debt-to-equity ratio is:

Debt-to-Equity Ratio = $4 million / $6 million = 0.67

This means that the company is financing its operations with 67% debt and 33% equity. A high debt-to-equity ratio indicates that the company is relying heavily on debt financing, which can be risky if the company is not able to generate sufficient cash flows to service its debt obligations.

d. Gross Profit Margin

The gross profit margin measures the profitability of the company's sales after deducting the cost of goods sold. It is calculated as follows:

Gross Profit Margin = (Net Sales - Cost of Goods Sold) / Net Sales

In the case of XYZ Corporation, the gross profit margin is:

Gross Profit Margin = ($12 million - $6 million) / $12 million = 0.5 or 50%

This means that for every dollar of sales, the company is earning 50 cents in gross profit after deducting the cost of goods sold. A high gross profit margin is generally desirable, as it indicates that the company is generating a healthy profit on its sales.

e. Return on Assets

The return on assets measures how efficiently the company is using its assets to generate profit. It is calculated as follows:

Return on Assets = Net Income / Total Assets

In the case of XYZ Corporation, the return on assets is:

Return on Assets = $1.2 million / $10 million = 0.12 or 12%

This means that for every dollar of assets, the company is earning 12 cents in profit. A high return on assets is generally desirable, as it indicates that the company is generating a healthy profit from its assets.

f. Current Ratio

The current ratio measures the company's ability to meet its short-term obligations. It is calculated as follows:

Current Ratio = Current Assets / Current Liabilities

In the case of XYZ Corporation, the current ratio is:

Current Ratio = ($2.5 million + $1.5 million) / $1.8 million = 2.22

This means that the company has $2.22 in current assets for every dollar of current liabilities. A high current ratio is generally desirable, as it indicates that the company has sufficient liquidity to meet its short-term obligations.

g. Quick Ratio

The quick ratio, also known as the acid-test ratio, measures the company's ability to meet its short-term obligations using its most liquid assets. It is calculated as follows:

Quick Ratio = (Current Assets - Inventory) / Current Liabilities

For XYZ Corporation, the quick ratio is:

Quick Ratio = ($12,000 + $1,500 - $6,000) / $4,000 = 2.375

This means that XYZ Corporation has $2.375 of liquid assets available to cover every dollar of its current liabilities. Generally, a quick ratio of 1 or higher is considered satisfactory, as it indicates that the company can meet its short-term obligations without having to rely on the sale of inventory.

h. Debt-to-Equity Ratio

The debt-to-equity ratio measures the extent to which the company is financed by debt versus equity. It is calculated as follows:

Debt-to-Equity Ratio = Total Liabilities / Total Equity

In the case of XYZ Corporation, the debt-to-equity ratio is:

Debt-to-Equity Ratio = $10,000 / $16,500 = 0.606

This means that for every dollar of equity, XYZ Corporation has 60.6 cents of debt. A high debt-to-equity ratio indicates that the company is heavily reliant on debt to finance its operations, which can be a cause for concern for investors and lenders.

i. Return on Equity (ROE)

The return on equity measures how much profit the company generates for every dollar of equity invested by shareholders. It is calculated as follows:

Return on Equity = Net Income / Total Equity

In the case of XYZ Corporation, the return on equity is:

Return on Equity = $3,000 / $16,500 = 0.182

This means that for every dollar of equity invested by shareholders, XYZ Corporation generates 18.2 cents of profit. A higher ROE indicates that the company is generating more profits per dollar of equity, which is generally seen as a positive sign by investors.

j. Exercise Summary

In this exercise, we calculated and analyzed several financial ratios for XYZ Corporation. These ratios provide important insights into the company's financial health and performance, including its liquidity, profitability, and solvency.

Overall, the financial ratios suggest that XYZ Corporation is a relatively healthy and stable company, with strong liquidity and profitability ratios. However, its high debt-to-equity ratio indicates that the company is heavily reliant on debt financing, which could be a concern for investors and lenders. It is important for investors and analysts to use a range of financial ratios and other metrics to gain a comprehensive understanding of a company's financial health and performance.

CHAPTER 5: TECHNIQUES FOR FINANCIAL ANALYSIS

Financial analysis is an important tool for businesses of all sizes and industries. It involves the use of various methods and techniques to analyze and interpret financial statements in order to assess a company's financial health and performance. This chapter will explore some of the most commonly used techniques for financial analysis, including ratio analysis, trend analysis, and common-size analysis. We will also discuss how these techniques can be applied to different industries and situations.

Section 1: Ratio Analysis

Ratio analysis is a popular method for analyzing a company's financial statements. Ratios are used to compare different aspects of a company's financial performance, such as its profitability, liquidity, and solvency, over time or against industry benchmarks. Here are some of the most commonly used ratios:

Profitability Ratios
Profitability ratios measure a company's ability to generate profits relative to its sales or assets. The most commonly used profitability ratios include:

Gross Profit Margin: This ratio measures the percentage of revenue that is left after deducting the cost of goods sold. A higher gross profit margin indicates that the company is generating more profit per dollar of sales.

Net Profit Margin: This ratio measures the percentage of revenue that is left after deducting all expenses, including taxes and interest. A higher net profit margin indicates that the company is generating more profit per dollar of sales.

Return on Assets (ROA): This ratio measures the company's ability to generate profits relative to its assets. It is calculated by dividing net income by total assets. A higher ROA indicates that the company is using its assets more efficiently to generate profits.

Liquidity Ratios
Liquidity ratios measure a company's ability to meet its short-term obligations. They indicate whether a company has enough cash and other liquid assets to pay off its debts as they come due. The most commonly used liquidity ratios include:

Current Ratio: This ratio measures the company's ability to pay its short-term debts with its current assets. It is calculated by dividing current assets by current liabilities. A higher current ratio indicates that the company has more current assets relative to its current liabilities and is therefore more able to meet its short-term obligations.

Quick Ratio: This ratio measures the company's ability to pay its short-term debts with its most liquid assets. It is calculated by subtracting inventory from current assets and then dividing the result by current liabilities. A higher quick ratio indicates that the company has more liquid assets relative to its current liabilities and is therefore more able to meet its short-term obligations.

Solvency Ratios

Solvency ratios measure a company's ability to meet its long-term obligations. They indicate whether a company has enough assets to cover its long-term debts. The most commonly used solvency ratios include:

Debt-to-Equity Ratio: This ratio measures the company's level of debt relative to its equity. It is calculated by dividing total liabilities by total equity. A higher debt-to-equity ratio indicates that the company is using more debt financing relative to its equity financing.

Interest Coverage Ratio: This ratio measures the company's ability to pay its interest expenses with its earnings before interest and taxes (EBIT). It is calculated by dividing EBIT by interest expenses. A higher interest coverage ratio indicates that the company is generating enough earnings to cover its interest expenses.

Section 2: Trend Analysis

Trend analysis involves analyzing financial data over time to identify patterns and trends. It can help businesses identify changes in their financial performance, both positive and negative, and make informed decisions about future operations. There are several ways to conduct trend analysis, including:

Horizontal Analysis

Horizontal analysis involves comparing financial data from one period to another. It can help businesses identify changes in their financial performance over time. For example, a company can compare its revenue, net income, or operating expenses from year to year to identify trends in its financial performance. Horizontal analysis is particularly useful for identifying changes in financial ratios and metrics over time.

Vertical Analysis

Vertical analysis involves analyzing financial data as a percentage of a base amount, such as total assets or total revenue. This can help businesses understand the relative importance of different items on their financial statements. For example, a company can analyze its income statement as a percentage of total revenue to identify the proportion of its revenue that is allocated to each expense category. This can help businesses identify areas where they can reduce costs or improve efficiency.

Common Size Analysis

Common size analysis is a form of vertical analysis that expresses financial data as a percentage of a common base, such as total assets or total revenue. This can help businesses compare their financial performance to industry benchmarks or competitors. For example, a company can analyze its income statement as a percentage of revenue and compare it to industry benchmarks to identify areas where it may be underperforming. Common size analysis can also be used to identify changes in a company's financial performance over time.

Ratio Analysis

Ratio analysis involves analyzing financial ratios and metrics to identify trends and make informed decisions about a company's financial health. This includes analyzing liquidity ratios, profitability ratios, solvency ratios, and efficiency ratios. Ratio analysis is particularly useful for identifying changes in a company's financial performance over time, and comparing a company's financial performance to industry benchmarks or competitors.

Limitations of Trend Analysis

While trend analysis is a useful tool for analyzing financial data over time, it is important to be aware of its limitations. First, trend analysis is based on historical data, which may not be an accurate predictor of future performance. Second, trend analysis does not take into account external factors that may impact a company's financial performance, such as changes in the economy or industry regulations. Finally, trend analysis is only as accurate as the data that is used to conduct it. If the data is incomplete or inaccurate, the results of the analysis may be unreliable.

Example of Trend Analysis

As an example of trend analysis, let's consider a fictional company, ABC Corporation, which manufactures and sells widgets. ABC Corporation wants to analyze its financial performance over the past three years to identify trends and make informed decisions about future operations.

First, ABC Corporation conducts horizontal analysis by comparing its revenue, net income, and operating expenses from year to year. The results of this analysis indicate that revenue has increased steadily over the past three years, while net income has remained relatively stable. However, operating expenses have increased significantly over the past year, which may indicate a need to reduce costs or improve efficiency.

Next, ABC Corporation conducts vertical analysis by analyzing its income statement as a percentage of total revenue. This analysis indicates that the proportion of revenue allocated to cost of goods sold has remained relatively stable over the past three years, while the proportion allocated to operating expenses has increased significantly. This suggests that ABC Corporation may need to focus on reducing operating expenses to improve profitability.

Finally, ABC Corporation conducts ratio analysis by analyzing its liquidity ratios, profitability ratios, solvency ratios, and efficiency ratios. This analysis indicates that ABC Corporation's liquidity ratios are strong, but its profitability ratios could be improved. In particular, the company's return on assets (ROA) has declined over the past three years, which may indicate a need to improve efficiency or reduce costs.

Based on the results of these analyses, ABC Corporation can make informed decisions about future operations. For example, the company may focus on reducing operating expenses, improving efficiency, or expanding its product line to increase revenue and profitability.

Analyzing trends in financial statements and ratios over time

Analyzing trends in financial statements and ratios over time is a critical aspect of financial analysis. This technique helps businesses identify changes in their financial performance over time and make informed decisions about future operations. In this section, we will discuss the importance of analyzing trends in financial statements and ratios, and how this technique can be used to identify key financial indicators and evaluate a company's financial health.

Importance of Analyzing Trends in Financial Statements and Ratios

Analyzing trends in financial statements and ratios over time is essential for businesses for several reasons. Firstly, it provides an insight into a company's financial performance over time. By comparing financial data from one period to another, businesses can identify trends, both positive and negative, in their financial performance. This information is essential for making informed decisions about future operations, such as investment decisions, expansion plans, and cost-cutting measures.

Secondly, analyzing trends in financial statements and ratios can help identify key financial indicators that may affect a company's financial health. For example, by analyzing the trend in a company's inventory turnover ratio over time, businesses can identify if there are any issues with inventory management. Similarly, by analyzing the trend in a company's debt-to-equity ratio, businesses can identify if the company is becoming too heavily leveraged.

Techniques for Analyzing Trends in Financial Statements and Ratios

There are several techniques that businesses can use to analyze trends in financial statements and ratios over time. These include:

Horizontal Analysis: Horizontal analysis involves comparing financial data from one period to another. It can help businesses identify changes in their financial performance over time. For example, a business may compare its revenue from the previous year to the current year to identify if there has been any growth or decline in revenue.

Vertical Analysis: Vertical analysis involves analyzing the composition of financial statements. It helps businesses understand how much each component of the financial statement contributes to the overall financial health of the business. For example, a business may use vertical analysis to identify the percentage of revenue that is generated from each product line.

Ratio Analysis: Ratio analysis involves analyzing financial ratios over time. It helps businesses identify changes in financial ratios that may affect their financial health. For example, a business may analyze the trend in its debt-to-equity ratio over time to identify if the company is becoming too heavily leveraged.

Common Size Analysis: Common size analysis involves expressing each item on the financial statement as a percentage of the total. It helps businesses understand the composition of the financial statement and identify changes in the composition over time. For example, a business may use common size analysis to identify the percentage of revenue that is generated from each product line.

Interpreting Trends in Financial Statements and Ratios

Interpreting trends in financial statements and ratios can be a complex process. However, there are several key indicators that businesses can look for when interpreting trends. These include:

Consistency: Businesses should look for consistency in their financial performance over time. A consistent trend in financial performance is an indicator of financial stability.

Growth: Businesses should look for growth in their financial performance over time. Growth is an indicator of financial health and can be a sign of a healthy business.

Decline: Businesses should be aware of any declines in their financial performance over time. Declines may be an indicator of underlying issues that need to be addressed.

Industry benchmarks: Businesses should compare their financial performance to industry benchmarks. This will help them identify if their financial performance is on par with industry standards.

Conclusion

Analyzing trends in financial statements and ratios over time is a critical aspect of financial analysis. This technique helps businesses identify changes in their financial performance, both positive and negative, and make informed decisions about future operations. It allows businesses to compare their financial performance to industry standards and identify areas for improvement. The insights gained from analyzing trends in financial statements and ratios over time can help businesses make strategic decisions that can ultimately lead to greater profitability.

It is important to note that trend analysis is not a one-time process. Businesses should conduct trend analysis regularly to track their financial performance over time and adjust their operations accordingly. Additionally, it is important to use multiple financial ratios and metrics to gain a comprehensive understanding of a company's financial health. No single ratio or metric can provide a complete picture of a company's financial performance.

In conclusion, analyzing trends in financial statements and ratios over time is a valuable tool for businesses seeking to understand their financial performance and make informed decisions about future operations. It provides a comprehensive understanding of a company's financial health and allows businesses to identify areas for improvement and take action to achieve greater profitability. Regularly conducting trend analysis is a critical aspect of financial management and should be incorporated into a business's financial planning process.

Benchmarking financial performance against industry standards and competitors

Benchmarking financial performance against industry standards and competitors is an essential aspect of financial analysis. It involves comparing a company's financial ratios and other performance metrics against those of other companies in the same industry or sector. This technique helps businesses identify areas where they are performing well and areas where they need to improve to remain competitive in the marketplace. In this section, we will explore the concept of benchmarking financial performance, its importance, and various approaches to benchmarking.

Understanding Industry Standards

Before we can benchmark financial performance against industry standards and competitors, we need to understand what industry standards are and how they are determined. Industry standards are financial performance metrics that are commonly used to evaluate companies within a specific industry or sector. They are typically based on data from financial statements and other sources and are calculated using ratios and other statistical measures.

Industry standards can vary depending on the industry or sector being evaluated. For example, the financial performance metrics used to evaluate a technology company may be different from those used to evaluate a manufacturing company. Some common financial performance metrics used as industry standards include:

Return on Equity (ROE)
Return on Assets (ROA)
Gross Margin
Operating Margin
Net Profit Margin
Inventory Turnover
Debt-to-Equity Ratio
Current Ratio
Quick Ratio

Industry standards can be obtained from a variety of sources, including industry associations, financial publications, and government agencies. It is important to ensure that the data used to calculate industry standards are accurate and up-to-date to obtain a reliable benchmark.

Approaches to Benchmarking Financial Performance

There are several approaches to benchmarking financial performance against industry standards and competitors. Some of the most common approaches include:

Peer Group Comparison: This approach involves comparing a company's financial ratios and other performance metrics to those of its competitors within the same industry or sector. Peer group comparison helps businesses identify areas where they are underperforming compared to their competitors and where they need to improve to remain competitive.

For example, suppose a company in the retail industry has a lower gross margin than its competitors. In that case, it may need to adjust its pricing strategy or reduce its cost of goods sold to improve its profitability.

Trend Analysis: Trend analysis involves analyzing a company's financial data over time to identify patterns and trends. This approach helps businesses identify changes in their financial performance, both positive and negative, and make informed decisions about future operations.

For example, suppose a company's net profit margin has been declining over the past few years. In that case, it may need to evaluate its cost structure, pricing strategy, or revenue streams to reverse the trend and improve profitability.

Best-in-Class Comparison: This approach involves comparing a company's financial ratios and other performance metrics to those of the best-performing companies in the same industry or sector. Best-in-class comparison helps businesses identify areas where they are underperforming compared to the top-performing companies and where they need to improve to achieve a competitive advantage.

For example, suppose a company in the technology industry has a lower return on equity than the best-performing companies in the same industry. In that case, it may need to evaluate its business strategy, capital structure, or operational efficiency to improve its return on equity and remain competitive.

Benefits of Benchmarking Financial Performance

Benchmarking financial performance against industry standards and competitors offers several benefits to businesses, including:

Improved Performance: Benchmarking helps businesses identify areas where they need to improve to remain competitive and achieve better financial results. By benchmarking financial performance, businesses can set performance targets and implement strategies to improve their financial performance over time.

Competitive Advantage: Benchmarking helps businesses identify areas where they are underperforming compared to their competitors and take action to close the gap. By identifying best practices and strategies used by industry leaders and competitors, businesses can gain a competitive advantage and improve their financial performance.

Better Decision Making: Benchmarking provides businesses with valuable insights into their financial performance and the financial performance of their competitors. This information can help businesses make better decisions about resource allocation, investment decisions, and other financial decisions.

Increased Efficiency: By benchmarking financial performance, businesses can identify areas where they can improve their efficiency and reduce costs. This can help them operate more efficiently and achieve better financial results.

Improved Customer Satisfaction: Benchmarking financial performance can also help businesses identify areas where they can improve customer satisfaction. By benchmarking customer satisfaction metrics such as customer retention rates and customer loyalty, businesses can identify areas where they need to improve their customer service and take action to improve it.

Enhanced Reputation: Benchmarking financial performance can help businesses enhance their reputation by demonstrating their commitment to financial excellence and continuous improvement. This can be particularly important in industries where financial stability and performance are important factors in customer decision making.

Overall, benchmarking financial performance against industry standards and competitors is a valuable tool for businesses looking to improve their financial performance, gain a competitive advantage, and make better financial decisions. By identifying areas for improvement and implementing strategies to close the gap, businesses can achieve better financial results and enhance their reputation in their industry.

Sensitivity analysis and scenario planning to evaluate the impact of different assumptions on financial performance

Financial analysis is an essential component of business decision-making. It helps businesses evaluate their financial performance and make informed decisions about future operations. One of the challenges that businesses face when conducting financial analysis is dealing with uncertainty. Financial forecasts and projections are based on assumptions about future events that may or may not happen. Sensitivity analysis and scenario planning are two techniques that businesses can use to evaluate the impact of different assumptions on financial performance. This section will provide an in-depth analysis of sensitivity analysis and scenario planning, including their benefits, drawbacks, and how businesses can use them to improve financial decision-making.

Sensitivity Analysis

Sensitivity analysis is a technique used to evaluate the impact of changes in assumptions on financial performance. It helps businesses understand the degree to which their financial projections are sensitive to changes in key assumptions. The process involves changing one or more assumptions and observing the impact on financial results. Sensitivity analysis is commonly used in financial modeling to evaluate the risk and uncertainty associated with different scenarios.

For example, a business might conduct sensitivity analysis on its revenue projections to evaluate the impact of changes in sales volume, price, and product mix. By changing these assumptions and observing the impact on revenue and profitability, the business can determine which factors are most important to its financial performance and adjust its strategy accordingly.

Sensitivity analysis can be performed using various methods, including:

One-way Sensitivity Analysis: This involves changing one assumption at a time and observing the impact on financial results. For example, a business might change the sales volume assumption and observe the impact on revenue and profitability.

Two-way Sensitivity Analysis: This involves changing two assumptions simultaneously and observing the impact on financial results. For example, a business might change both the sales volume and price assumptions and observe the impact on revenue and profitability.

Multi-way Sensitivity Analysis: This involves changing multiple assumptions simultaneously and observing the impact on financial results. For example, a business might change the sales volume, price, and product mix assumptions and observe the impact on revenue and profitability.

Monte Carlo Simulation: This involves running multiple scenarios with different assumptions and probabilities assigned to each scenario. This method is useful for evaluating the range of possible outcomes based on various assumptions and their probabilities.

Sensitivity analysis can be used to evaluate different aspects of a business's financial performance, including revenue, expenses, cash flow, and profitability. By identifying the key drivers of financial performance and assessing their sensitivity to changes in assumptions, businesses can develop more accurate financial projections and make informed decisions about their operations.

However, sensitivity analysis has its limitations. It relies on assumptions that may not accurately reflect the future, and changes in one assumption may impact other assumptions, making it difficult to isolate the true impact of each assumption. Additionally, sensitivity analysis does not consider external factors that may impact financial performance, such as changes in the economy or industry trends.

To overcome these limitations, businesses can use scenario planning in conjunction with sensitivity analysis. Scenario planning involves developing multiple scenarios based on different assumptions and evaluating the impact of each scenario on financial performance. By considering a range of possible outcomes and the likelihood of each scenario, businesses can develop a more comprehensive understanding of their financial risks and opportunities.

In the next section, we will discuss scenario planning and how it can be used to evaluate the impact of different assumptions on financial performance.

Forecasting financial performance based on historical trends and future expectations

Forecasting financial performance is a critical task for businesses of all sizes. The ability to accurately predict future financial results enables businesses to plan for the future, make strategic decisions, and allocate resources effectively. Financial forecasts are essential for obtaining funding, negotiating contracts, and maintaining investor confidence. Forecasting can be done by analyzing historical trends and future expectations.

Analyzing Historical Trends
Analyzing historical trends is an important part of financial forecasting. Historical data can provide valuable insights into a business's past performance, which can be used to make informed predictions about its future performance. This data can include financial statements, such as income statements, balance sheets, and cash flow statements, as well as other performance metrics, such as sales volume and market share.

When analyzing historical trends, businesses should consider several factors, including:

a. Revenue Growth: Revenue growth is a critical factor in financial forecasting. Businesses should consider their historical revenue growth rates and evaluate whether they are likely to continue at the same rate or slow down in the future. For example, a business that has experienced consistent revenue growth of 10% per year over the past five years may expect similar growth rates in the future. However, if the business has recently entered a more competitive market, it may need to adjust its growth projections accordingly.

b. Cost Trends: Understanding cost trends is essential for financial forecasting. Businesses should consider their historical cost trends, including changes in the cost of goods sold, labor costs, and overhead expenses. Cost trends can help businesses identify areas where they can reduce costs to improve their profitability.

c. Profitability: Profitability is a critical factor in financial forecasting. Businesses should consider their historical profitability metrics, such as gross profit margin, net profit margin, and return on investment (ROI). Understanding profitability trends can help businesses make informed decisions about pricing, product mix, and cost reduction initiatives.

Future Expectations

In addition to analyzing historical trends, businesses must also consider future expectations when forecasting financial performance. Future expectations can be influenced by a variety of factors, including changes in the market, shifts in consumer preferences, and technological advancements.

When considering future expectations, businesses should consider the following factors:

a. Market Conditions: Market conditions play a significant role in financial forecasting. Businesses should consider the current state of the market, including trends in the industry, the competitive landscape, and consumer behavior. By understanding market conditions, businesses can make informed decisions about pricing, product mix, and market expansion.

b. Business Strategy: A business's strategy can have a significant impact on its future financial performance. Businesses should consider their strategic goals and evaluate whether they are likely to achieve them. For example, if a business plans to enter a new market, it may need to adjust its growth projections accordingly.

c. Technological Advances: Technological advances can significantly impact a business's financial performance. Businesses should consider emerging technologies in their industry and evaluate their potential impact on their operations. For example, the rise of e-commerce has transformed the retail industry, and businesses that have not adapted to this change may struggle to remain competitive.

Forecasting Methods

There are several methods businesses can use to forecast financial performance. The most common methods include:

a. Trend Analysis: Trend analysis involves analyzing historical trends to identify patterns and make informed predictions about future performance. This method is relatively simple and can be useful for short-term forecasting.

b. Regression Analysis: Regression analysis involves analyzing historical data to identify relationships between variables and make predictions about future performance. This method is more complex than trend analysis but can provide more accurate long-term forecasts.

c. Scenario Analysis: Scenario analysis involves creating multiple scenarios based on different assumptions to evaluate the impact of each scenario on financial performance. This method is useful for evaluating the potential risks and opportunities associated with different future events and helps businesses prepare for potential outcomes.

d. Monte Carlo Simulation: Monte Carlo simulation involves generating random variables based on probability distributions to simulate potential future outcomes. This method can be useful for evaluating the probability of different financial outcomes based on a range of assumptions and is commonly used in risk management.

e. Expert Opinion: Expert opinion involves seeking input from industry experts or experienced professionals to make informed predictions about future performance. This method can be useful for forecasting financial performance in industries that are rapidly changing or difficult to analyze using historical data.

Each of these methods has its strengths and weaknesses, and businesses may choose to use a combination of methods to forecast financial performance accurately. It's essential to select the appropriate method based on the available data, the time horizon for the forecast, and the specific business's industry and competitive landscape.

One of the most critical factors in forecasting financial performance is the quality of data used in the analysis. Businesses need to ensure they are using accurate and up-to-date financial data to make informed predictions. Data quality can be improved by implementing robust data collection processes, using reliable data sources, and performing regular data validation checks.

Another crucial factor in forecasting financial performance is the ability to adjust the forecast based on new information or changes in the business environment. It's essential to review and update financial forecasts regularly to reflect changing circumstances and make adjustments to the forecast assumptions as necessary.

Forecasting financial performance is a critical aspect of financial management, and businesses that can accurately predict future performance are better equipped to make informed decisions and achieve long-term success. By using a combination of forecasting methods and ensuring data quality, businesses can create accurate and reliable financial forecasts that enable them to make informed strategic decisions.

Case study: Analyzing financial performance and creating a forecast for a start-up business

Analyzing financial performance and creating a forecast for a start-up business is critical for entrepreneurs and investors alike. In this section, we will explore a case study of a start-up business and use various methods to analyze its financial performance and create a financial forecast. This case study will provide a practical example of how to use different financial analysis tools and techniques to assess the financial health of a start-up business and make informed decisions about its future prospects.

Case Study:
Imagine that you are an investor who is considering investing in a start-up business called "GreenTech Innovations Inc." GreenTech Innovations Inc. is a technology company that specializes in the development of environmentally friendly products. The company has been in operation for two years and has experienced steady growth. However, the company's founders are seeking additional funding to expand their operations and launch new products.

Financial Statements Analysis:
The first step in analyzing the financial performance of GreenTech Innovations Inc. is to examine its financial statements. The company has provided you with its income statement and balance sheet for the past two years.

Income Statement:

	Year 2	Year 1
Revenue	$1,000,000	$750,000
Cost of Goods Sold	$600,000	$450,000

Gross Profit	$400,000	$300,000
Operating Expenses	$200,000	$150,000
Net Income	$200,000	$150,000

Balance Sheet:

	Year 2	Year 1
Cash	$100,000	$50,000
Accounts Receivable	$200,000	$150,000
Inventory	$300,000	$225,000
Property, Plant, and Equipment	$400,000	$300,000
Total Assets	$1,000,000	$725,000
Accounts Payable	$100,000	$75,000
Accrued Expenses	$50,000	$40,000
Short-term Debt	$50,000	$25,000
Long-term Debt	$300,000	$200,000
Equity	$500,000	$385,000
Total Liabilities and Equity	$1,000,000	$725,000

Ratio Analysis:

The next step in analyzing GreenTech Innovations Inc.'s financial performance is to perform ratio analysis. Ratio analysis is a valuable tool that helps investors and managers evaluate a company's financial health by comparing different financial metrics. The following ratios will be analyzed:

Liquidity Ratios: Liquidity ratios measure a company's ability to meet its short-term obligations. The most common liquidity ratios are the current ratio and the quick ratio.

a. Current Ratio: The current ratio is calculated by dividing current assets by current liabilities. A current ratio of 2:1 is considered healthy.

	Year 2	Year 1
Current Ratio		2.0

GreenTech Innovations Inc.'s current ratio has remained stable over the past two years, indicating that the company has sufficient current assets to cover its short-term liabilities.

b. Quick Ratio: The quick ratio is calculated by dividing quick assets by current liabilities. Quick assets include cash, accounts receivable, and marketable securities. A quick ratio of 1:1 is considered healthy.

	ear 2	Year 1
Quick Ratio		1.6

GreenTech Innovations Inc.'s quick ratio has decreased slightly over the past year, In addition to analyzing liquidity ratios, GreenTech Innovations Inc. should also analyze profitability and efficiency ratios to evaluate its financial performance.

Profitability ratios, such as gross profit margin and net profit margin, measure the company's ability to generate profits from its operations. Gross profit margin is calculated by subtracting the cost of goods sold from revenue and then dividing the result by revenue. Net profit margin, on the other hand, is calculated by subtracting all expenses, including taxes and interest, from revenue and then dividing the result by revenue.

Efficiency ratios, such as inventory turnover and accounts receivable turnover, measure the company's ability to efficiently manage its resources. Inventory turnover is calculated by dividing the cost of goods sold by average inventory, while accounts receivable turnover is calculated by dividing revenue by average accounts receivable.

By analyzing these ratios, GreenTech Innovations Inc. can gain a more comprehensive understanding of its financial performance and identify areas where it can improve. For example, if the company's gross profit margin is low, it may need to re-evaluate its pricing strategy or look for ways to reduce the cost of goods sold. Similarly, if the company's inventory turnover is low, it may need to implement better inventory management practices to improve efficiency.

After analyzing its liquidity, profitability, and efficiency ratios, GreenTech Innovations Inc. can use this information to create a financial forecast for the next year. This forecast should take into account any expected changes in the company's operations, such as new product launches or changes in the competitive landscape.

To create a financial forecast, the company can use any of the forecasting methods discussed earlier in this chapter, such as trend analysis, regression analysis, or scenario analysis. The forecast should include projected income statements, balance sheets, and cash flow statements for the next year, as well as a detailed explanation of the assumptions and methods used to create the forecast.

In conclusion, analyzing financial performance and creating a forecast is essential for any business, whether it's a start-up or an established company. By analyzing key ratios and using forecasting methods, businesses can gain a better understanding of their financial position and make informed decisions to improve their performance.

Exercise: Analyzing financial trends and creating a forecast for a hypothetical business

In this exercise, we will analyze financial trends and create a forecast for a hypothetical business. The business we will be analyzing is a start-up software company called Tech Innovations Inc. The company provides customized software solutions to small and medium-sized businesses.

Step 1: Analyzing Historical Financial Statements

The first step in analyzing financial trends is to review the historical financial statements of the company. We will analyze the company's income statement, balance sheet, and cash flow statement for the past three years to identify any trends or patterns in the company's financial performance.

Income Statement Analysis:

Looking at Tech Innovations Inc.'s income statement, we can see that the company has experienced steady revenue growth over the past three years. In 20X1, the company had revenue of $500,000. This increased to $750,000 in 20X2 and then to $1,000,000 in 20X3.

However, the company's net income has been inconsistent over the past three years. In 20X1, the company had a net loss of $50,000. In 20X2, the company had a net income of $25,000, and in 20X3, the company had a net income of $100,000. This inconsistency in net income is a cause for concern and needs further analysis.

Balance Sheet Analysis:

The balance sheet of Tech Innovations Inc. reveals that the company has experienced steady growth in its assets and liabilities over the past three years. The company's total assets increased from $250,000 in 20X1 to $500,000 in 20X3. The liabilities also increased from $100,000 in 20X1 to $300,000 in 20X3. The equity of the company has also increased from $150,000 in 20X1 to $200,000 in 20X3.

Cash Flow Statement Analysis:

The cash flow statement of Tech Innovations Inc. shows that the company has been generating positive cash flows from operating activities over the past three years. In 20X1, the company generated cash flow from operating activities of $100,000. This increased to $150,000 in 20X2 and $200,000 in 20X3. The company has also been investing in its business with cash flows used in investing activities, which have been increasing over the years.

Identifying Financial Trends

Based on the analysis of Tech Innovations Inc.'s financial statements, we can identify several trends in the company's financial performance:

Steady revenue growth over the past three years.
Inconsistent net income over the past three years.
Steady growth in assets and liabilities over the past three years.
Positive cash flows from operating activities over the past three years.

Creating a Forecast

Using the trends identified in step 2, we can create a forecast for Tech Innovations Inc. for the next three years. We will use the following assumptions for our forecast:

Revenue will continue to grow at a rate of 25% per year for the next three years.
Net income will be consistent at 10% of revenue for the next three years.
The company will continue to invest in its business with cash flows used in investing activities of $50,000 per year for the next three years.
The company will not issue any new debt or equity over the next three years.
Based on these assumptions, the forecasted income statement, balance sheet, and cash flow statement for Tech Innovations Inc. for the next three years are as follows:

Forecasted Income Statement:

	2022	2023	2024
Revenue	$750,000	$937,500	$1,171,875
Cost of Goods Sold	$375,000	$468,750	$585,938

Gross Profit	$375,000	$468,750	$585,938
Operating Expenses	$250,000	$312,500	$390,625
Net Income	$125,000	$156,250	$195,313

Forecasted Balance Sheet:

	2022	2023	2024
Assets			
Cash	$125,000	$156,250	$195,313
Accounts Receivable	$187,500	$234,375	$292,969
Inventory	$187,500	$234,375	$292,969
Property, Plant, and Equipment	$1,000,000	$1,000,000	$1,000,000
Total Assets	$1,500,000	$1,625,000	$1,781,251
Liabilities and Equity			
Accounts Payable	$112,500	$140,625	$175,781
Long-Term Debt	$500,000	$500,000	$500,000
Total Liabilities	$612,500	$640,625	$675,781
Common Stock	$600,000	$600,000	$600,000
Retained Earnings	$287,500	$384,375	$505,470
Total Equity	$887,500	$984,375	$1,105,470
Total Liabilities and Equity	$1,500,000	$1,625,000	$1,781,251

Forecasted Cash Flow Statement:

	2022	2023	2024
Cash Flows from Operating Activities			
Net Income	$125,000	$156,250	$195,313
Depreciation	$125,000	$125,000	$125,000
Changes in Operating Assets and Liabilities	$0	$0	$0
Net Cash Flows from Operating Activities	$250,000	$281,250	$320,313
Cash Flows from Investing Activities			
Purchase of Property, Plant, and	-$0	-$50,000	-$50,000

Equipment			
Net Cash Flows from Investing Activities	-$0	-$50,000	-$50,000
Cash Flows from Financing Activities			
Issuance of Long-Term Debt	$0	$0	$0
Issuance of Common Stock	$0	$0	$0
Net Cash Flows from Financing Activities	$0	$0	$0
Net Increase in Cash	$250,000	$231,250	$270,313
Beginning Cash	$125,000	$375,000	$606,250
Ending Cash	$375,000	$606,250	$876,563

This forecast shows that Tech Innovations Inc. is expected to experience significant revenue growth over the next three years, resulting in increased net income. The company is also expected to continue investing in its business, which is necessary for future growth and expansion.

However, it is important to note that forecasts are only predictions and are subject to change based on unforeseen events and changes in the business environment. For example, if there is a significant economic downturn or an unexpected shift in consumer behavior, the forecasted revenue and net income for Tech Innovations Inc. may not be accurate.

Additionally, it is important for companies to regularly review and update their forecasts to ensure they are still relevant and accurate. This can involve adjusting assumptions or incorporating new information as it becomes available.

Overall, forecasting is an important tool for businesses to use in order to plan for the future and make informed decisions. By analyzing past trends and making assumptions about future performance, companies can gain valuable insights into their financial health and identify potential areas for growth and improvement.

PART 3: MARKETING AND FINANCE

Marketing and finance are two critical components of any business. While marketing is responsible for creating a demand for products and services, finance is responsible for managing the resources necessary to meet that demand. The interplay between marketing and finance is essential to the success of any business, regardless of its size or industry.

Marketing is the process of identifying, anticipating, and satisfying customer needs and wants. It involves creating, communicating, and delivering value to customers through the development and promotion of products and services. The goal of marketing is to generate revenue by attracting and retaining customers. Successful marketing campaigns can lead to increased brand recognition, customer loyalty, and market share.

Finance, on the other hand, involves managing the financial resources of a business. This includes financial planning, budgeting, accounting, and investing. The goal of finance is to maximize shareholder value by using resources effectively and efficiently. Financial decisions impact all areas of a business, including marketing. Effective financial management can help ensure that marketing efforts are well-funded and targeted towards the most profitable opportunities.

The relationship between marketing and finance is a two-way street. Marketing efforts must be financially viable and generate sufficient revenue to justify the costs. Finance must support marketing by providing the necessary resources and measuring the effectiveness of marketing efforts. In this way, marketing and finance are inextricably linked, and both must work together to achieve the company's goals.

In this section, we will explore the intersection of marketing and finance in more detail. We will discuss how marketing and finance can work together to achieve business objectives, such as maximizing profitability and increasing market share. We will also examine the different financial tools and techniques that marketers can use to measure the effectiveness of their campaigns and make data-driven decisions.

Ultimately, the success of any business depends on its ability to create value for its customers while managing its financial resources effectively. Marketing and finance are two key functions that must work in harmony to achieve this goal. By understanding the relationship between these two critical components, businesses can develop strategies that drive growth, increase revenue, and enhance shareholder value.

CHAPTER 6: BUDGETING FOR MARKETING ACTIVITIES

Marketing is an essential function of any business. It helps businesses to identify and meet the needs of their customers, differentiate their products and services from those of their competitors, and create brand awareness. Marketing activities include advertising, public relations, sales promotions, personal selling, and direct marketing. However, marketing activities require resources such as money, time, and personnel. Therefore, it is important for businesses to plan and budget for their marketing activities.

Budgeting for marketing activities involves estimating the costs associated with each marketing activity and allocating resources accordingly. This requires an understanding of the marketing mix, which includes product, price, promotion, and place. Businesses must also consider the target market, competition, and market trends when developing their marketing budget.

This chapter will provide an overview of the budgeting process for marketing activities. It will cover the different types of marketing budgets, how to develop a marketing budget, and how to monitor and control marketing expenditures.

Types of Marketing Budgets:

There are several types of marketing budgets that businesses can use, including:

Percentage of Sales Budget: This budget allocates a percentage of the previous year's sales revenue to the marketing budget. For example, if a business had sales of $1 million last year and allocated 5% of sales to marketing, the marketing budget for this year would be $50,000.

Objective and Task Budget: This budget is based on the objectives and tasks that need to be accomplished in the marketing plan. It involves estimating the costs associated with each objective and task and allocating resources accordingly.

Competitive Parity Budget: This budget allocates resources based on what competitors are spending on marketing. The assumption is that if competitors are spending a certain amount on marketing, then the business should spend a similar amount to remain competitive.

Available Funds Budget: This budget allocates resources based on the amount of funds available. This budget is often used by small businesses or startups with limited resources.

Developing a Marketing Budget:

Developing a marketing budget requires an understanding of the business's marketing objectives and the resources available. The following steps can be used to develop a marketing budget:

Define Marketing Objectives: The first step in developing a marketing budget is to define the marketing objectives. These objectives should be specific, measurable, achievable, relevant, and time-bound (SMART). For example, an objective could be to increase sales by 10% within the next year.

Identify Target Market: The next step is to identify the target market. This includes demographic and psychographic information about the target market, as well as their needs and preferences.

Develop Marketing Strategy: Once the target market has been identified, the next step is to develop a marketing strategy. This involves identifying the marketing mix (product, price, promotion, and place) and developing a plan for each element.

Estimate Costs: The next step is to estimate the costs associated with each marketing activity. This includes costs for advertising, public relations, sales promotions, personal selling, and direct marketing.

Allocate Resources: The final step is to allocate resources to each marketing activity based on the estimated costs and the business's overall budget. This involves deciding which activities are most important and allocating resources accordingly.

Monitoring and Controlling Marketing Expenditures:

Once the marketing budget has been developed and resources allocated, it is important to monitor and control marketing expenditures. This involves tracking actual expenditures against the budget and making adjustments as necessary. The following steps can be used to monitor and control marketing expenditures:

Set Performance Metrics: The first step is to set performance metrics for each marketing activity. These metrics should be specific, measurable, achievable, relevant, and time-bound (SMART).

Track Actual Expenditures: The next step is to track actual expenditures against the budget. This can be done by reviewing financial reports on a regular basis, such as monthly or quarterly. Any discrepancies between actual expenditures and the budget should be identified and analyzed.

Analyze Variances: Once discrepancies are identified, it is important to analyze the variances to understand why they occurred. Was the budget unrealistic, or did the marketing team overspend? Were there unforeseen expenses or changes in the market that affected spending?

Make Adjustments: Based on the analysis of variances, adjustments can be made to the budget or the marketing plan. If the budget was unrealistic, adjustments can be made for future periods. If overspending occurred, the marketing team may need to adjust their tactics or find ways to reduce costs.

Communicate Results: Finally, it is important to communicate the results of the monitoring and controlling process to all stakeholders, including management, the marketing team, and other relevant departments. This helps to ensure transparency and accountability, and can also lead to improvements in future budgeting and planning processes.

Overall, monitoring and controlling marketing expenditures is critical to ensuring that resources are used effectively and efficiently. By setting performance metrics, tracking actual expenditures, analyzing variances, making adjustments, and communicating results, companies can ensure that their marketing activities are contributing to the overall success of the organization.

The importance of budgeting for marketing activities

In today's business environment, marketing plays a crucial role in the success of any organization. Marketing activities involve a variety of expenses such as advertising, promotions, research and development, and branding. Budgeting for marketing activities is important because it helps organizations to plan and manage their expenses effectively. A well-constructed marketing budget can also help organizations to maximize their return on investment (ROI) and achieve their marketing objectives. This chapter will explore the importance of budgeting for marketing activities and provide insights on how organizations can develop, manage, and monitor their marketing budgets.

Why is Budgeting for Marketing Activities Important?

Planning and Forecasting
A well-constructed marketing budget provides a framework for planning and forecasting. By setting clear objectives and allocating resources to specific marketing activities, organizations can plan for the future and make informed decisions based on their projected income and expenses. A marketing budget can help organizations to avoid overspending and identify areas where they need to invest more to achieve their marketing goals. Planning and forecasting can also help organizations to adapt to changes in the market and respond to new opportunities quickly.

Resource Allocation
Marketing budgets help organizations to allocate resources effectively. By setting clear priorities, organizations can ensure that their resources are being used efficiently. Marketing budgets can help organizations to make difficult decisions about which marketing activities to pursue and which ones to avoid. For example, if an organization has limited resources, it may need to prioritize certain marketing activities over others to achieve the best possible ROI.

ROI Maximization
Marketing budgets help organizations to maximize their ROI. By setting clear objectives and measuring the success of each marketing activity, organizations can identify which activities are providing the best ROI. Marketing budgets also allow organizations to identify areas where they can reduce expenses without compromising the quality of their marketing efforts. By monitoring and analyzing their marketing expenses, organizations can continually optimize their marketing budgets and improve their ROI.

Performance Evaluation
Marketing budgets help organizations to evaluate the performance of their marketing activities. By setting specific performance metrics and tracking actual expenses against the budget, organizations can determine whether their marketing activities are achieving their objectives. Marketing budgets can help organizations to identify areas where they need to make adjustments and improve their performance. Marketing budgets also provide a basis for comparing the performance of different marketing activities and determining which activities are providing the best ROI.

Competitive Advantage

Marketing budgets can help organizations to gain a competitive advantage. By investing in marketing activities that are aligned with their strategic objectives, organizations can differentiate themselves from their competitors and build brand recognition. Marketing budgets can also help organizations to respond to new opportunities and emerging trends in the market quickly.

Developing a Marketing Budget

Developing a marketing budget involves several steps, including:

Establishing Marketing Objectives

The first step in developing a marketing budget is to establish marketing objectives. Marketing objectives should be specific, measurable, achievable, relevant, and time-bound (SMART). Organizations should identify their target market, determine their marketing goals, and establish a budget that aligns with their overall business strategy.

Estimating Marketing Expenses

The next step is to estimate marketing expenses. This involves identifying the marketing activities that will be required to achieve the marketing objectives and estimating the cost of each activity. Organizations should consider all expenses associated with each marketing activity, including direct expenses such as advertising and promotions, as well as indirect expenses such as overhead costs and labor costs.

Allocating Resources

Once marketing expenses have been estimated, organizations need to allocate resources to each marketing activity. This involves prioritizing marketing activities based on their expected ROI and available resources. Organizations should consider the cost and expected ROI of each marketing activity when making allocation decisions.

Monitoring and Controlling Marketing Expenditures

After the marketing budget has been developed and resources allocated, it is important to monitor and control marketing expenditures. This involves tracking actual expenditures against the budget and making adjustments as necessary. The following steps can be used to monitor and control marketing expenditures:

Set Performance Metrics: The first step is to set performance metrics for each marketing activity. These metrics should be specific, measurable, achievable, relevant, and time-bound (SMART). By setting clear performance metrics, marketers can track their progress and identify areas that require improvement.

Track Actual Expenditures: The next step is to track actual expenditures against the budget. This can be done using a budget tracking tool or software, which allows marketers to compare actual expenditures to the budget in real-time. By monitoring actual expenditures, marketers can identify areas where they are overspending and take corrective action.

Analyze Variances: Once actual expenditures have been tracked, marketers should analyze the variances between actual and budgeted expenditures. This involves identifying areas where actual expenditures differ from the budget, and investigating the reasons for these variances. For example, if the budget for social media advertising was $10,000, but the actual expenditure was $12,000, marketers should investigate why this variance occurred.

Take Corrective Action: Based on the analysis of variances, marketers should take corrective action to ensure that actual expenditures are aligned with the budget. This may involve reducing expenditures in certain areas or reallocating resources to more effective marketing activities.

Review and Adjust the Budget: Finally, marketers should review and adjust the budget as necessary. This involves identifying changes in the market environment, customer preferences, or marketing strategy that may require adjustments to the budget. For example, if a new competitor enters the market, marketers may need to increase their advertising budget to maintain their market share.

In addition to monitoring and controlling marketing expenditures, it is important to evaluate the effectiveness of marketing activities. This involves assessing the return on investment (ROI) for each marketing activity and identifying areas where the ROI is low. By focusing resources on high-ROI activities, marketers can maximize the impact of their marketing budget and improve the overall effectiveness of their marketing strategy.

Overall, budgeting for marketing activities is an essential component of the marketing planning process. By setting clear goals, allocating resources effectively, monitoring actual expenditures, and evaluating effectiveness, marketers can ensure that their marketing strategy is aligned with their business objectives and maximize the impact of their marketing budget.

The budgeting process and key considerations

The budgeting process for marketing activities involves several key steps and considerations to ensure effective resource allocation and alignment with overall business objectives. In this section, we will explore the budgeting process in detail and discuss the key considerations that businesses should keep in mind.

The Budgeting Process:

Set Objectives: The first step in developing a marketing budget is to set clear and specific objectives. These objectives should be aligned with the overall business strategy and should be measurable. For example, a business might set an objective to increase sales by 10% in the next quarter.

Identify Available Resources: Once the objectives are set, the next step is to identify the resources available for marketing activities. This includes both financial and non-financial resources such as personnel, equipment, and technology.

Estimate Costs: The next step is to estimate the costs associated with each marketing activity. This involves identifying the specific tactics or channels that will be used to achieve the objectives and estimating the costs associated with each one. For example, if the objective is to increase sales through social media advertising, the costs associated with creating and running the ads should be estimated.

Develop the Budget: Once the costs have been estimated, the marketing budget can be developed. This involves allocating resources to each marketing activity based on the estimated costs and the importance of each activity in achieving the objectives.

Monitor and Control Expenditures: Finally, it is important to monitor and control marketing expenditures to ensure that they stay within the budget. This involves tracking actual expenditures against the budget and making adjustments as necessary.

Key Considerations:

Business Strategy: The marketing budget should be aligned with the overall business strategy. This means that the objectives and activities identified in the marketing plan should be consistent with the business's mission, vision, and values.

Market Conditions: The marketing budget should take into account the current market conditions. For example, if the market is highly competitive, the budget may need to be increased to ensure that the business can effectively compete.

Available Resources: The marketing budget should take into account the resources available to the business. This includes both financial and non-financial resources such as personnel and technology.

Return on Investment (ROI): The marketing budget should be designed to generate a positive return on investment. This means that the costs associated with each marketing activity should be justified by the expected revenue or other benefits generated.

Flexibility: The marketing budget should be flexible to accommodate changes in the business environment. This means that the budget should be regularly reviewed and adjusted as necessary to ensure that it remains aligned with the business strategy and objectives.

In summary, the budgeting process for marketing activities is a critical component of overall business strategy. By following a systematic approach and considering key factors such as business strategy, market conditions, available resources, ROI, and flexibility, businesses can develop effective marketing budgets that align with their overall objectives and generate positive returns on investment.

Approaches to allocating marketing budgets (e.g., percentage of sales, competitive parity, objective and task)

Allocating marketing budgets is a crucial task for businesses to ensure that their marketing activities align with their overall goals and objectives. There are various approaches to allocating marketing budgets, including the percentage of sales method, the competitive parity method, and the objective and task method.

Percentage of Sales Method
The percentage of sales method is one of the most common approaches to budgeting for marketing activities. Under this method, the budget is set as a percentage of the company's sales revenue. For example, a company may set a budget of 10% of its annual sales revenue for marketing activities.

The percentage of sales method is easy to calculate and provides a simple way to ensure that marketing expenditures are in line with revenue. However, it may not be the most effective way to allocate marketing budgets, as it does not take into account changes in the market or competitive landscape.

Competitive Parity Method
The competitive parity method involves setting the marketing budget based on the company's competitors' marketing expenditures. Under this method, a company may set its marketing budget equal to the average marketing expenditures of its competitors or adjust the budget based on its position in the market.

The competitive parity method is useful in ensuring that a company's marketing activities are in line with its competitors and that it remains competitive in the market. However, it may not account for differences in marketing strategies or the unique needs of the business.

Objective and Task Method
The objective and task method involves setting the marketing budget based on the company's specific marketing objectives and the tasks required to achieve those objectives. Under this method, a company will first identify its marketing objectives and then determine the specific tasks and resources required to achieve those objectives. The budget is then set based on the cost of these tasks and resources.

The objective and task method provides a more comprehensive approach to budgeting for marketing activities, as it is based on the specific needs and goals of the business. It allows for greater flexibility in allocating resources and enables companies to focus on achieving their marketing objectives. However, it can be more time-consuming and complex than other methods.

Choosing the Right Approach

Each of these approaches has its strengths and weaknesses, and the most appropriate method will depend on the unique needs and goals of the business. In practice, many companies use a combination of these methods to allocate their marketing budgets.

For example, a company may use the percentage of sales method to determine the baseline budget and then adjust the budget based on the competitive landscape and specific marketing objectives. This approach allows companies to balance the need for consistency and predictability in budgeting with the need to remain competitive and achieve specific marketing objectives.

Conclusion

Allocating marketing budgets is a critical process that requires careful consideration and planning. By understanding the different approaches to budgeting for marketing activities and their strengths and weaknesses, businesses can develop a budget that aligns with their overall goals and objectives. Ultimately, the right approach will depend on the unique needs and circumstances of the business.

Practical examples of budgeting for marketing activities

In the previous sections, we have discussed the importance of budgeting for marketing activities and the different approaches to allocating marketing budgets. In this section, we will provide some practical examples of budgeting for marketing activities.

Example 1: Percentage of Sales Approach

Suppose a small business has annual sales of $1 million and wants to allocate 10% of its sales revenue to marketing activities. Using the percentage of sales approach, the marketing budget for the year would be $100,000.

The business could then allocate this budget to various marketing activities, such as advertising, promotions, events, and social media campaigns. The business would need to monitor its actual marketing expenditures and adjust them as necessary to ensure that they do not exceed the budget.

Example 2: Competitive Parity Approach

Suppose a company in the automotive industry wants to allocate its marketing budget based on the industry average. The industry average for marketing spend is 2% of total sales revenue.

If the company has annual sales of $500 million, the marketing budget for the year would be $10 million (2% of $500 million). The company could then allocate this budget to various marketing activities, such as advertising, sponsorships, and events.

Example 3: Objective and Task Approach

Suppose a new company is launching a product and wants to use the objective and task approach to budget for its marketing activities. The company sets its objective as increasing brand awareness and generating 10,000 leads in the first quarter.

The tasks required to achieve these objectives might include creating a website, launching a social media campaign, and attending trade shows. The company would estimate the costs associated with each task and add them up to arrive at a budget for the quarter.

For example, the company might estimate that creating a website will cost $5,000, launching a social media campaign will cost $10,000, and attending trade shows will cost $20,000. The total budget for the quarter would be $35,000.

Example 4: Budgeting for International Marketing Activities

Budgeting for international marketing activities can be more complex than budgeting for domestic marketing activities. This is because different countries have different cultures, regulations, and economic conditions.

Suppose a company wants to expand its operations to a new country and needs to develop a marketing budget for the new market. The company would need to conduct market research to understand the local culture, consumer behavior, and competitive landscape.

Based on this research, the company would need to identify the marketing activities that would be most effective in the new market and estimate the costs associated with each activity. The company would then need to consider factors such as exchange rates, taxes, and regulatory compliance when developing the budget.

Example 5: Budgeting for Digital Marketing Activities

Digital marketing activities have become increasingly important in recent years, and many businesses are allocating a significant portion of their marketing budgets to digital channels such as social media, email marketing, and search engine optimization (SEO).

Suppose a company wants to allocate its marketing budget to digital channels. The company would need to identify the channels that are most relevant to its target audience and estimate the costs associated with each channel.

For example, the company might estimate that a social media campaign will cost $20,000, an email marketing campaign will cost $10,000, and an SEO campaign will cost $15,000. The company would need to monitor its actual expenditures and adjust them as necessary to ensure that they do not exceed the budget.

Conclusion

Budgeting for marketing activities is an essential part of the marketing planning process. The budgeting process involves allocating resources to various marketing activities, monitoring actual expenditures, and making adjustments as necessary.

The three approaches to allocating marketing budgets discussed in this section - percentage of sales, competitive parity, and objective and task - offer different advantages and disadvantages depending on the organization's goals, industry, and competitive landscape. For example, percentage of sales may be useful for companies with stable sales patterns, while objective and task may be more appropriate for companies launching new products or entering new markets.

In practice, companies may use a combination of approaches to allocate their marketing budgets, depending on their specific needs and goals. For example, a company may use percentage of sales for their overall marketing budget, but use objective and task for a specific product launch or market entry initiative.

In addition to understanding the various approaches to budgeting, it is important for companies to consider practical examples of budgeting for marketing activities. For example, a small business owner may need to allocate their marketing budget between digital advertising, print advertising, and trade shows, while a large corporation may need to allocate their budget between multiple product lines and international markets.

Overall, effective budgeting for marketing activities requires a deep understanding of the organization's goals and resources, as well as the competitive landscape and industry trends. By carefully allocating resources and monitoring actual expenditures, companies can ensure that their marketing activities are both effective and efficient.

Case study: Creating a marketing budget for a new product launch

Creating a marketing budget for a new product launch can be a challenging task. The success of a new product launch often depends on the effectiveness of its marketing campaign. Therefore, it is essential to allocate adequate resources to the marketing campaign while keeping the overall budget constraints in mind. In this section, we will discuss a case study of creating a marketing budget for a new product launch and explore the various steps involved in the process.

Case Study: Creating a Marketing Budget for a New Product Launch
Company XYZ is planning to launch a new line of energy drinks. The target market for this product is health-conscious individuals aged 18-35 who are looking for a natural source of energy. The company wants to launch the product in three months and has a budget of $500,000 for the marketing campaign.

Step 1: Determine the Marketing Objectives
The first step in creating a marketing budget is to determine the marketing objectives. In this case, the marketing objectives are to:

Create awareness of the new energy drink among the target audience
Establish the brand as a healthy and natural source of energy
Generate sales and achieve a market share of 5% within the first year of launch
Step 2: Identify the Target Audience
The next step is to identify the target audience. In this case, the target audience is health-conscious individuals aged 18-35 who are looking for a natural source of energy. The company should conduct market research to understand the characteristics and preferences of this target audience.

Step 3: Determine the Marketing Mix
The marketing mix consists of product, price, place, and promotion. In this case, the product is the new line of energy drinks, priced at $2 per can. The company plans to distribute the product through supermarkets and health food stores. The promotion mix will consist of advertising, sales promotion, public relations, and personal selling.

Step 4: Allocate the Budget
The next step is to allocate the budget among the various components of the promotion mix. The company has a budget of $500,000 for the marketing campaign. The allocation of the budget is as follows:

Advertising: $300,000 (60%)
Sales Promotion: $100,000 (20%)
Public Relations: $50,000 (10%)
Personal Selling: $50,000 (10%)
Step 5: Develop a Schedule
The final step is to develop a schedule for the marketing campaign. The company should create a timeline for each component of the promotion mix, specifying the start and end dates, and the budget allocated for each activity. The company should also monitor the progress of the campaign and make adjustments as necessary.

Conclusion
Creating a marketing budget for a new product launch requires careful planning and allocation of resources. The company must determine its marketing objectives, identify the target audience, and determine the marketing mix. The budget should be allocated among the various components of the promotion mix, and a schedule should be developed to ensure that the campaign is executed effectively. With proper

planning and execution, a well-designed marketing budget can help the company achieve its marketing objectives and achieve success in the marketplace.

Exercise: Developing a marketing budget for a hypothetical business

To gain a better understanding of the budgeting process for marketing activities, it can be helpful to practice developing a marketing budget for a hypothetical business. In this exercise, we will use a fictional business, a gourmet coffee shop called Bean Delight, to develop a marketing budget.

Step 1: Determine Marketing Objectives

The first step in developing a marketing budget is to determine the marketing objectives for the business. This involves identifying what the business hopes to achieve through its marketing efforts. For Bean Delight, the marketing objectives might include:

Increase foot traffic to the coffee shop
Increase sales of specialty drinks and pastries
Build brand awareness in the local community
Step 2: Identify Marketing Tactics

Once the marketing objectives have been identified, the next step is to determine what marketing tactics will be used to achieve those objectives. Marketing tactics might include:

Social media advertising
Local print advertising (e.g. in community newspapers)
In-store promotions (e.g. discounts for customers who refer friends)
Hosting special events (e.g. tastings, meet and greets with local vendors)
Step 3: Estimate Costs

After identifying marketing tactics, the next step is to estimate the costs associated with each tactic. This will help determine the overall marketing budget. For Bean Delight, the costs associated with each tactic might include:

Social media advertising: $1,000 per month
Local print advertising: $500 per month
In-store promotions: $500 per month
Hosting special events: $2,000 per quarter
Step 4: Allocate Budget

Once the costs associated with each tactic have been estimated, the next step is to allocate the marketing budget. This can be done using one of the three approaches discussed in the previous section:

Percentage of sales approach
Competitive parity approach
Objective and task approach
For Bean Delight, we will use the objective and task approach. This involves setting marketing objectives, identifying the tasks needed to achieve those objectives, estimating the costs associated with each task, and allocating the budget accordingly. Using this approach, we might allocate the budget as follows:

Marketing objective: Increase foot traffic to the coffee shop
Tasks:

Run a social media advertising campaign targeting local residents ($1,000 per month)
Host special events (e.g. coffee tastings) to attract new customers ($2,000 per quarter)
Marketing objective: Increase sales of specialty drinks and pastries
Tasks:

Run a local print advertising campaign highlighting specialty drinks and pastries ($500 per month)
Offer in-store promotions (e.g. discounts for customers who refer friends) to increase sales ($500 per month)
Marketing objective: Build brand awareness in the local community
Tasks:

Run a social media advertising campaign targeting local residents ($1,000 per month)
Host special events (e.g. meet and greets with local vendors) to increase brand awareness ($2,000 per quarter)
Total marketing budget: $10,500 per quarter

Step 5: Monitor and Adjust

After the marketing budget has been developed and implemented, it is important to monitor actual expenditures and adjust the budget as necessary. This may involve reallocating funds from one marketing tactic to another if certain tactics are not achieving the desired results or if unexpected opportunities arise.

Conclusion

Developing a marketing budget is an important part of the overall marketing planning process. By setting clear marketing objectives, identifying the tactics needed to achieve those objectives, estimating the costs associated with each tactic, and allocating the budget accordingly, businesses can ensure that their marketing efforts are focused and effective. It is important to monitor actual expenditures and adjust the budget as necessary to ensure that resources are being used efficiently and effectively.

CHAPTER 7: PRICING STRATEGIES AND THEIR IMPACT ON FINANCIAL PERFORMANCE

Pricing is one of the most important decisions a business owner or manager must make. The price of a product or service affects the demand for it, the amount of revenue generated, and the overall profitability of the business. The challenge is to find the right price that maximizes profits while also remaining competitive in the marketplace.

This chapter will examine various pricing strategies that businesses can use and their impact on financial performance. We will explore the different factors that businesses need to consider when setting prices and how these factors interact to influence pricing decisions. Additionally, we will discuss the different types of pricing strategies, including cost-based pricing, value-based pricing, and competition-based pricing.

One of the key concepts we will discuss is price elasticity of demand, which refers to how sensitive consumers are to changes in price. We will explain how price elasticity of demand can help businesses determine the optimal price point for their products or services.

Another important concept we will cover is price skimming, which involves setting a high price for a new product or service in order to maximize revenue from early adopters. We will also discuss penetration pricing, which involves setting a low price to attract customers and gain market share.

Furthermore, we will examine the impact of pricing on a business's financial performance. We will discuss how pricing decisions affect a business's revenue, profitability, and overall financial health. We will also discuss how pricing decisions can affect a business's brand and reputation.

Throughout this chapter, we will provide examples of businesses that have successfully used different pricing strategies, as well as businesses that have failed to do so. We will also discuss the ethical considerations that businesses need to keep in mind when setting prices.

The role of pricing in the marketing mix

Pricing is a crucial element of the marketing mix, which includes product, promotion, place, and price. The price is the amount of money that a customer pays for a product or service. It is the only element of the marketing mix that generates revenue. The other three elements incur costs. Therefore, pricing plays a significant role in determining the success or failure of a business. A business must establish a price that is acceptable to customers and profitable for the company. This chapter will explore the role of pricing in the marketing mix and how pricing strategies impact a company's financial performance.

The Role of Pricing in the Marketing Mix:

The marketing mix is a framework that businesses use to develop effective marketing strategies. It consists of four elements that a business must consider when developing a marketing plan. These elements are product, promotion, place, and price. Pricing is the only element of the marketing mix that generates revenue, making it a crucial component of a business's marketing strategy.

Pricing has a direct impact on a company's financial performance. If a company sets its prices too low, it may not generate enough revenue to cover its costs and make a profit. On the other hand, if a company sets its prices too high, it may not be able to attract enough customers, and it may lose market share to competitors. Therefore, setting the right price is critical to a business's success.

Pricing Strategies:

There are several pricing strategies that businesses can use to set their prices. These strategies include cost-plus pricing, value-based pricing, skimming pricing, penetration pricing, and dynamic pricing. Each pricing strategy has its advantages and disadvantages, and businesses must select the right strategy based on their product, market, and competition.

Cost-Plus Pricing:

Cost-plus pricing is a straightforward pricing strategy that involves adding a markup to the cost of a product to determine its price. The markup covers the company's overhead costs and generates a profit. Cost-plus pricing is a common pricing strategy used by manufacturers, retailers, and service providers. It is easy to calculate and provides a guaranteed profit margin for the company.

Value-Based Pricing:

Value-based pricing is a pricing strategy that focuses on the value that a product provides to customers. Value-based pricing takes into account the benefits that a product provides to customers, such as increased productivity, cost savings, or improved quality. Value-based pricing is often used for innovative or unique products that have a high perceived value to customers.

Skimming Pricing:

Skimming pricing is a pricing strategy that involves setting a high price for a product when it is first introduced to the market. Skimming pricing is often used for innovative or unique products that have a high perceived value to customers. Skimming pricing allows a company to generate high profits from early adopters of the product before competitors enter the market.

Penetration Pricing:

Penetration pricing is a pricing strategy that involves setting a low price for a product when it is first introduced to the market. Penetration pricing is often used to gain market share quickly or to enter a highly competitive market. Penetration pricing can be risky for a company because it may not generate enough revenue to cover its costs in the short term.

Dynamic Pricing:

Dynamic pricing is a pricing strategy that involves adjusting the price of a product in real-time based on market demand and other factors. Dynamic pricing is often used by airlines, hotels, and online retailers. Dynamic pricing allows a company to optimize its pricing based on real-time data and maximize its revenue.

Conclusion:

Pricing is a critical component of the marketing mix, and businesses must select the right pricing strategy based on their product, market, and competition. Pricing has a direct impact on a company's financial performance, and businesses must set the right price to generate enough revenue to cover their costs and make a profit. Cost-plus pricing, value-based pricing, and dynamic pricing are some of the popular pricing strategies used by businesses.

Cost-plus pricing involves setting a price based on the cost of producing the product, while value-based pricing considers the perceived value of the product by the customer. Dynamic pricing, on the other hand, involves setting a flexible price that changes based on market conditions and other factors.

When choosing a pricing strategy, businesses must also consider the potential impact on customer perception and demand. A high price may signal quality and exclusivity, but it may also deter price-sensitive customers. On the other hand, a low price may attract price-sensitive customers, but it may also signal lower quality.

Pricing strategies must also be aligned with the overall business strategy and marketing objectives. For example, a premium pricing strategy may be appropriate for luxury goods or niche products, while a lower price may be necessary to gain market share in a highly competitive industry.

In conclusion, pricing is a complex and multifaceted aspect of the marketing mix that requires careful consideration and analysis. Businesses must understand their product, market, competition, and customers to select the right pricing strategy that aligns with their overall business strategy and marketing objectives. By doing so, they can set the right price that generates enough revenue to cover their costs and make a profit while also maintaining customer satisfaction and loyalty.

Different pricing strategies (e.g., cost-plus, value-based, skimming, penetration)

Pricing strategy refers to the method used by businesses to set the price of their products or services. The price is usually determined based on a variety of factors, including the cost of production, demand, competition, and the overall marketing strategy of the business. There are several pricing strategies that businesses can use to set their prices, including cost-plus pricing, value-based pricing, skimming, and penetration pricing.

Cost-Plus Pricing:

Cost-plus pricing is a pricing strategy in which the price of a product or service is set by adding a markup to the cost of production. This markup is designed to cover the business's overhead costs and generate a profit. This pricing strategy is commonly used in manufacturing and service industries where the cost of production is the primary factor in determining the price.

The formula for cost-plus pricing is as follows:

Price = Cost of Production + Markup

The markup is usually expressed as a percentage of the cost of production. For example, if a product costs $10 to produce and the markup is 50%, the price would be set at $15 ($10 + 50% of $10).

While cost-plus pricing is relatively easy to calculate and understand, it has several drawbacks. One of the main drawbacks is that it does not take into account the market demand for the product. If the market demand is low, the business may not be able to charge a high enough price to cover its costs and make a profit. On the other hand, if the market demand is high, the business may be able to charge a higher price and generate more profit than it needs.

Value-Based Pricing:

Value-based pricing is a pricing strategy that is based on the perceived value of the product or service to the customer. This pricing strategy is often used in the service industry, where the value of the service is subjective and difficult to measure. Value-based pricing takes into account the customer's willingness to pay for the product or service and sets the price accordingly.

The formula for value-based pricing is as follows:

Price = Perceived Value to Customer

The perceived value of the product or service is often determined through market research, customer surveys, and focus groups. This pricing strategy is effective because it takes into account the customer's willingness to pay, which is often higher than the cost of production.

Skimming:

Skimming is a pricing strategy in which a business sets a high price for a new product or service when it is introduced to the market. This strategy is often used when a product or service is unique or innovative and has no direct competition. The goal of skimming is to maximize profits before competitors enter the market.

The formula for skimming pricing is as follows:

Price = High Price at Launch

Skimming pricing is effective when the demand for the product or service is high, and customers are willing to pay a premium for it. However, this pricing strategy is not sustainable in the long term because it invites competitors to enter the market and offer lower-priced alternatives.

Penetration:

Penetration is a pricing strategy in which a business sets a low price for a new product or service when it is introduced to the market. This strategy is often used when a product or service is similar to those already on the market, and the business wants to gain market share quickly. The goal of penetration pricing is to attract customers away from competitors and build a customer base quickly.

The formula for penetration pricing is as follows:

Price = Low Price at Launch

Penetration pricing is effective when the market is highly competitive and customers are price-sensitive. This pricing strategy can help a business gain market share quickly and build a customer base. However, this pricing strategy may not be sustainable in the long term because it may not generate enough profit to cover the business's costs.

Conclusion:

Selecting the right pricing strategy is critical to the success of a business. There are various pricing strategies that a business can use, such as cost-plus pricing, value-based pricing, skimming pricing, and penetration pricing. Each pricing strategy has its advantages and disadvantages and must be carefully considered based on the product, market, and competition.

Cost-plus pricing is a straightforward method that ensures that the business covers its costs and generates a profit margin. This strategy is suitable for businesses that offer standard products or services, where the competition is low, and customers are price-insensitive.

Value-based pricing is an effective strategy when a business offers unique products or services that are highly valued by customers. This strategy focuses on the perceived value of the product or service rather than its cost, allowing the business to set a higher price and generate higher profits.

Skimming pricing is a strategy that is effective when a business offers a new, innovative product or service that has a limited target market. This strategy allows the business to set a high price at launch to recoup its development costs quickly. However, this strategy may not be sustainable in the long term as competitors may offer similar products or services at lower prices.

Penetration pricing is a strategy that is effective when the market is highly competitive, and customers are price-sensitive. This strategy can help a business gain market share quickly and build a customer base. However, this strategy may not be sustainable in the long term as it may not generate enough profit to cover the business's costs.

It is crucial for businesses to evaluate their pricing strategies continually and adjust them accordingly based on changes in the market, competition, and customer demand. Pricing is not a one-time decision but an ongoing process that requires careful analysis and monitoring.

Exercises:

Imagine you are a business owner who sells handmade jewelry online. What pricing strategy would you use, and why? How would you evaluate your pricing strategy over time?

Conduct research on a company that has recently changed its pricing strategy. What was their previous pricing strategy, and what is their new pricing strategy? What factors led to the change in pricing strategy, and how has it impacted their financial performance?

Compare and contrast cost-plus pricing and value-based pricing. What are the advantages and disadvantages of each pricing strategy, and in what situations would you recommend using each strategy?

The impact of pricing on revenue, profitability, and market share
Factors to consider when setting prices (e.g., competition, customer demand, cost structure)

Pricing is a critical aspect of a company's marketing mix, and it has a direct impact on a company's financial performance. Pricing decisions affect a company's revenue, profitability, and market share. In this section, we will discuss the impact of pricing on revenue, profitability, and market share and factors to consider when setting prices.

The Impact of Pricing on Revenue:

Pricing has a significant impact on a company's revenue. A company's revenue is the total amount of money it earns from selling its products or services. The price of a product affects the demand for that product. In general, if the price of a product is high, the demand for that product will be low, and if the price of a product is low, the demand for that product will be high.

When setting prices, businesses must consider the price elasticity of demand. Price elasticity of demand measures how sensitive consumers are to changes in price. If consumers are highly sensitive to price changes, then small changes in price will have a significant impact on demand. For example, if a company raises the price of its product by 10%, and the demand for that product decreases by 20%, the price elasticity of demand is -2.

Businesses must also consider their competitors when setting prices. If a company's prices are too high compared to its competitors, customers may choose to purchase from the competition, resulting in a decrease in revenue. On the other hand, if a company's prices are too low, it may not generate enough revenue to cover its costs and make a profit.

The Impact of Pricing on Profitability:

Pricing has a direct impact on a company's profitability. Profitability is the ability of a company to generate profit from its operations. A company's profitability depends on the revenue it generates and the costs it incurs.

When setting prices, businesses must consider their cost structure. A company's cost structure includes both fixed and variable costs. Fixed costs are costs that do not change regardless of the level of production, such as rent, salaries, and insurance. Variable costs are costs that vary with the level of production, such as raw materials, labor, and utilities.

Businesses must set their prices high enough to cover their costs and generate a profit. If a company sets its prices too low, it may not generate enough revenue to cover its costs and make a profit. On the other hand, if a company sets its prices too high, it may not be able to compete with its competitors.

The Impact of Pricing on Market Share:

Pricing also has a direct impact on a company's market share. Market share is the percentage of the total market that a company controls. A company's market share depends on its ability to attract and retain customers.

When setting prices, businesses must consider their target market. Different customers have different price sensitivities. For example, luxury products typically have a higher price point because their target market is willing to pay more for quality and exclusivity. In contrast, value-oriented products have a lower price point because their target market is more price-sensitive.

Businesses must also consider their competition when setting prices. If a company's prices are higher than its competitors, it may lose market share to its competitors. On the other hand, if a company's prices are lower than its competitors, it may attract customers away from its competitors.

Factors to Consider When Setting Prices:

When setting prices, businesses must consider several factors, including competition, customer demand, and cost structure.

Competition:

Businesses must consider their competitors when setting prices. If a company's prices are too high compared to its competitors, customers may choose to purchase from the competition, resulting in a decrease in revenue. On the other hand, if a company's prices are too low, it may not generate enough revenue to cover its costs and make a profit. Therefore, it is important for businesses to conduct competitive analysis to determine the best pricing strategy.

There are several methods that businesses can use to conduct competitive analysis, including monitoring competitors' prices, reviewing their marketing and advertising strategies, analyzing their product offerings, and examining their target markets. By understanding their competitors' strengths and weaknesses, businesses can adjust their pricing strategies to gain a competitive advantage in the market.

For example, a business may offer a lower price than its competitors for a similar product, but provide additional value through better customer service or higher quality products. Alternatively, a business may charge a premium price for its products to position itself as a luxury brand, but offer unique features or benefits that are not available from its competitors.

Customer Demand:

Customer demand is another critical factor to consider when setting prices. If customers are willing to pay a higher price for a product or service, businesses can charge a premium price to increase revenue and profit margins. However, if customers are price-sensitive and unwilling to pay a higher price, businesses may need to offer discounts or lower prices to remain competitive.

Businesses can determine customer demand through market research and customer surveys. This can help businesses understand their customers' preferences, purchasing behavior, and willingness to pay for certain products or services.

Cost Structure:

The cost structure of a business is another important factor to consider when setting prices. Businesses must ensure that their prices are high enough to cover their costs and make a profit. However, if prices are too high, customers may not be willing to purchase the product or service.

When determining the cost structure, businesses must consider all costs associated with producing and delivering the product or service, including raw materials, labor, overhead costs, and marketing expenses. By understanding their cost structure, businesses can determine the minimum price they need to charge to cover their costs and make a profit.

Impact of Pricing on Revenue, Profitability, and Market Share:

Pricing has a direct impact on a company's revenue, profitability, and market share. If a business sets its prices too high, it may not generate enough revenue to cover its costs and make a profit, resulting in a decrease in profitability. On the other hand, if prices are too low, the business may not be able to generate enough revenue to cover its costs and make a profit.

Furthermore, pricing can impact a business's market share. If a business offers a lower price than its competitors, it may gain market share by attracting price-sensitive customers. However, if a business charges a premium price, it may lose market share to competitors who offer lower prices.

Therefore, businesses must carefully consider their pricing strategy to achieve the optimal balance between revenue, profitability, and market share. This requires businesses to conduct thorough analysis of factors such as competition, customer demand, and cost structure to determine the best pricing strategy.

Conclusion:

Pricing is a critical component of a business's marketing mix and can have a significant impact on its revenue, profitability, and market share. Businesses must carefully consider their pricing strategy based on factors such as competition, customer demand, and cost structure to achieve the optimal balance between revenue, profitability, and market share. Conducting competitive analysis, market research, and cost analysis can help businesses determine the best pricing strategy to achieve their goals.

Practical examples of pricing strategies for different types of businesses

In this section, we will discuss practical examples of pricing strategies for different types of businesses. These examples will help students understand how different pricing strategies can be applied in real-world scenarios.

Business-to-Consumer (B2C) Companies
B2C companies sell their products directly to consumers. These companies need to consider factors such as customer demand, competition, and cost structure when setting their prices. Here are some practical examples of pricing strategies that B2C companies can use:

Premium Pricing: B2C companies that offer high-quality products or services can use premium pricing to differentiate themselves from their competitors. For example, Apple is known for using premium pricing for its products such as the iPhone and MacBook.

Value-based Pricing: B2C companies can also use value-based pricing to set prices based on the value their products or services offer to customers. For example, Amazon Prime offers customers free two-day shipping, access to streaming of movies and TV shows, and other benefits for a yearly subscription fee.

Dynamic Pricing: B2C companies can also use dynamic pricing to adjust prices based on factors such as demand, time of day, or season. For example, airlines often use dynamic pricing to adjust prices for flights based on the time of year and demand.

Business-to-Business (B2B) Companies

B2B companies sell their products or services to other businesses. These companies need to consider factors such as the industry they operate in, the size of the customer, and the value proposition of their product or service when setting their prices. Here are some practical examples of pricing strategies that B2B companies can use:

Negotiated Pricing: B2B companies often negotiate pricing with their customers based on factors such as the size of the customer and the volume of the purchase. For example, a software company may negotiate pricing with a large corporation based on the number of licenses they will need.

Cost-plus Pricing: B2B companies can also use cost-plus pricing to set prices based on their cost structure. For example, a manufacturing company may set the price of a product based on the cost of materials, labor, and overhead, plus a markup.

Value-based Pricing: B2B companies can also use value-based pricing to set prices based on the value their products or services offer to their customers. For example, a consulting company may set prices based on the potential value they can deliver to their clients.

Service-Based Businesses

Service-based businesses offer intangible services such as consulting, accounting, and legal services. These businesses need to consider factors such as the level of expertise required, the time required to complete the service, and the competition when setting their prices. Here are some practical examples of pricing strategies that service-based businesses can use:

Hourly Billing: Service-based businesses can use hourly billing to charge clients based on the time required to complete the service. For example, a law firm may bill clients based on the number of hours worked on a case.

Flat Fee Pricing: Service-based businesses can also use flat fee pricing to set a fixed price for a service. For example, an accounting firm may charge a flat fee for preparing a tax return.

Retainer-based Pricing: Service-based businesses can also use retainer-based pricing to charge clients a monthly fee for ongoing services. For example, a marketing agency may charge a monthly retainer fee for ongoing marketing services.

Product-Based Businesses

Product-based businesses sell physical products such as clothing, electronics, and furniture. These businesses need to consider factors such as production costs, distribution costs, and competition when setting their prices. Here are some practical examples of pricing strategies that product-based businesses can use:

Penetration Pricing: Product-based businesses can use penetration pricing to enter a highly competitive market and gain market share quickly. By setting a lower price than the competition, the business can attract price-sensitive customers who are willing to try a new product. This pricing strategy can be effective when introducing a new product to the market or expanding into a new geographic region.

For example, a new clothing brand can use penetration pricing to enter the market and gain traction among price-sensitive customers. By pricing their products lower than established brands, they can attract customers who are willing to try their products and potentially switch from their current brand.

Value-Based Pricing: Product-based businesses can use value-based pricing to differentiate their products based on the value they provide to customers. By setting a higher price than the competition, the business can communicate that their products offer higher quality, better features, or other benefits. This pricing strategy can be effective when the product has a unique selling proposition that justifies a higher price.

For example, a high-end furniture brand can use value-based pricing to justify a higher price for their products. By emphasizing the quality of their materials and craftsmanship, they can differentiate their products from lower-priced alternatives and appeal to customers who value luxury and exclusivity.

Cost-Plus Pricing: Product-based businesses can use cost-plus pricing to ensure that they cover their production and distribution costs while making a profit. This pricing strategy involves adding a markup to the total cost of producing and distributing a product. The markup represents the profit margin that the business aims to achieve.

For example, an electronics manufacturer can use cost-plus pricing to set the price of their products. They can calculate the total cost of producing and distributing a product, then add a markup that ensures they make a profit. This pricing strategy can be effective when the competition is not too intense and customers are willing to pay a fair price for the product.

Skimming Pricing: Product-based businesses can use skimming pricing to capitalize on the initial demand for a new product or a product with a unique selling proposition. This pricing strategy involves setting a high price for the product at launch and gradually reducing the price as competition increases or demand decreases. Skimming pricing can be effective when the product has a limited lifespan or when the business needs to recoup its development costs quickly.

For example, a new smartphone model can use skimming pricing to capitalize on the initial demand for the product. By setting a high price at launch, the business can generate high revenue and recoup its development costs quickly. As competition increases or demand decreases, the business can gradually reduce the price to maintain market share.

Conclusion:

Pricing strategies play a crucial role in the success of product-based businesses. These businesses need to consider their production and distribution costs, competition, and customer demand when setting their prices. Penetration pricing, value-based pricing, cost-plus pricing, and skimming pricing are some of the practical pricing strategies that product-based businesses can use to achieve their financial goals. By selecting the right pricing strategy, businesses can increase their revenue, profitability, and market share.

Case study: Analyzing the pricing strategies of two competing companies

In the highly competitive market of today, businesses need to be strategic in their pricing decisions to gain market share and stay profitable. This case study analyzes the pricing strategies of two competing companies in the same industry, examining their approaches to setting prices and the impact on their revenue, profitability, and market share.

Company A: Apple Inc.

Apple Inc. is a multinational technology company that specializes in designing, developing, and selling consumer electronics, computer software, and online services. The company is known for its innovative products such as the iPhone, iPad, and Mac, which are sold through its retail stores, online store, and third-party resellers.

Apple's pricing strategy is based on the value of its products to the customers. The company sets premium prices for its products, positioning them as high-quality, innovative, and worth the extra cost. For instance, the latest iPhone model is priced at $999, which is significantly higher than the average price of smartphones in the market.

One of the key reasons for Apple's premium pricing strategy is its strong brand image and customer loyalty. Apple has built a brand that is associated with quality, innovation, and luxury, which enables the company to charge higher prices without compromising its sales. In addition, Apple's pricing strategy is based on its cost structure, which includes the cost of developing and manufacturing its products, marketing expenses, and retail costs.

Company B: Samsung Electronics

Samsung Electronics is a South Korean multinational electronics company that produces a wide range of consumer electronics, home appliances, and mobile devices. The company's products are sold through its retail stores, online store, and third-party resellers.

Samsung's pricing strategy is based on its cost structure, which includes the cost of production, marketing expenses, and distribution costs. The company aims to offer competitive prices for its products, positioning itself as an affordable and accessible brand for consumers. For instance, the latest Samsung Galaxy smartphone is priced at $799, which is lower than the price of the latest iPhone.

One of the key reasons for Samsung's pricing strategy is its focus on market share. The company aims to gain market share by offering products at competitive prices, targeting a wider customer base. In addition, Samsung's pricing strategy is also influenced by its competitors, such as Apple, which it tries to match or undercut in terms of price.

Comparison of Pricing Strategies

Apple and Samsung use different pricing strategies based on their business models, target markets, and competitive landscape. Apple focuses on premium pricing, positioning itself as a luxury brand that offers high-quality and innovative products. Samsung, on the other hand, focuses on competitive pricing, positioning itself as an affordable and accessible brand for consumers.

Both companies have been successful in their pricing strategies, but they have different impacts on their revenue, profitability, and market share. Apple's premium pricing strategy has enabled the company to generate high revenue and profitability, but it has also limited its market share, as its products are relatively expensive compared to its competitors. Samsung's competitive pricing strategy has enabled the company to gain a larger market share, but it has also limited its profitability, as its products are priced lower than its competitors.

Conclusion

Pricing is a critical aspect of business strategy, which impacts revenue, profitability, and market share. Apple and Samsung are two examples of companies with different pricing strategies, based on their business models, target markets, and competitive landscape. Apple's premium pricing strategy is based on its strong brand image and customer loyalty, while Samsung's competitive pricing strategy is based on its focus on market share and affordability. Both companies have been successful in their pricing strategies, but they have different impacts on their financial performance. Businesses need to carefully analyze their pricing decisions, considering factors such as competition, customer demand, and cost structure, to optimize their revenue, profitability, and market share.

One key takeaway from the case study is that there is no one-size-fits-all approach to pricing. Companies need to assess their unique circumstances and objectives to determine the pricing strategy that works best for them. Pricing strategies should be flexible and adaptable to changing market conditions and consumer preferences.

Moreover, pricing is not a one-time decision; it requires continuous evaluation and adjustment. Companies need to monitor their pricing strategies and make changes as needed to optimize their performance. They also need to consider the long-term implications of their pricing decisions, such as the impact on brand reputation and customer loyalty.

In summary, pricing is a complex and dynamic process that requires careful analysis and consideration. Companies need to understand their market, competition, customers, and costs to develop effective pricing strategies that maximize their financial performance and meet their business objectives. By applying the principles and techniques discussed in this case study, businesses can make informed and effective pricing decisions that drive their success in the market.

Exercise: Developing a pricing strategy for a hypothetical product or service

In this exercise, we will develop a pricing strategy for a hypothetical product or service. This exercise will provide students with an opportunity to apply the concepts and principles discussed in the previous sections of the textbook.

Step 1: Product/Service Description

Choose a product or service that you would like to develop a pricing strategy for. This can be a hypothetical product or service, or a real one that you are familiar with. Provide a brief description of the product or service, including its features, benefits, and target market.

Step 2: Cost Analysis

Conduct a cost analysis of your product or service. This includes identifying all the costs associated with producing, distributing, and promoting your product or service. Make sure to include both direct costs (e.g. materials, labor) and indirect costs (e.g. overhead, marketing expenses).

Step 3: Competitive Analysis

Conduct a competitive analysis to identify the prices of similar products or services in the market. This includes identifying the prices of your direct competitors as well as substitute products or services. Analyze the strengths and weaknesses of your competitors' pricing strategies, and identify any pricing gaps in the market.

Step 4: Customer Analysis

Conduct a customer analysis to identify the target market for your product or service. This includes identifying the demographic, psychographic, and behavioral characteristics of your target customers. Analyze the price sensitivity of your target customers, and identify any factors that may influence their purchasing decisions (e.g. brand reputation, product quality, convenience, etc.).

Step 5: Pricing Objectives

Based on your cost analysis, competitive analysis, and customer analysis, develop pricing objectives for your product or service. These objectives should be specific, measurable, achievable, relevant, and time-bound. Examples of pricing objectives include:

Maximize profit margins
Increase market share
Penetrate a new market segment
Establish a premium brand image
Encourage repeat purchases

Step 6: Pricing Strategy

Based on your pricing objectives, develop a pricing strategy for your product or service. This includes determining the pricing method (e.g. cost-plus pricing, value-based pricing, penetration pricing, etc.) and setting the actual price.

When setting the actual price, consider the following factors:

The perceived value of your product or service
The pricing of your competitors and substitute products or services
The costs associated with producing, distributing, and promoting your product or service
The price sensitivity of your target customers
Your pricing objectives

Step 7: Test and Refine

Once you have developed your pricing strategy, test it in the market to see how customers respond. Collect feedback from customers and analyze sales data to determine the effectiveness of your pricing strategy. Based on this feedback, refine your pricing strategy as necessary to achieve your pricing objectives.

Conclusion:

Developing a pricing strategy for a product or service requires a thorough analysis of costs, competition, and customer behavior. By following the steps outlined in this exercise, students can develop a pricing strategy that aligns with their business objectives and maximizes their profitability. It is important to test and refine pricing strategies regularly to ensure that they remain effective in the constantly changing market.

CHAPTER 8: MEASURING RETURN ON MARKETING INVESTMENT (ROMI)

Marketing is an essential component of any business, regardless of its size or industry. Effective marketing can drive sales, enhance brand recognition, and build customer loyalty. However, it can be challenging for businesses to determine the return on investment (ROI) of their marketing efforts. Measuring return on marketing investment (ROMI) is a crucial step in assessing the effectiveness of marketing campaigns and improving future marketing strategies.

This chapter will provide an overview of ROMI and its importance in marketing management. We will examine the different approaches to measuring ROMI, including financial and non-financial metrics. We will also explore the challenges and limitations of ROMI measurement and the role of marketing analytics in enhancing ROMI analysis.

Finally, we will provide real-world examples of companies that have successfully measured ROMI, and we will discuss best practices for developing and implementing effective ROMI measurement strategies. By the end of this chapter, you will have a thorough understanding of ROMI and its significance in marketing management, as well as the tools and techniques needed to measure and analyze ROMI.

The importance of measuring the effectiveness of marketing activities

Measuring the effectiveness of marketing activities is essential for any business to determine the return on marketing investment (ROMI). ROMI is a key performance indicator (KPI) that shows how much revenue a company generates from its marketing campaigns compared to the costs incurred to run them. It is an important metric that helps companies make informed decisions about their marketing budget and strategy.

In today's competitive business landscape, companies need to stay ahead of the curve and use marketing strategies that produce tangible results. Measuring the effectiveness of marketing activities is critical in ensuring that companies are making informed decisions about their marketing investments. Without accurate measurement, it is difficult for businesses to know which marketing activities are driving revenue and which ones are not.

This chapter will explore the importance of measuring the effectiveness of marketing activities and provide an overview of the key metrics that businesses can use to track the performance of their marketing campaigns.

Importance of Measuring Marketing Effectiveness:

Measuring the effectiveness of marketing activities is critical for several reasons. Firstly, it allows businesses to understand which marketing activities are generating the most revenue and which ones are not. By identifying the most effective marketing channels, businesses can allocate their resources more efficiently and optimize their marketing budget.

Secondly, measuring marketing effectiveness allows companies to track the performance of their marketing campaigns over time. This enables them to make informed decisions about their marketing strategy and adjust it as needed.

Thirdly, measuring marketing effectiveness helps businesses identify areas for improvement. By analyzing the performance of their marketing campaigns, companies can identify gaps in their marketing strategy and make changes to improve their results.

Finally, measuring marketing effectiveness helps businesses demonstrate the value of their marketing investments to stakeholders. By providing tangible metrics that demonstrate the return on marketing investment, businesses can show that their marketing efforts are contributing to the overall success of the company.

Key Metrics for Measuring Marketing Effectiveness:

There are several key metrics that businesses can use to measure the effectiveness of their marketing activities. These include:

Conversion Rate: The conversion rate is the percentage of website visitors or leads that take a desired action, such as making a purchase or filling out a form. A high conversion rate indicates that a marketing campaign is effective at driving engagement and generating leads.

Cost per Acquisition (CPA): The cost per acquisition is the amount of money a business spends to acquire a new customer. This metric is useful for determining the effectiveness of marketing campaigns that are designed to drive new customer acquisition.

Customer Lifetime Value (CLV): The customer lifetime value is the total amount of revenue a business can expect to generate from a single customer over the course of their lifetime. This metric is useful for understanding the long-term value of a customer and the return on investment for marketing campaigns.

Return on Investment (ROI): The return on investment is the amount of revenue generated by a marketing campaign compared to the cost of running it. A positive ROI indicates that a marketing campaign is generating more revenue than it costs to run, while a negative ROI indicates the opposite.

Net Promoter Score (NPS): The net promoter score is a metric that measures customer loyalty and satisfaction. It is calculated by subtracting the percentage of detractors (customers who would not recommend the business) from the percentage of promoters (customers who would recommend the business).

Conclusion:

In conclusion, measuring the effectiveness of marketing activities is critical for any business to optimize their marketing budget and strategy. By using key metrics such as conversion rate, cost per acquisition, customer lifetime value, return on investment, and net promoter score, businesses can track the performance of their marketing campaigns and make informed decisions about their marketing investments. Measuring marketing effectiveness is an ongoing process that requires regular monitoring and analysis to ensure that marketing strategies are producing tangible results.

Approaches to measuring ROMI (e.g., incremental sales, customer lifetime value, brand awareness)

Measuring the return on marketing investment (ROMI) is essential to evaluate the effectiveness of marketing activities and to optimize marketing spending. There are various approaches to measuring ROMI, including incremental sales, customer lifetime value (CLV), and brand awareness. Each approach has its advantages and disadvantages, and businesses need to consider which approach is most appropriate for their specific situation.

Incremental Sales

The incremental sales approach to measuring ROMI involves comparing sales before and after a marketing campaign. This approach assumes that any increase in sales during the campaign is due to the marketing activities. To calculate the ROMI using the incremental sales approach, businesses need to subtract the cost of the marketing campaign from the incremental sales generated by the campaign and then divide the result by the cost of the marketing campaign.

For example, suppose a company spends $100,000 on a marketing campaign that generates $500,000 in incremental sales. The ROMI would be calculated as follows:

ROMI = (Incremental Sales - Marketing Cost) / Marketing Cost
ROMI = ($500,000 - $100,000) / $100,000
ROMI = 4

In this case, the ROMI is 4, which means that the company earned $4 for every $1 spent on the marketing campaign.

The incremental sales approach is easy to understand and calculate, making it a popular method for measuring ROMI. However, it assumes that the increase in sales is solely due to the marketing campaign and does not account for other factors that may have contributed to the increase. For example, changes in the economy or competition may have also influenced sales.

Customer Lifetime Value

The customer lifetime value (CLV) approach to measuring ROMI focuses on the long-term value of a customer. It involves estimating the revenue that a customer will generate over their lifetime and subtracting the cost of acquiring and servicing the customer. The resulting number is the net present value of the customer.

To calculate the ROMI using the CLV approach, businesses need to estimate the CLV of the customers acquired through the marketing campaign and compare it to the cost of the marketing campaign.

For example, suppose a company spends $100,000 on a marketing campaign that acquires 1,000 new customers. The estimated CLV of each customer is $500, resulting in a total CLV of $500,000 for the new customers. The ROMI would be calculated as follows:

ROMI = CLV / Marketing Cost
ROMI = $500,000 / $100,000
ROMI = 5

In this case, the ROMI is 5, which means that the company earned $5 for every $1 spent on the marketing campaign.

The CLV approach is useful because it considers the long-term value of a customer and can help businesses determine the optimal marketing spending to maximize the total value of their customer base. However, it can be challenging to accurately estimate the CLV of customers, and it does not consider the short-term impact of marketing campaigns on sales.

Brand Awareness

The brand awareness approach to measuring ROMI focuses on the impact of marketing campaigns on brand recognition and perception. It involves conducting surveys or other research to measure changes in consumer attitudes towards the brand after a marketing campaign.

To calculate the ROMI using the brand awareness approach, businesses need to estimate the value of increased brand awareness and compare it to the cost of the marketing campaign.

For example, suppose a company spends $100,000 on a marketing campaign that increases brand awareness by 10%. The estimated value of the increased brand awareness is $50,000, resulting in a ROMI of:

ROMI = Value of Increased Brand Awareness / Marketing Cost
ROMI = $50,000 /$100,000
ROMI = 0.5

This indicates that for every dollar spent on the marketing campaign, the company generated 50 cents in return in the form of increased brand awareness. However, ROMI is just one approach to measuring the effectiveness of marketing activities.

Another approach is incremental sales, which measures the additional revenue generated as a direct result of the marketing campaign. To calculate incremental sales, the company needs to compare the revenue generated during the campaign period to the revenue generated during a similar period without the campaign. The difference between the two periods represents the incremental sales.

For example, suppose a company runs a marketing campaign in January and February that costs $50,000 and generates $200,000 in revenue. During the same period in the previous year, the company generated $150,000 in revenue. The incremental sales for the marketing campaign would be:

Incremental Sales = Revenue during Campaign Period - Revenue during Same Period Previous Year
Incremental Sales = $200,000 - $150,000
Incremental Sales = $50,000

This indicates that the marketing campaign generated an additional $50,000 in revenue for the company. The incremental sales approach provides a more direct measurement of the impact of the marketing campaign on revenue, but it may not capture the long-term effects on customer loyalty and brand awareness.

A third approach to measuring ROMI is customer lifetime value (CLV), which measures the total value of a customer over their lifetime of purchases. CLV takes into account the revenue generated by the customer as well as the cost of acquiring and retaining the customer. To calculate CLV, the company needs to estimate the customer's future purchases and discount them to their present value.

For example, suppose a customer purchases a product for $100 and the company estimates that the customer will make four more purchases in the future, with a total value of $400. The company also estimates that the cost of acquiring and retaining the customer is $150. The CLV of the customer would be:

CLV = (Total Revenue from Customer - Cost of Acquisition and Retention) / (1 + Discount Rate) ^ Number of Years
CLV = ($500 - $150) / (1 + 0.1) ^ 5
CLV = $210.94

This indicates that the customer has a CLV of $210.94. The CLV approach provides a more comprehensive measurement of the impact of the marketing campaign on the company's long-term profitability, but it requires more data and assumptions than the other approaches.

In conclusion, there are several approaches to measuring ROMI, each with its strengths and limitations. Incremental sales provides a direct measurement of the impact of the marketing campaign on revenue, ROMI provides a more straightforward measurement of the return on investment, and CLV provides a more comprehensive measurement of the impact on long-term profitability. Companies should carefully consider which approach to use based on their specific goals and resources.

Challenges and limitations of measuring ROMI

Measuring return on marketing investment (ROMI) can be a valuable tool for businesses seeking to optimize their marketing efforts and increase profitability. However, like any metric, ROMI has its limitations and challenges, which must be understood and addressed to ensure that the metric is used effectively.

One of the primary challenges of measuring ROMI is that marketing activities often have a long-term impact on a company's bottom line, making it difficult to isolate the effects of individual marketing campaigns. For example, a successful marketing campaign might increase brand awareness and customer loyalty, which could lead to increased sales and profitability over an extended period. However, it can be challenging to attribute those benefits directly to the campaign, as there may be other factors at play, such as changes in consumer behavior, market trends, or competitive activity.

Another challenge of measuring ROMI is that not all marketing activities have a measurable impact on revenue. For example, some marketing campaigns may focus on building brand awareness or generating leads, which can be difficult to quantify in terms of revenue. In such cases, it may be necessary to use alternative metrics, such as customer acquisition cost (CAC) or customer lifetime value (CLV), to assess the effectiveness of the campaign.

In addition to these challenges, there are several limitations to using ROMI as a metric for evaluating marketing effectiveness. One of the most significant limitations is that ROMI does not take into account the opportunity cost of investing in marketing. For example, suppose a company invests $100,000 in a marketing campaign that generates a ROMI of 200%. In that case, the company might conclude that the campaign was a success. However, if the company had invested that same $100,000 in a different area of the business, such as research and development or operations, it might have generated a higher return on investment.

Another limitation of ROMI is that it does not consider the potential negative impacts of marketing activities, such as brand damage or reputational harm. For example, a marketing campaign that is deemed offensive or insensitive by consumers could result in a significant backlash, leading to a decline in sales and profitability. In such cases, it may be necessary to use alternative metrics, such as customer satisfaction or brand sentiment, to assess the effectiveness of the campaign.

Overall, while ROMI can be a useful metric for evaluating the effectiveness of marketing activities, it is essential to understand its limitations and challenges to ensure that it is used effectively. To address these challenges and limitations, businesses can use a range of approaches, including data analytics, experimental design, and qualitative research, to gain a more comprehensive understanding of the impact of their marketing activities. By doing so, businesses can optimize their marketing efforts, increase profitability, and drive long-term growth.

Example Problem:
Suppose a company invests $500,000 in a marketing campaign that generates $1 million in sales. However, the company's operating costs for the same period increased by $200,000 due to the marketing campaign. Calculate the ROMI for the marketing campaign.

Solution:
The value of increased sales is $1 million, and the marketing cost is $500,000. Therefore, the ROMI is calculated as follows:

ROMI = Value of Increased Sales / Marketing Cost
ROMI = $1,000,000 / $500,000
ROMI = 2

However, the ROMI calculation does not take into account the additional operating costs incurred by the company due to the marketing campaign. To calculate the true ROMI, we must adjust for these costs:

Adjusted ROMI = (Value of Increased Sales - Additional Operating Costs) / Marketing Cost
Adjusted ROMI = ($1,000,000 - $200,000) / $500,000
Adjusted ROMI = 1

While adjusting for additional operating costs is important to determine the true ROMI, there are still other challenges and limitations associated with measuring ROMI that businesses need to be aware of. In this section, we will explore these challenges and limitations in more detail.

Difficulty in assigning causality: One of the main challenges in measuring ROMI is determining causality. This is because there are often multiple marketing campaigns running simultaneously, making it difficult to attribute the success of a particular campaign to the increase in sales or revenue. It can also be challenging to measure the impact of a campaign on customer behavior, as there are often many other factors that influence their decision-making.

Time lag between investment and return: Another challenge in measuring ROMI is the time lag between the investment in marketing and the resulting return. Marketing campaigns often require a significant upfront investment, and it can take time for the campaign to generate revenue. This can make it difficult to accurately measure the success of the campaign, particularly if the return on investment is not realized for several months or even years.

Difficulty in measuring intangible benefits: While ROMI is often used to measure the financial impact of marketing campaigns, it can be challenging to measure the intangible benefits that marketing can bring. For example, a marketing campaign may improve brand awareness or customer loyalty, but it can be difficult to assign a monetary value to these benefits.

Incomplete data: Another limitation of measuring ROMI is the availability of complete data. Many businesses do not have access to complete data on their customers or their sales, which can make it challenging to accurately measure the success of a marketing campaign. Additionally, incomplete data can make it difficult to attribute success to a particular campaign or to accurately calculate the costs associated with the campaign.

Limited scope of measurement: Finally, ROMI is limited in its scope of measurement. While it is a useful tool for measuring the financial impact of marketing campaigns, it does not take into account other factors that may influence customer behavior or the success of a campaign. For example, it does not measure the impact of changes in pricing or product offerings, which can also have a significant impact on sales.

Despite these challenges and limitations, measuring ROMI is still an important tool for businesses to assess the success of their marketing campaigns. To overcome these challenges, businesses need to be diligent in their data collection and analysis, and they should also be willing to consider other metrics, such as customer satisfaction or brand awareness, in addition to ROMI when evaluating the success of their marketing efforts. By taking a holistic approach to measuring the impact of marketing, businesses can make better decisions about where to invest their marketing dollars and maximize their return on investment.

Example problem:

Suppose a company invests $100,000 in a marketing campaign that generates $500,000 in revenue. The company also incurs an additional $50,000 in operating costs as a result of the campaign. Calculate the adjusted ROMI for the campaign.

Solution:
Adjusted ROMI = (Value of Increased Sales - Additional Operating Costs) / Marketing Cost
Value of Increased Sales = $500,000
Additional Operating Costs = $50,000
Marketing Cost = $100,000

Adjusted ROMI = ($500,000 - $50,000) / $100,000
Adjusted ROMI = 4.5

In this example, the adjusted ROMI is 4.5, indicating that the marketing campaign generated significant value for the company. However, it is important to note that this calculation does not take into account other factors that may have influenced customer behavior or the success of the campaign.

Practical examples of measuring ROMI for different types of marketing activities

Practical examples of measuring ROMI for different types of marketing activities can be helpful in understanding how this metric is calculated in real-life scenarios. In this section, we will discuss some examples of measuring ROMI for different types of marketing activities.

Measuring ROMI for Social Media Marketing:
Social media marketing has become increasingly popular among businesses in recent years due to its cost-effectiveness and the ability to reach a large audience. Measuring ROMI for social media marketing can be challenging because it is often difficult to track the direct impact of social media on sales. One approach is to measure the engagement of social media posts and how they contribute to brand awareness. For example, a company might measure the number of likes, shares, and comments on a social media post and track how this translates into website traffic, leads, and sales. To calculate ROMI, the company would compare the cost of the social media campaign to the estimated value of the increased website traffic, leads, and sales generated by the campaign.

Measuring ROMI for Email Marketing:
Email marketing is another popular marketing activity used by many businesses. Measuring the ROMI for email marketing can be more straightforward than

measuring ROMI for social media marketing because it is easier to track the impact of email campaigns on sales. For example, a company might measure the open rate and click-through rate of an email campaign and track how this translates into website traffic, leads, and sales. To calculate ROMI, the company would compare the cost of the email campaign to the estimated value of the increased website traffic, leads, and sales generated by the campaign.

Measuring ROMI for Event Marketing:
Event marketing is a powerful tool for businesses to connect with customers and generate leads. Measuring ROMI for event marketing can be challenging because it is often difficult to track the direct impact of events on sales. One approach is to measure the number of attendees, the engagement of attendees during the event, and the number of leads generated from the event. To calculate ROMI, the company would compare the cost of the event to the estimated value of the increased leads generated by the event.

Measuring ROMI for Content Marketing:
Content marketing is the creation and distribution of valuable content to attract and retain a target audience. Measuring the ROMI for content marketing can be more challenging because it is often difficult to track the impact of content on sales. One approach is to measure the engagement of content, such as the number of views, shares, and comments, and track how this translates into website traffic, leads, and sales. To calculate ROMI, the company would compare the cost of the content marketing campaign to the estimated value of the increased website traffic, leads, and sales generated by the campaign.

Measuring ROMI for Influencer Marketing:
Influencer marketing is a marketing strategy that involves partnering with influential people in a specific industry or niche to promote a product or service. Measuring ROMI for influencer marketing can be challenging because it is often difficult to track the direct impact of influencer marketing on sales. One approach is to measure the engagement of influencer posts, such as the number of likes, shares, and comments, and track how this translates into website traffic, leads, and sales. To calculate ROMI, the company would compare the cost of the influencer marketing campaign to the estimated value of the increased website traffic, leads, and sales generated by the campaign.

Measuring ROMI for Search Engine Marketing:
Search engine marketing involves promoting a website by increasing its visibility in search engine results pages (SERPs) through the use of paid advertising. Measuring ROMI for search engine marketing can be more straightforward than measuring ROMI for some other types of marketing activities because it is easier to track the

impact of search engine marketing on website traffic and conversions. There are several key metrics that can be used to measure the effectiveness of search engine marketing, including click-through rates (CTRs), conversion rates, and cost per acquisition (CPA).

CTRs are a measure of how many users click on a particular ad relative to the number of times the ad is displayed. A high CTR indicates that the ad is effective at attracting users to the website. Conversion rates, on the other hand, measure the percentage of website visitors who complete a desired action, such as making a purchase or filling out a form. A high conversion rate indicates that the website is effectively converting visitors into customers.

CPA is a measure of how much it costs to acquire a customer through search engine marketing. It is calculated by dividing the total cost of the marketing campaign by the number of conversions. A low CPA indicates that the campaign is cost-effective and generating a positive ROMI.

For example, suppose a company spends $10,000 on a search engine marketing campaign that generates 10,000 clicks and 100 conversions. The cost per click (CPC) is $1, and the CPA is $100 ($10,000 / 100 conversions). If the average customer generates $500 in revenue, the ROMI is:

ROMI = (Revenue - Marketing Cost) / Marketing Cost
ROMI = ($50,000 - $10,000) / $10,000
ROMI = 4

This indicates that the search engine marketing campaign is generating a positive return on investment.

Measuring ROMI for Social Media Marketing:
Social media marketing involves promoting a brand or product through social media platforms such as Facebook, Twitter, and Instagram. Measuring ROMI for social media marketing can be more challenging than measuring ROMI for search engine marketing because it is often difficult to track the impact of social media on website traffic and conversions.

One way to measure the effectiveness of social media marketing is through engagement metrics, such as likes, shares, and comments. These metrics can provide insight into how users are interacting with the brand on social media and can help to identify areas for improvement.

Another way to measure the effectiveness of social media marketing is through sentiment analysis. Sentiment analysis involves analyzing social media posts and comments to determine the overall sentiment towards a brand or product. A positive sentiment indicates that the social media marketing campaign is effective at building brand awareness and generating positive associations with the brand.

For example, suppose a company spends $5,000 on a social media marketing campaign that generates 1,000 likes and 100 shares. If the sentiment analysis indicates a positive sentiment towards the brand, this can be an indication that the campaign is generating a positive ROMI.

Measuring ROMI for Content Marketing:
Content marketing involves creating and distributing content, such as blog posts, videos, and infographics, to attract and engage a target audience. Measuring ROMI for content marketing can be challenging because it is often difficult to directly attribute website traffic and conversions to specific pieces of content.

One way to measure the effectiveness of content marketing is through engagement metrics, such as page views, time spent on page, and social shares. These metrics can provide insight into how users are interacting with the content and can help to identify areas for improvement.

Another way to measure the effectiveness of content marketing is through lead generation metrics, such as the number of downloads of a white paper or the number of sign-ups for a newsletter. These metrics can provide insight into how effective the content is at generating leads and nurturing potential customers.

For example, suppose a company spends $7,500 on a content marketing campaign that generates 10,000 page views and 50 leads. If the average customer generates $1,000 in revenue, the ROMI is:

ROMI = (Revenue - Marketing Cost) / Marketing Cost
ROMI = (50 * $1,000 - $7,500) / $7,500
ROMI = 0.33

This indicates that for every dollar spent on the content marketing campaign, the company generated 33 cents in revenue. While this may seem low, it is important to consider the long-term benefits of content marketing, such as improved brand awareness and customer loyalty, which may not be captured in the short-term ROMI calculation.

Another example of measuring ROMI for content marketing is through social media. Social media marketing involves using social media platforms to promote a company's products or services. Measuring ROMI for social media marketing can be more challenging because it is difficult to directly attribute revenue to social media efforts. However, companies can track engagement metrics such as likes, shares, and comments, which can provide insight into the effectiveness of the social media campaign.

For example, suppose a company spends $10,000 on a social media campaign that generates 1,000 likes, 500 shares, and 200 comments. The ROMI can be calculated using a variety of metrics, such as the cost per engagement or the cost per conversion (e.g., website visits, lead forms submitted).

Overall, measuring ROMI for different types of marketing activities requires careful consideration of the costs and benefits associated with each activity. Companies must use a combination of quantitative and qualitative metrics to accurately measure the impact of their marketing efforts on their bottom line.

Case study: Analyzing the ROMI of a recent marketing campaign

In this case study, we will examine the return on marketing investment (ROMI) for a recent marketing campaign. This case study will provide students with a real-world example of how to calculate ROMI and analyze the results.

Background
ABC Corporation is a technology company that sells software products to businesses. The company recently launched a marketing campaign to promote a new software product, which aimed to increase sales and generate leads. The campaign was a mix of digital and traditional marketing activities, including email marketing, social media advertising, print advertising, and events.

Marketing Costs
The total cost of the marketing campaign was $150,000, which was allocated across different marketing activities as follows:

Email Marketing: $50,000
Social Media Advertising: $30,000
Print Advertising: $20,000
Events: $50,000
Revenue and Lead Generation

The marketing campaign generated 500 leads, of which 100 converted into paying customers. The average revenue per customer was $10,000, resulting in total revenue of $1,000,000.

Calculating ROMI

To calculate the ROMI of the marketing campaign, we need to determine the value of the increased sales generated by the campaign and compare it to the marketing costs. We can use the following formula:

ROMI = (Value of Increased Sales - Marketing Cost) / Marketing Cost

Value of Increased Sales = Total Revenue - Baseline Revenue

Baseline Revenue refers to the revenue that would have been generated without the marketing campaign. It is important to establish this baseline to accurately calculate the impact of the marketing campaign. In this case, ABC Corporation's baseline revenue was $500,000, which was the revenue generated from the same product in the previous year.

Using the above information, we can calculate the ROMI for the marketing campaign as follows:

Value of Increased Sales = $1,000,000 - $500,000 = $500,000

ROMI = ($500,000 - $150,000) / $150,000 = 2.33

Interpreting the Results

The ROMI for the marketing campaign is 2.33, which means that for every dollar spent on the campaign, ABC Corporation generated $2.33 in revenue. This is a positive outcome and suggests that the marketing campaign was successful.

However, it is important to note that the ROMI does not take into account the additional operating costs incurred by the company due to the marketing campaign. To calculate the true ROMI, we need to adjust for these costs. For example, if the marketing campaign resulted in an increase in customer support costs or a need for additional staff, these costs should be subtracted from the revenue generated by the campaign.

Conclusion

In this case study, we have analyzed the ROMI of a recent marketing campaign for ABC Corporation. We have seen how to calculate the ROMI using the value of increased sales and marketing costs, and how to interpret the results. We have also discussed the importance of establishing a baseline revenue and adjusting for additional operating costs to accurately calculate the ROMI.

Exercise: Calculating and analyzing ROMI for a hypothetical marketing campaign

In this exercise, we will walk through the process of calculating and analyzing the return on marketing investment (ROMI) for a hypothetical marketing campaign.

Scenario: A company is launching a new product and has decided to invest in a marketing campaign to promote the product. The company has allocated a budget of $100,000 for the campaign, which will run for 3 months. The campaign includes a mix of digital and traditional marketing tactics, such as social media advertising, email marketing, print ads, and a product launch event. The company expects the campaign to generate $500,000 in revenue over the next year.

Step 1: Determine the Value of Increased Sales
To calculate the ROMI, we first need to determine the value of the increased sales generated by the campaign. In this scenario, the company expects the campaign to generate $500,000 in revenue over the next year. This represents the value of the increased sales.

Step 2: Calculate the Marketing Cost
Next, we need to calculate the cost of the marketing campaign. In this scenario, the company has allocated a budget of $100,000 for the campaign, which will run for 3 months. To calculate the marketing cost, we can use the following formula:

Marketing Cost = Campaign Budget / Campaign Duration

Marketing Cost = $100,000 / 3 months

Marketing Cost = $33,333 per month

Step 3: Calculate the ROMI
With the value of increased sales and marketing cost determined, we can now calculate the ROMI using the following formula:

ROMI = (Value of Increased Sales - Marketing Cost) / Marketing Cost

ROMI = ($500,000 - $100,000) / $100,000

ROMI = 4

Step 4: Analyze the ROMI
A ROMI of 4 indicates that for every dollar spent on the marketing campaign, the company generated $4 in additional revenue over the next year. This is a positive ROI, indicating that the campaign was successful in generating a return on the company's investment.

However, the ROMI alone does not provide a complete picture of the success of the campaign. It is important to analyze the ROMI in the context of the company's goals and objectives, as well as the industry benchmarks and competition.

For example, if the company's goal was to generate $1 million in revenue from the campaign, a ROMI of 4 falls short of that goal. In this case, the company may need to reevaluate its marketing strategy and tactics to achieve its goals.

Additionally, if the industry benchmark for ROMI in the company's sector is 6, a ROMI of 4 may indicate that the company's campaign was not as successful as its competitors. This may require the company to invest more in its marketing efforts or explore new tactics to improve its ROI.

Conclusion
Calculating and analyzing the ROMI of a marketing campaign is an important step in evaluating its success and determining future marketing strategies. By following the steps outlined in this exercise, businesses can gain a better understanding of the value of their marketing efforts and make data-driven decisions to optimize their marketing ROI.

CHAPTER 9: CUSTOMER PROFITABILITY ANALYSIS

Customer profitability analysis (CPA) is an essential tool for businesses to evaluate and understand the profitability of their customer segments. It provides insights into the financial performance of each customer group and enables businesses to make informed decisions about their marketing, sales, and pricing strategies. In this chapter, we will explore the concept of customer profitability analysis and its significance for businesses. We will discuss how CPA can help organizations gain a competitive edge and improve their financial performance.

Understanding Customer Profitability Analysis

Definition of Customer Profitability Analysis

Customer profitability analysis is the process of determining the profitability of each customer or customer group. It involves evaluating the revenues generated by a customer group against the costs incurred in serving that group. CPA can be used to identify the most profitable customer segments, evaluate the effectiveness of marketing and sales strategies, and assess the impact of changes in pricing or product offerings.

Importance of Customer Profitability Analysis

CPA is essential for businesses because it helps them make informed decisions about how to allocate resources and which customers to prioritize. By understanding the profitability of each customer segment, businesses can focus their efforts on the most profitable groups and develop targeted marketing strategies to attract and retain those customers.

Additionally, CPA can help businesses identify unprofitable customers and take steps to either improve their profitability or discontinue their services. This can result in significant cost savings for the organization and can help improve overall profitability.

Benefits of Customer Profitability Analysis

The benefits of customer profitability analysis are numerous. Some of the key benefits include:

Improved financial performance: CPA can help businesses improve their financial performance by identifying the most profitable customer segments and focusing resources on those groups.

More informed decision-making: By understanding the profitability of each customer group, businesses can make more informed decisions about marketing, sales, and pricing strategies.

Cost savings: CPA can help businesses identify unprofitable customers and take steps to reduce costs associated with serving those customers.

Improved customer satisfaction: By focusing on the most profitable customer segments, businesses can develop targeted marketing strategies that are more likely to resonate with those customers, resulting in increased customer satisfaction.

Conducting a Customer Profitability Analysis

Steps in Conducting a Customer Profitability Analysis

The following are the steps involved in conducting a customer profitability analysis:

Step 1: Determine the relevant customer segments: The first step in conducting a CPA is to determine the relevant customer segments. This can be based on various criteria such as demographics, geography, or purchasing behavior.

Step 2: Determine the costs associated with serving each customer segment: Once the customer segments have been identified, the costs associated with serving each segment need to be determined. These costs may include sales and marketing expenses, production costs, and customer service costs.

Step 3: Calculate the revenues generated by each customer segment: The next step is to calculate the revenues generated by each customer segment. This can be based on factors such as the number of customers, the frequency of purchases, and the average purchase value.

Step 4: Calculate the profitability of each customer segment: Once the revenues and costs associated with each customer segment have been determined, the profitability of each segment can be calculated by subtracting the costs from the revenues.

Step 5: Analyze the results: The final step in conducting a CPA is to analyze the results and use them to make informed decisions about marketing, sales, and pricing strategies.

Tools for Conducting a Customer Profitability Analysis

There are several tools that businesses can use to conduct a CPA. These include:

Customer relationship management (CRM) software: CRM software can be used to track customer behavior and purchases, which can be used to calculate customer profitability. CRM software can also provide valuable insights into customer preferences and needs, which can inform marketing and sales strategies.

Activity-based costing (ABC): ABC is a method of costing that assigns costs to specific activities and then allocates those costs to products or services based on how much of each activity they require. This approach can be useful in calculating the costs associated with serving different customers.

Data analytics software: Data analytics software can be used to analyze customer data and identify trends and patterns that can inform customer profitability analysis. This software can also be used to segment customers based on their profitability and develop targeted marketing strategies for each segment.

Customer profitability analysis software: There are several software programs specifically designed for conducting CPA. These programs can automate the process of collecting and analyzing customer data, making it easier and more efficient for businesses to conduct this type of analysis.

It's important to note that while these tools can be useful in conducting a CPA, they are not a substitute for careful analysis and interpretation of the data. Businesses must also take into account other factors that may impact customer profitability, such as customer retention rates, marketing and advertising expenses, and overhead costs.

In addition, it's important to consider the limitations of these tools. For example, CRM software may not capture all relevant customer data, and data analytics software may not be able to account for all the complexities of customer behavior. As a result, it's important to use multiple tools and approaches to conduct a comprehensive customer profitability analysis.

Overall, businesses that conduct a CPA are better equipped to make informed decisions about their sales and marketing strategies. By understanding which customers are most profitable, businesses can develop targeted marketing campaigns and tailor their products and services to meet the needs of their most valuable customers.

The importance of understanding customer profitability

In today's highly competitive business environment, it is important for companies to understand the profitability of their customers. Understanding customer profitability allows businesses to make informed decisions about pricing, marketing, and product development. This chapter will explore the importance of understanding customer profitability, and how businesses can use customer profitability analysis to improve their bottom line.

The Benefits of Understanding Customer Profitability

Improved Pricing Strategies

One of the primary benefits of understanding customer profitability is the ability to develop better pricing strategies. By understanding which customers are more profitable, businesses can adjust their prices to optimize profitability. For example, businesses can offer discounts to low-profit customers to encourage them to spend more or raise prices for high-profit customers.

Enhanced Marketing Efforts

Another benefit of understanding customer profitability is the ability to target marketing efforts more effectively. By identifying the most profitable customers, businesses can create more targeted marketing campaigns and offers to attract and retain these customers. Additionally, businesses can avoid wasting resources on customers who are unlikely to generate significant profits.

Improved Product Development

Understanding customer profitability can also inform product development efforts. By analyzing customer behavior and preferences, businesses can develop products and services that are more likely to appeal to their most profitable customers. This can result in higher sales and profits.

Section 2: Conducting a Customer Profitability Analysis

Data Collection

To conduct a customer profitability analysis, businesses must first collect data on customer behavior and purchases. This can be done using a variety of tools, including CRM software, customer surveys, and transaction records.

Tools for Conducting a Customer Profitability Analysis

There are several tools that businesses can use to conduct a CPA. These include:

Customer relationship management (CRM) software: CRM software can be used to track customer behavior and purchases, which can help businesses identify their most profitable customers.

Customer surveys: Surveys can be used to gather data on customer preferences and behavior, which can inform product development and marketing efforts.

Transaction records: Transaction records can provide valuable data on customer purchases and behavior, which can be used to identify profitable customers and inform marketing and pricing strategies.

Calculating Customer Profitability

To calculate customer profitability, businesses must first calculate the revenue generated by each customer. This includes all purchases made by the customer over a specific period of time. Next, businesses must calculate the costs associated with serving each customer, including the cost of goods sold and any marketing or customer service expenses. The difference between revenue and costs represents the profit generated by each customer.

Analyzing Customer Profitability

Once customer profitability has been calculated, businesses can analyze the data to identify trends and patterns. This can help businesses identify their most profitable customers, as well as areas for improvement in their pricing, marketing, and product development strategies.

Section 3: Challenges and Limitations of Customer Profitability Analysis

Data Collection Challenges

One of the main challenges of conducting a CPA is collecting accurate and comprehensive data on customer behavior and purchases. This can be particularly challenging for businesses that rely on multiple data sources, which may not always be consistent or easily accessible.

Cost Allocation Issues

Another challenge of conducting a CPA is allocating costs to individual customers. This can be particularly challenging for businesses that serve a large number of customers or offer a wide range of products and services.

Limitations of Traditional CPA Methods

Traditional CPA methods, such as activity-based costing, may not be appropriate for all businesses. For example, businesses that offer services rather than products may struggle to allocate costs accurately.

Conclusion

In conclusion, understanding customer profitability is essential for businesses that want to optimize their pricing strategies, maximize profits, and stay competitive in today's market. By analyzing the profitability of each customer, businesses can identify which customers are generating the most value and focus their efforts on retaining and expanding those relationships, while also identifying which customers may be unprofitable and need to be either dropped or re-engaged in a more profitable way.

Furthermore, a customer profitability analysis provides businesses with a more accurate picture of their overall financial performance and can reveal valuable insights that are not apparent from traditional financial statements. It also helps businesses make informed decisions regarding their marketing and sales strategies, product offerings, and pricing structures.

While conducting a CPA can be complex and time-consuming, it is an investment that can pay significant dividends in the long run. Businesses that prioritize customer profitability and use the tools and techniques discussed in this chapter to conduct a thorough analysis are more likely to succeed in today's competitive marketplace.

In summary, understanding customer profitability is a critical component of any business strategy. It enables businesses to focus on the customers that generate the most value, optimize pricing and product strategies, and ultimately improve overall profitability. By conducting a thorough customer profitability analysis, businesses can gain valuable insights into their financial performance and make informed decisions that will drive long-term success.

Approaches to calculating customer profitability (e.g., contribution margin, customer lifetime value)

Customer profitability analysis (CPA) is a crucial tool for businesses that want to understand the profitability of individual customers or customer segments. However, there is no one-size-fits-all approach to calculating customer profitability. In fact, there are several different approaches that businesses can take, each with its own strengths and weaknesses. This section will explore two common approaches to calculating customer profitability: contribution margin analysis and customer lifetime value (CLV) analysis.

Contribution Margin Analysis

Contribution margin analysis is a simple and straightforward approach to calculating customer profitability. It involves calculating the contribution margin for each customer or customer segment, which is the difference between the revenue generated by the customer and the variable costs associated with serving that customer.

To calculate contribution margin, businesses need to first identify all of the costs associated with serving a particular customer or customer segment. This includes direct costs such as raw materials, labor, and shipping costs, as well as indirect costs such as overhead expenses. Once these costs have been identified, businesses can subtract them from the revenue generated by the customer to arrive at the contribution margin.

One of the key benefits of contribution margin analysis is that it provides a clear and concise picture of the profitability of individual customers or customer segments. This information can be used to make informed decisions about pricing, marketing, and customer acquisition. However, contribution margin analysis has some limitations. For example, it does not take into account the long-term value of a customer or the cost of acquiring new customers.

Customer Lifetime Value (CLV) Analysis

Customer lifetime value (CLV) analysis is a more sophisticated approach to calculating customer profitability. It takes into account not only the revenue generated by a customer but also the costs associated with acquiring and retaining that customer over the course of their lifetime.

To calculate CLV, businesses need to first estimate the revenue that a customer will generate over their lifetime. This involves forecasting the customer's purchasing behavior, such as how frequently they will make purchases and how much they will spend each time. Once this has been estimated, businesses can subtract the costs associated with acquiring and retaining the customer from the estimated revenue to arrive at the customer's lifetime value.

One of the key benefits of CLV analysis is that it provides a more comprehensive view of customer profitability that takes into account both short-term and long-term factors. This information can be used to make more informed decisions about marketing, customer acquisition, and customer retention. However, CLV analysis can be complex and time-consuming, requiring businesses to make assumptions about customer behavior and future market conditions.

Conclusion

In conclusion, there are several approaches that businesses can take to calculating customer profitability, each with its own strengths and weaknesses. Contribution margin analysis is a simple and straightforward approach that provides a clear picture of short-term profitability. CLV analysis is a more sophisticated approach that takes into account both short-term and long-term factors. Businesses should carefully consider which approach is best suited to their specific needs and goals, and use this information to make informed decisions about pricing, marketing, and customer acquisition.

Factors to consider when analyzing customer profitability (e.g., acquisition cost, retention cost, referral value)

Customer profitability analysis is a vital component of any business's strategy to maximize profits and drive growth. However, analyzing customer profitability is not a one-size-fits-all approach, and there are many factors to consider when undertaking such an analysis. In this section, we will discuss the various factors to consider when analyzing customer profitability, such as acquisition cost, retention cost, and referral value.

Acquisition Cost

Acquisition cost refers to the cost a business incurs to acquire a new customer. This cost may include marketing and advertising expenses, sales commissions, and other expenses related to bringing new customers on board. To calculate customer profitability accurately, it is essential to factor in acquisition costs.

For example, suppose a company spends $1,000 on marketing to acquire a new customer who makes a one-time purchase of $100. In that case, the company has a negative return on investment (ROI). However, if that same customer makes multiple purchases over time, the ROI can increase significantly, making it a profitable acquisition.

When calculating acquisition cost, businesses must consider the lifetime value of the customer. A customer who makes only one purchase may not be as valuable as a customer who makes multiple purchases over time. Therefore, businesses should factor in the potential lifetime value of a customer when calculating acquisition costs.

Retention Cost

Retaining customers is just as important as acquiring new ones. However, retaining customers can be challenging and may require significant investment. Retention costs may include customer service costs, loyalty programs, and other expenses related to keeping customers engaged with the business.

To calculate customer profitability accurately, it is essential to factor in retention costs. A customer who makes multiple purchases over time may be more profitable than a customer who makes only one purchase. Therefore, businesses must invest in retaining customers to maximize profitability.

Referral Value

Referral value refers to the value of a customer who refers new customers to the business. Referral marketing can be a powerful tool for driving growth, as customers who are referred by existing customers tend to be more loyal and more likely to make repeat purchases.

To calculate customer profitability accurately, it is essential to factor in referral value. Referral marketing can be a cost-effective way to acquire new customers, as referred customers tend to have a higher lifetime value than non-referred customers.

Conclusion

In conclusion, analyzing customer profitability is an essential component of any business strategy. When analyzing customer profitability, businesses must consider various factors, such as acquisition cost, retention cost, and referral value. By factoring in these costs, businesses can make data-driven decisions that maximize profitability and drive growth.

Practical examples of customer profitability analysis for different types of businesses

Understanding customer profitability is crucial for businesses of all types and sizes. In this section, we will examine practical examples of how different types of businesses can use customer profitability analysis to optimize their operations and increase their bottom line.

Retail Businesses

Retail businesses rely heavily on customer traffic and volume to generate revenue. Understanding customer profitability can help retailers identify which customers are generating the most revenue and which customers may be costing more than they are worth.

For example, a retail business can use customer lifetime value (CLV) analysis to determine which customers are most valuable to their business. By analyzing customer behavior such as purchase history, frequency of purchases, and amount spent per purchase, a retailer can determine the CLV of each customer.

A retailer can also use contribution margin analysis to determine the profitability of individual products. By calculating the contribution margin for each product, a retailer can determine which products are generating the most profit and which products may be costing more than they are worth.

Service-Based Businesses

Service-based businesses, such as consulting firms or law firms, may not have physical products to sell, but they still rely on generating revenue from their clients. Understanding customer profitability can help service-based businesses identify which clients are generating the most revenue and which clients may be costing more than they are worth.

For example, a consulting firm can use customer acquisition cost (CAC) analysis to determine which clients are most valuable to their business. By calculating the CAC for each client, a consulting firm can determine which clients are generating the most revenue and which clients may not be worth the cost of acquisition.

A law firm can also use customer retention cost (CRC) analysis to determine which clients are most valuable to their business. By analyzing the cost of retaining each client, a law firm can determine which clients are generating the most revenue and which clients may not be worth the cost of retention.

Manufacturing Businesses

Manufacturing businesses rely on producing and selling physical products to generate revenue. Understanding customer profitability can help manufacturing businesses identify which products are generating the most revenue and which products may be costing more than they are worth.

For example, a manufacturing business can use product profitability analysis to determine the profitability of individual products. By calculating the cost of goods sold (COGS) and the selling price for each product, a manufacturing business can determine which products are generating the most profit and which products may be costing more than they are worth.

A manufacturing business can also use customer referral value (CRV) analysis to determine which customers are most valuable to their business. By analyzing the referral value of each customer, a manufacturing business can determine which customers are generating the most revenue and which customers may not be worth the cost of acquisition.

E-commerce Businesses
E-commerce businesses rely on generating revenue through online sales. Understanding customer profitability can help e-commerce businesses identify which customers are generating the most revenue and which customers may be costing more than they are worth.

For example, an e-commerce business can use conversion rate analysis to determine which customers are most valuable to their business. By analyzing the conversion rates of individual customers, an e-commerce business can determine which customers are more likely to purchase products and which customers may not be worth the cost of acquisition.

An e-commerce business can also use customer satisfaction analysis to determine which customers are most valuable to their business. By analyzing the satisfaction levels of individual customers, an e-commerce business can determine which customers are more likely to make repeat purchases and refer new customers to the business.

Conclusion

In conclusion, understanding customer profitability is essential for businesses of all types and sizes. By analyzing customer behavior and profitability, businesses can identify which customers are generating the most revenue and which customers may be costing more than they are worth. With this information, businesses can optimize their operations and increase their overall profitability.

There are several approaches to calculating customer profitability, including contribution margin analysis and customer lifetime value. Each approach has its advantages and disadvantages, and businesses should carefully consider which approach is best suited to their needs.

In addition to the approaches to calculating customer profitability, there are also several factors to consider when analyzing customer profitability. These include the acquisition cost, retention cost, and referral value of customers. By taking these factors into account, businesses can gain a more comprehensive understanding of customer profitability and make more informed decisions about pricing and marketing strategies.

Practical examples of customer profitability analysis can vary depending on the type of business. For example, a retail store may analyze customer profitability based on sales volume and frequency of visits, while a software company may analyze customer profitability based on the lifetime value of a customer. In each case, the goal is the same: to identify which customers are generating the most revenue and which customers are costing more than they are worth.

Overall, understanding customer profitability is a key component of successful business operations. By analyzing customer behavior and profitability, businesses can optimize their operations and increase their overall profitability. By taking the time to carefully consider the approaches to calculating customer profitability and the factors to consider when analyzing customer profitability, businesses can make more informed decisions and ultimately achieve greater success.

Case study: Analyzing the profitability of different customer segments for a retail business

In this case study, we will examine how a retail business can analyze the profitability of different customer segments. We will focus on a fictional clothing store called "Fashionista," which sells trendy clothes and accessories for women. Fashionista operates both online and offline stores across the United States. The company has been experiencing a decline in sales and profitability in recent years due to increasing competition from other fashion retailers.

Fashionista's management team is looking for ways to improve the company's profitability. One idea is to focus on the most profitable customer segments and adjust the marketing strategy accordingly. To do this, Fashionista's management team has decided to analyze the profitability of different customer segments.

Step 1: Define Customer Segments

The first step in analyzing customer profitability is to define customer segments. Fashionista's management team decided to define three customer segments based on the customers' shopping behavior:

High-Value Customers: These are customers who make large purchases and have a high lifetime value for the company.

Regular Customers: These are customers who shop at Fashionista regularly but do not make large purchases.

Low-Value Customers: These are customers who rarely shop at Fashionista and typically only purchase items on sale.

Step 2: Calculate Customer Profitability

The next step is to calculate the profitability of each customer segment. To do this, Fashionista's management team used the following metrics:

Customer Acquisition Cost (CAC): The cost of acquiring a new customer, including marketing, advertising, and promotional expenses.

Customer Retention Cost (CRC): The cost of retaining a customer, including loyalty programs, customer service, and retention campaigns.

Customer Lifetime Value (CLV): The total revenue a customer generates over the course of their relationship with the company, minus the CAC and CRC.

Based on these metrics, Fashionista's management team calculated the profitability of each customer segment as follows:

High-Value Customers:

CAC: $50

CRC: $20

Average CLV: $2,500

Profitability: $2,430 ($2,500 - $50 - $20)

Regular Customers:

CAC: $30

CRC: $10

Average CLV: $500

Profitability: $460 ($500 - $30 - $10)

Low-Value Customers:

CAC: $10

CRC: $5

Average CLV: $50

Profitability: $35 ($50 - $10 - $5)

Step 3: Analyze Results

After calculating the profitability of each customer segment, Fashionista's management team analyzed the results to determine the most profitable customer segment. The analysis showed that High-Value Customers were the most profitable segment, with a profitability of $2,430 per customer. In contrast, Regular and Low-Value Customers were less profitable, with profitabilities of $460 and $35, respectively.

Step 4: Adjust Marketing Strategy

Based on these results, Fashionista's management team decided to adjust the company's marketing strategy to focus on High-Value Customers. They developed targeted marketing campaigns, loyalty programs, and promotions aimed at attracting and retaining these customers. They also increased the product lines and offerings that were popular among High-Value Customers and decreased those that were not.

The results of this customer profitability analysis were significant for Fashionista. The company saw an increase in sales and profits, and the management team was able to make informed decisions about the company's marketing strategy. This case study highlights the importance of analyzing customer profitability and adjusting marketing strategies accordingly. By focusing on the most profitable customer segments, businesses can optimize their operations and increase profitability.

Exercise: Calculating and analyzing customer profitability for a hypothetical business

In this exercise, we will be calculating and analyzing the customer profitability for a hypothetical business. The business is a retail store that sells clothing, accessories, and home goods. The business has been operating for one year and has a total of 1,000 customers. The business has collected data on each customer's purchases, returns, and discounts. The business's financial statements are as follows:

Income Statement:

Revenue: $500,000
Cost of goods sold: $200,000
Gross profit: $300,000
Operating expenses: $250,000
Net profit: $50,000

Balance Sheet:

Cash: $20,000
Accounts receivable: $40,000
Inventory: $100,000
Fixed assets: $200,000
Total assets: $360,000
Accounts payable: $50,000
Long-term debt: $100,000
Equity: $210,000
Total liabilities and equity: $360,000

Instructions:

Calculate the acquisition cost for each customer.
To calculate the acquisition cost for each customer, we need to divide the total marketing and advertising expenses by the total number of customers. Let's assume that the total marketing and advertising expenses for the year were $50,000. Therefore, the acquisition cost per customer is $50.

Calculate the retention cost for each customer.
To calculate the retention cost for each customer, we need to divide the total sales and marketing expenses by the total number of customers. Let's assume that the total sales and marketing expenses for the year were $100,000. Therefore, the retention cost per customer is $100.

Calculate the referral value for each customer.

To calculate the referral value for each customer, we need to divide the total revenue generated from referrals by the total number of customers. Let's assume that the total revenue generated from referrals for the year was $20,000. Therefore, the referral value per customer is $20.

Calculate the total revenue and cost for each customer.
To calculate the total revenue and cost for each customer, we need to gather data on each customer's purchases, returns, and discounts. Let's assume that customer A had the following transactions:

Purchases: $500
Returns: $50
Discounts: $0
Therefore, customer A's total revenue is $450.

Let's also assume that the cost of goods sold for the items purchased by customer A was $250. Therefore, the gross profit for customer A is $200.

To calculate the operating expenses associated with customer A, we need to gather data on the expenses incurred to serve this customer. Let's assume that the operating expenses associated with customer A were $50. Therefore, the net profit for customer A is $150.

Analyze the customer profitability.
Using the information gathered from the previous steps, we can calculate the customer profitability for each customer. Let's assume that the customer profitability for customer A is as follows:

Acquisition cost: $50
Retention cost: $100
Referral value: $20
Total revenue: $450
Total cost: $250
Gross profit: $200
Operating expenses: $50
Net profit: $150
Based on this analysis, customer A is generating a net profit of $150 for the business. The acquisition cost and retention cost for customer A are lower than the average customer, indicating that customer A is more profitable for the business. However, the referral value for customer A is lower than the average customer, indicating that customer A is less likely to refer new customers to the business.

By analyzing the profitability of each customer, the business can make informed decisions about how to allocate resources and develop strategies to increase profitability. In the case of customer A, the business may want to focus on ways to increase their referral value, such as offering incentives for referrals or improving customer satisfaction.

In addition to analyzing individual customer profitability, businesses can also use customer profitability analysis to segment their customers and develop targeted strategies for each segment. For example, a business may identify high-value customers who generate significant revenue and have low acquisition and retention costs, and develop loyalty programs or personalized marketing campaigns to retain these customers.

On the other hand, a business may also identify low-value customers who are not profitable for the business, and consider either increasing their profitability through upselling or cross-selling, or focusing resources on acquiring higher-value customers.

Overall, customer profitability analysis is a powerful tool for businesses to understand their customer base and make data-driven decisions to optimize their operations and increase profitability. By taking a strategic approach to customer profitability analysis and using the insights gained to develop targeted strategies, businesses can maximize the lifetime value of their customers and achieve long-term success.

Now let's move on to the exercise where we will calculate and analyze customer profitability for a hypothetical business.

Exercise: Calculating and Analyzing Customer Profitability for a Hypothetical Business

Assume you are a financial analyst for a business that sells a variety of consumer products, including clothing, home goods, and electronics. Your manager has asked you to analyze the profitability of the business's customers and provide recommendations for how the business can increase profitability.

The following table provides data on the revenue, cost of goods sold, acquisition cost, retention cost, and referral value for each customer:

Customer ID	Revenue	Cost of Goods Sold	Acquisition Cost	Retention Cost	Referral Value
1	$500	$300	$50	$75	$25

2	$200	$100	$40	$50	$10
3	$300	$200	$60	$40	$5
4	$400	$250	$70	$60	$15

Using this data, calculate the net profit for each customer and analyze the results.

Solution:

To calculate the net profit for each customer, we subtract the cost of goods sold, acquisition cost, retention cost, and referral value from the revenue. The results are shown in the following table:

Customer ID	Revenue	Cost of Goods Sold	Acquisition Cost	Retention Cost	Referral Value	Net Profit
1	$500	$300	$50	$75	$25	$50
2	$200	$100	$40	$50	$10	$0
3	$300	$200	$60	$40	$5	-$5
4	$400	$250	$70	$60	$15	$5

Based on the net profit calculations, customer 1 generates the highest net profit for the business, followed by customer 4, while customers 2 and 3 are not profitable.

However, analyzing customer profitability involves more than just looking at the net profit. For example, customer 1 has a high acquisition cost, indicating that the business may be spending too much on acquiring this type of customer. Additionally, customer 4 has a high retention cost, which means the business may need to focus on reducing costs associated with retaining this type of customer.

Furthermore, customer 1 has a low referral value, indicating that this type of customer may not be likely to refer new customers to the business. On the other hand, customer 4 has a high referral value, which could make them a valuable asset in terms of bringing in new customers.

Therefore, in order to optimize customer profitability, the business may need to take a more holistic approach and consider factors beyond just the net profit. For example, the business could explore ways to reduce acquisition costs for high-profit customers or find ways to increase referral values for customers with low referral values.

In addition, the business could consider segmenting its customer base and developing different strategies for each segment. For instance, customers who are not profitable could be dropped or targeted for specific retention strategies. High-profit customers could be given special treatment or incentives to encourage them to continue doing business with the company. Customers with high referral values could be targeted for referral marketing campaigns.

Overall, the exercise of calculating and analyzing customer profitability highlights the importance of understanding the profitability of each individual customer in order to make informed decisions about marketing and customer retention strategies. By taking a holistic approach to customer profitability analysis and considering factors beyond just the net profit, businesses can optimize their operations and maximize their profitability.

PART 4:
CUSTOMER SERVICE
AND FINANCE

In any business, customer service is critical to the success and longevity of the enterprise. Customers are the lifeblood of any business, and it is their satisfaction that ultimately determines whether or not a business will succeed. However, while customer service is an essential aspect of any business, it is often overlooked or undervalued, particularly when it comes to its relationship with finance.

The relationship between customer service and finance is not always immediately apparent. However, the two are intrinsically linked, and understanding this link is crucial to the success of any business. On the one hand, customer service plays a crucial role in generating revenue for a business. It is through excellent customer service that businesses can attract new customers, retain existing ones, and increase customer loyalty. On the other hand, finance is critical to the sustainability and profitability of a business. By managing cash flow, keeping costs under control, and maximizing revenue, finance ensures that a business can continue to operate and grow.

The intersection between customer service and finance is where the most significant opportunities for business success lie. By optimizing the customer experience and leveraging financial tools and strategies, businesses can generate sustainable growth and profitability. This section of the textbook will explore the intersection between customer service and finance, providing students with a comprehensive understanding of how these two areas can work together to drive business success.

In this section, we will start by examining the importance of customer service in driving business success. We will look at how excellent customer service can generate revenue, increase customer loyalty, and drive business growth. We will then move on to explore the financial aspects of customer service, including the cost of customer acquisition and retention, customer lifetime value, and customer profitability.

We will then examine several key financial tools and strategies that businesses can use to optimize their customer service operations. These tools and strategies include financial analysis, budgeting and forecasting, performance metrics, and pricing strategies.

Finally, we will conclude this section by examining the ethical and legal considerations that businesses must take into account when managing the intersection between customer service and finance. We will look at issues such as customer privacy, data protection, and financial regulation, providing students with a comprehensive understanding of the legal and ethical framework that underpins business operations.

Overall, this section of the textbook will provide students with a comprehensive understanding of how customer service and finance intersect and how businesses can leverage this intersection to drive sustainable growth and profitability. Through a combination of theoretical concepts, practical examples, and problem-solving exercises, students will gain a deep understanding of the critical role that customer service and finance play in the success of any business.

CHAPTER 10: UNDERSTANDING THE FINANCIAL IMPACT OF CUSTOMER SERVICE

Customer service plays a critical role in any business, as it directly impacts customer satisfaction and loyalty. However, the financial impact of customer service is often overlooked, as it is not always easy to quantify. In this chapter, we will explore the financial impact of customer service, and how it affects a business's bottom line.

Customer service involves all activities that businesses undertake to meet the needs of their customers. This can range from answering customer queries, to handling customer complaints and providing after-sales support. The quality of customer service provided by a business can have a significant impact on the customer's perception of the business and ultimately, their buying behavior.

Businesses that provide excellent customer service tend to have loyal customers who are more likely to make repeat purchases, recommend the business to others, and even pay a premium for the products or services offered by the business. Conversely, businesses that provide poor customer service are likely to lose customers and suffer reputational damage.

However, the financial impact of customer service is not limited to customer retention and acquisition. It also has an impact on the business's operational costs and profitability. For example, poor customer service can result in increased costs due to returns and complaints. Additionally, businesses that have poor customer service may have to spend more on marketing and advertising to attract new customers.

In this chapter, we will examine the various financial metrics that businesses can use to measure the impact of customer service, such as customer lifetime value, customer acquisition cost, and customer retention cost. We will also explore the different strategies that businesses can employ to improve their customer service and maximize their financial returns.

Overall, understanding the financial impact of customer service is critical for businesses to make informed decisions about their customer service strategies. By measuring the financial impact of customer service, businesses can identify areas for improvement and optimize their resources to maximize profitability.

The importance of customer service in business success

In today's business world, customer service is not just a buzzword but a key driver of business success. It has become increasingly clear that businesses cannot survive without customers, and customer satisfaction is a vital aspect of customer retention. Therefore, providing high-quality customer service is essential for businesses to maintain their customer base, attract new customers, and ultimately increase revenue. In this chapter, we will explore the importance of customer service in business success and how it impacts a company's financial performance.

The Importance of Customer Service in Business Success:
A business that provides excellent customer service creates a competitive advantage in the marketplace. Customers who are satisfied with a company's customer service are more likely to become loyal customers, and they will share their positive experiences with friends and family, which can lead to new customers. On the other hand, customers who have negative experiences with a company's customer service are more likely to share their experiences with others, which can harm the company's reputation and ultimately lead to a loss of business.

In addition to the direct impact on customer loyalty and retention, customer service also plays a crucial role in brand perception. A business that provides poor customer service can damage its reputation and brand image, while a company that provides excellent customer service can enhance its reputation and differentiate itself from competitors. Therefore, it is essential to invest in customer service to establish a positive brand image and reputation.

The Financial Impact of Customer Service:

The impact of customer service on a company's financial performance cannot be overstated. Studies have shown that companies that invest in customer service outperform their competitors in terms of revenue growth and profitability. For example, a study by Harvard Business Review found that companies that prioritize customer service have higher customer retention rates, which leads to a 5% to 10% increase in revenue growth.

In addition, providing excellent customer service can lead to cost savings. For example, businesses that provide proactive customer service, such as identifying and resolving issues before customers even know they exist, can reduce the number of customer complaints and support requests, which can lead to cost savings. By investing in customer service, businesses can reduce their overall costs and increase their profitability.

Moreover, customer service can also impact a company's ability to attract new customers. Positive reviews and word-of-mouth recommendations can lead to new customers, which can ultimately lead to increased revenue. Conversely, negative reviews and poor customer service experiences can harm a company's reputation and deter potential customers from doing business with the company.

Conclusion:
In conclusion, customer service is a critical component of business success, and companies that invest in customer service have a competitive advantage in the marketplace. The impact of customer service on a company's financial performance is significant, as it can lead to increased revenue growth, cost savings, and the ability to attract new customers. Therefore, businesses must prioritize customer service and invest in providing high-quality customer experiences to remain competitive in today's marketplace.

The impact of poor customer service on financial performance

Customer service is one of the most important factors that contribute to business success. It is the process of providing assistance, support, and information to customers in a manner that meets or exceeds their expectations. Businesses that prioritize their customers and provide excellent customer service are more likely to achieve success than those that don't. In this section, we will explore the impact of poor customer service on financial performance.

Poor Customer Service and Its Impact on Financial Performance:

Businesses that provide poor customer service are likely to experience a number of negative consequences that can negatively impact their financial performance. Below are some of the ways poor customer service can affect a business financially:

Decreased Sales:
Poor customer service can lead to decreased sales. When customers have a negative experience with a business, they are less likely to return and more likely to share their negative experience with others. This can lead to a decrease in sales and revenue.

Loss of Customers:
Poor customer service can also lead to the loss of customers. When customers have a negative experience, they are less likely to return and may choose to take their business elsewhere. This can result in a loss of revenue and market share.

Damage to Reputation:
Poor customer service can damage a business's reputation. When customers have a negative experience, they are likely to share their experience with others. This can damage the business's reputation and make it more difficult to attract and retain customers.

Increased Customer Acquisition Costs:
Poor customer service can also result in increased customer acquisition costs. When a business loses a customer due to poor customer service, it must spend more money to acquire a new customer to replace the lost one.

Decreased Customer Lifetime Value:
Poor customer service can also lead to a decreased customer lifetime value. When customers have a negative experience with a business, they are less likely to remain a customer over the long term. This can result in a decrease in the customer lifetime value, which can negatively impact the business's financial performance.

Examples of Poor Customer Service:

There are many examples of poor customer service that can negatively impact a business's financial performance. Below are some of the most common examples:

Long Wait Times:
Long wait times can frustrate customers and lead to a negative experience. This can result in a loss of customers and revenue.

Poor Communication:

Poor communication can lead to misunderstandings and mistakes. This can lead to a negative experience for customers and damage the business's reputation.

Lack of Personalization:
Customers expect businesses to personalize their experience. When businesses fail to do so, customers may feel unimportant and undervalued. This can lead to a negative experience and a loss of customers.

Poor Quality Products or Services:
When businesses provide poor quality products or services, customers are likely to have a negative experience. This can result in a loss of customers and revenue.

Lack of Follow-Up:
When businesses fail to follow up with customers, it can lead to a negative experience. Customers expect businesses to follow up and address their concerns. When businesses fail to do so, it can damage their reputation and lead to a loss of customers.

Conclusion:

In conclusion, poor customer service can have a significant impact on a business's financial performance. It can lead to a decrease in sales, loss of customers, damage to reputation, increased customer acquisition costs, decreased customer lifetime value, and more. Therefore, it is important for businesses to prioritize their customers and provide excellent customer service in order to achieve financial success. By doing so, businesses can increase customer satisfaction, retention, and loyalty, which can ultimately lead to increased revenue and profitability.

Case studies of companies that have improved their financial performance through customer service improvements

Customer service is a critical component of business success, and its impact on financial performance cannot be overstated. Companies that prioritize customer service tend to have higher levels of customer loyalty and retention, which ultimately lead to increased revenue and profitability. On the other hand, companies that provide poor customer service risk losing customers, damaging their reputation, and incurring financial losses.

In this section, we will examine case studies of companies that have improved their financial performance through customer service improvements. We will explore the strategies they employed to enhance customer service, the challenges they faced, and the outcomes they achieved.

Case Study 1: Zappos

Zappos is an online retailer that specializes in shoes and clothing. The company has become known for its exceptional customer service, which is built around its core values of delivering WOW through service, embracing and driving change, creating fun and a little weirdness, being adventurous, creative, and open-minded, pursuing growth and learning, building open and honest relationships with communication, and being passionate and determined.

Zappos' customer service strategy focuses on exceeding customer expectations and building relationships. The company offers free shipping and returns, a 365-day return policy, and a 24/7 customer service hotline. Zappos also invests heavily in employee training, with new employees going through four weeks of customer service training and being offered a $2,000 bonus to quit if they don't feel they are a good fit for the company.

Zappos' commitment to customer service has paid off in terms of financial performance. In 2009, the company was acquired by Amazon for $1.2 billion, and its revenue has continued to grow since then.

Case Study 2: Ritz-Carlton

Ritz-Carlton is a luxury hotel chain that is known for its exceptional customer service. The company's customer service strategy is built around its motto, "We are Ladies and Gentlemen serving Ladies and Gentlemen." This motto emphasizes the importance of treating customers with respect and dignity, and providing personalized service.

Ritz-Carlton invests heavily in employee training, with new employees going through an intensive three-day orientation program, and ongoing training throughout their tenure with the company. The company also empowers its employees to resolve customer issues on their own, without needing to seek approval from their managers.

Ritz-Carlton's commitment to customer service has paid off in terms of financial performance. The company has consistently ranked highly in customer satisfaction surveys, and its revenue has continued to grow.

Case Study 3: Nordstrom

Nordstrom is a high-end department store that is known for its exceptional customer service. The company's customer service strategy is built around its core value of providing a superior customer experience. Nordstrom offers a 24/7 customer service hotline, free shipping and returns, and a 90-day return policy. The company also invests heavily in employee training, with new employees going through a two-week training program, and ongoing training throughout their tenure with the company.

Nordstrom's commitment to customer service has paid off in terms of financial performance. The company consistently ranks highly in customer satisfaction surveys, and its revenue has continued to grow. In 2018, Nordstrom reported $15.5 billion in revenue.

Conclusion:

The case studies of Zappos, Ritz-Carlton, and Nordstrom illustrate the importance of customer service in driving financial performance. These companies have invested heavily in customer service, with a focus on exceeding customer expectations, building relationships, and empowering employees to resolve customer issues. The result has been increased customer loyalty and retention, and ultimately, increased revenue and profitability.

Business owners and managers should take note of these case studies and consider how they can improve their own customer service strategies. This may involve investing in employee training, developing customer-centric policies, and implementing technologies that enable personalized and efficient interactions with customers.

However, it is important to note that improving customer service is not a one-time effort, but an ongoing process. Customer needs and expectations evolve over time, and businesses must continuously adapt to meet these changes. This requires a commitment to customer service excellence at all levels of the organization, from the CEO down to frontline employees.

Furthermore, companies should not view customer service as a cost center, but as an opportunity to create value and differentiate themselves from competitors. By providing exceptional customer experiences, businesses can build brand equity and generate positive word-of-mouth, which can lead to new customer acquisition and increased revenue.

In conclusion, the financial impact of customer service cannot be understated. Companies that prioritize customer service and invest in their employees and technologies to enhance it have the potential to reap significant financial rewards. As such, businesses should view customer service as a strategic priority and allocate the necessary resources to make it a core component of their operations.

Practical examples of how customer service can be measured and analyzed for financial impact

In the previous sections, we explored the importance of customer service in driving financial performance and discussed case studies of companies that have improved their financial performance through customer service improvements. In this section, we will delve into practical examples of how customer service can be measured and analyzed for financial impact.

Customer service is a critical aspect of any business, and its impact on financial performance can be significant. Therefore, it is essential to measure and analyze customer service performance regularly to identify areas of improvement and ensure that customer service is contributing to the company's financial success.

There are several ways to measure and analyze customer service performance, and we will explore some of the most commonly used methods below.

Customer Satisfaction Surveys
One of the most popular ways to measure customer service performance is through customer satisfaction surveys. These surveys are conducted to collect feedback from customers about their experience with the company's products or services.

Customer satisfaction surveys can be conducted through various channels, such as email, phone, or online surveys. The feedback received from customers can be analyzed to identify areas where the company is performing well and areas where improvement is needed.

For example, a financial services company may conduct a customer satisfaction survey to assess the quality of their customer service. The survey may ask questions about the timeliness and accuracy of responses, the friendliness and professionalism of the customer service representatives, and the overall satisfaction with the service provided.

The results of the survey can be analyzed to identify areas where the company is performing well and areas where improvement is needed. If the company finds that customers are dissatisfied with the timeliness of responses, it may consider investing in technology that can improve response times.

Net Promoter Score (NPS)

Net Promoter Score (NPS) is another commonly used method to measure customer service performance. The NPS is a metric that measures customer loyalty and satisfaction by asking customers how likely they are to recommend the company to others on a scale of 0-10.

Customers who score 9-10 are considered promoters and are likely to recommend the company to others, while those who score 0-6 are considered detractors and are unlikely to recommend the company.

To calculate the NPS, the percentage of detractors is subtracted from the percentage of promoters. The result is a score that ranges from -100 to 100.

For example, a software company may use NPS to measure its customer service performance. The company may ask customers how likely they are to recommend the software to others and then calculate the NPS score based on the responses.

If the company finds that the NPS score is low, it may consider investing in customer service training to improve the quality of service provided.

Customer Retention Rate

Customer retention rate is another important metric for measuring customer service performance. This metric measures the percentage of customers who continue to use the company's products or services over a specified period.

A high customer retention rate indicates that the company is providing high-quality products or services and that customers are satisfied with their experience.

For example, a telecommunications company may measure its customer retention rate by calculating the percentage of customers who continue to use its services after a year.

If the company finds that the customer retention rate is low, it may consider investing in customer service improvements to address the issues that are causing customers to leave.

First Contact Resolution (FCR)

First Contact Resolution (FCR) measures the percentage of customer inquiries that are resolved on the first contact with the company. A high FCR rate indicates that the company is providing efficient and effective customer service.

For example, a retail company may measure its FCR rate by tracking the percentage of customer inquiries that are resolved during the first call to customer service.

If the company finds that the FCR rate is low, it may indicate that there are issues with the quality of customer service. This could lead to lower customer satisfaction, which in turn could impact revenue and profitability.

Another metric that can be used to measure customer service is Net Promoter Score (NPS). NPS is a customer loyalty metric that measures how likely a customer is to recommend a company's products or services to others. It is based on a scale of 0 to 10, with 0 being "not at all likely" and 10 being "extremely likely."

Customers who rate a company as a 9 or 10 are considered promoters, while those who rate the company as a 6 or below are considered detractors. The NPS score is calculated by subtracting the percentage of detractors from the percentage of promoters.

NPS is a valuable metric because it provides insight into customer loyalty and the likelihood of repeat business. Companies with high NPS scores tend to have higher customer retention rates and increased revenue.

In addition to FCR and NPS, customer service can also be measured through customer satisfaction surveys. These surveys can be sent out after a customer has interacted with the company's customer service department, and they provide valuable feedback on the customer's experience.

Customer satisfaction surveys can be used to identify areas where the company is excelling in terms of customer service, as well as areas where improvements can be made. For example, if a survey reveals that customers are consistently dissatisfied with the company's response time to inquiries, the company may need to invest in additional customer service resources to address this issue.

Finally, companies can use social media monitoring tools to track customer sentiment and identify potential issues with customer service. By monitoring social media platforms such as Twitter and Facebook, companies can quickly identify and respond to customer complaints and concerns.

Overall, there are a variety of metrics and tools that can be used to measure and analyze the financial impact of customer service. By tracking these metrics and making data-driven decisions to improve customer service, companies can increase customer loyalty, retention, and ultimately, profitability.

CHAPTER 11: MEASURING CUSTOMER SATISFACTION AND ITS IMPACT ON FINANCIAL PERFORMANCE

Customer satisfaction is an essential aspect of any business, and it is closely linked to financial performance. When customers are satisfied with a company's products or services, they are more likely to remain loyal and make repeat purchases, which can translate into increased revenue and profits. In contrast, poor customer satisfaction can result in lost business, negative word-of-mouth, and damage to a company's reputation.

Therefore, measuring customer satisfaction is critical to understanding how a company is performing and identifying areas for improvement. In this chapter, we will discuss the various methods and metrics that companies can use to measure customer satisfaction and analyze its impact on financial performance.

We will begin by defining customer satisfaction and exploring its significance in the business world. We will then discuss various approaches to measuring customer satisfaction, including surveys, focus groups, and social media monitoring. Next, we will explore the relationship between customer satisfaction and financial performance, including how customer satisfaction impacts revenue, profitability, and shareholder value.

Finally, we will examine some case studies of companies that have successfully used customer satisfaction metrics to drive financial performance, as well as some common challenges and limitations associated with measuring customer satisfaction.

Defining Customer Satisfaction:

Customer satisfaction refers to the degree to which a customer is pleased with a company's products or services. It is a subjective measure that can be influenced by a variety of factors, including product quality, price, customer service, and brand reputation.

The importance of customer satisfaction in the business world cannot be overstated. Satisfied customers are more likely to remain loyal and make repeat purchases, which can lead to increased revenue and profitability. In contrast, dissatisfied customers are likely to take their business elsewhere, resulting in lost revenue and a damaged reputation.

Measuring Customer Satisfaction:

There are several approaches that companies can use to measure customer satisfaction, including surveys, focus groups, and social media monitoring.

Surveys are perhaps the most common method of measuring customer satisfaction. Surveys can be conducted via phone, email, or web-based platforms, and they can be designed to gather both quantitative and qualitative data. Common survey questions might include "How satisfied are you with our product/service?" or "How likely are you to recommend our product/service to a friend?"

Focus groups are another method of measuring customer satisfaction. Focus groups involve bringing together a group of customers to discuss their experiences with a company's products or services. Focus groups can provide valuable qualitative data and insights into customer attitudes and behaviors.

Social media monitoring involves tracking and analyzing customer feedback and conversations on social media platforms such as Twitter, Facebook, and Instagram. Social media monitoring can provide real-time insights into customer sentiment and opinions, as well as identify potential issues and areas for improvement.

Measuring the Impact of Customer Satisfaction on Financial Performance:

Customer satisfaction has a direct impact on a company's financial performance. Satisfied customers are more likely to remain loyal and make repeat purchases, leading to increased revenue and profitability. In contrast, dissatisfied customers are more likely to take their business elsewhere, resulting in lost revenue and a damaged reputation.

One common metric used to measure the financial impact of customer satisfaction is the Net Promoter Score (NPS). The NPS measures the likelihood that a customer will recommend a company's products or services to others. The NPS is calculated by subtracting the percentage of detractors (customers who are unlikely to recommend the company) from the percentage of promoters (customers who are likely to recommend the company).

Other metrics that can be used to measure the financial impact of customer satisfaction include customer lifetime value (CLV), customer acquisition cost (CAC), and customer churn rate.

Case Studies:

There are several examples of companies that have successfully used customer satisfaction metrics to drive financial performance. For example, Amazon has built its business on a foundation of customer satisfaction, and uses metrics such as Net Promoter Score (NPS) and Customer Effort Score (CES) to measure customer satisfaction and loyalty. Amazon's focus on customer satisfaction has contributed to its success and growth, with the company consistently ranking highly in customer satisfaction surveys.

Another example is Apple, which uses customer satisfaction metrics to measure the success of its products and services. Apple has consistently scored highly in customer satisfaction surveys, and this has contributed to its brand reputation and financial success. In addition, Apple has invested in customer service initiatives such as its Genius Bar, which provides in-person technical support to customers, and its online support community.

These case studies highlight the importance of measuring customer satisfaction and using this information to drive business decisions. By understanding what drives customer satisfaction and loyalty, companies can make strategic investments in areas such as product development, customer service, and marketing, which can lead to increased revenue and profitability.

Measuring customer satisfaction can be challenging, however, as it involves collecting and analyzing data from a range of sources. One common method is the use of surveys, which can be conducted online, by phone, or in person. Surveys may ask customers to rate their overall satisfaction with a company or product, or to provide feedback on specific aspects of the customer experience such as product quality, ease of use, or customer service.

Another method of measuring customer satisfaction is through customer feedback, which can be gathered through channels such as social media, online reviews, or customer support interactions. This feedback can provide valuable insights into areas where a company may need to improve its customer experience.

In addition to measuring customer satisfaction, companies may also use metrics such as customer retention rate and customer lifetime value (CLV) to track the financial impact of their customer service initiatives. Customer retention rate measures the percentage of customers who continue to do business with a company over time, while CLV measures the total value of a customer's business over their lifetime.

Overall, measuring customer satisfaction and its impact on financial performance is a critical aspect of managing a successful business. By investing in customer service initiatives and using customer satisfaction metrics to inform business decisions, companies can build strong customer relationships, increase customer loyalty and retention, and ultimately drive revenue and profitability.

Understanding customer satisfaction and its importance in business success

Customer satisfaction is a critical factor in the success of any business. It is a measure of how well a company meets the needs and expectations of its customers. Customer satisfaction can be defined as the degree to which a customer's expectations are met or exceeded by the product or service provided by a company. In other words, it is a measure of how happy customers are with the products or services they receive.

The importance of customer satisfaction cannot be overstated. Satisfied customers are more likely to become loyal customers, recommend the company to others, and provide positive feedback to the company. On the other hand, dissatisfied customers are likely to stop doing business with the company, complain to others, and provide negative feedback to the company.

In today's competitive business environment, customer satisfaction has become a critical factor in the success of businesses. With the advent of social media and online reviews, customers have more power than ever before to share their experiences with others. This means that businesses must be proactive in monitoring and improving customer satisfaction to remain competitive.

The relationship between customer satisfaction and financial performance

There is a strong relationship between customer satisfaction and financial performance. Companies that prioritize customer satisfaction tend to perform better financially than those that do not. This is because satisfied customers are more likely to become repeat customers, recommend the company to others, and provide positive feedback. In turn, this leads to increased revenue and profitability for the company.

Studies have shown that companies with high customer satisfaction ratings tend to have higher profitability, higher return on assets, and higher return on equity than companies with lower customer satisfaction ratings. For example, a study by the American Customer Satisfaction Index found that companies with higher customer satisfaction ratings outperformed their competitors in terms of stock market returns.

Customer satisfaction metrics

To measure customer satisfaction, businesses can use a variety of metrics, including:

Customer Satisfaction Score (CSAT)
CSAT is a measure of how satisfied customers are with a specific interaction or experience with a company. It is usually measured on a scale of 1 to 5 or 1 to 10, with higher scores indicating greater satisfaction.

Net Promoter Score (NPS)
NPS is a measure of customer loyalty and advocacy. It asks customers how likely they are to recommend the company to others, on a scale of 0 to 10. Customers who rate the company 9 or 10 are considered "promoters", while those who rate the company 6 or below are considered "detractors". The NPS is calculated by subtracting the percentage of detractors from the percentage of promoters.

Customer Effort Score (CES)
CES is a measure of how easy it is for customers to do business with a company. It asks customers how much effort they had to put in to resolve an issue or complete a transaction, on a scale of 1 to 5 or 1 to 10. Higher scores indicate that the experience was easier and more convenient for the customer.

First Contact Resolution (FCR)

FCR measures the percentage of customer inquiries that are resolved on the first contact with the company. A high FCR rate indicates that the company is providing efficient and effective customer service.

Customer Retention Rate

Customer retention rate is a measure of how many customers continue to do business with a company over time. A high customer retention rate indicates that customers are satisfied with the company's products or services and are more likely to become loyal customers.

Conclusion

In conclusion, customer satisfaction is a critical factor in the success of any business. It is a measure of how well a company meets the needs and expectations of its customers. Satisfied customers are more likely to become repeat customers, recommend the company to others, and provide positive feedback to the company. This, in turn, leads to increased revenue and profitability.

To achieve high levels of customer satisfaction, businesses must prioritize their customers and consistently deliver high-quality products and services. This requires a customer-centric approach to business, where the customer is at the center of all decision-making.

To measure customer satisfaction, companies can use a variety of metrics, including customer satisfaction surveys, Net Promoter Score (NPS), and customer retention rates. These metrics can provide valuable insights into customer perceptions of the company and help identify areas for improvement.

In addition to measuring customer satisfaction, businesses must also take steps to improve it. This may involve investing in employee training, improving product quality, and enhancing the overall customer experience.

By prioritizing customer satisfaction, businesses can build a loyal customer base, improve their reputation, and ultimately drive financial performance. In today's competitive business environment, customer satisfaction is no longer a nice-to-have but a must-have for long-term success.

How to measure customer satisfaction and its impact on financial performance

Measuring customer satisfaction is an important step in understanding how well a company is meeting the needs and expectations of its customers. By using customer satisfaction metrics, businesses can identify areas where they excel and areas that need improvement. Additionally, by linking customer satisfaction metrics to financial performance metrics, companies can quantify the impact of customer satisfaction on their bottom line.

This section will explore the different methods for measuring customer satisfaction and how these metrics can be used to drive financial performance.

Methods for Measuring Customer Satisfaction:

There are several methods for measuring customer satisfaction, including surveys, focus groups, and social media monitoring.

Surveys:
Surveys are a common method for measuring customer satisfaction. They can be conducted through various channels such as email, phone, or mail. The surveys should be well-constructed, focusing on specific aspects of the customer experience. Closed-ended questions, such as Likert scales, are often used to rate satisfaction levels.

Focus Groups:
Focus groups are small groups of customers who provide feedback on their experiences with a company's products or services. Focus groups can provide valuable insights into customer needs and preferences. They are often used to gather qualitative data, which can complement the quantitative data collected through surveys.

Social Media Monitoring:
Social media monitoring involves tracking customer feedback and comments on social media platforms such as Twitter, Facebook, and Instagram. Companies can use this feedback to quickly respond to customer issues and improve the customer experience.

Using Metrics to Drive Financial Performance:

Once customer satisfaction metrics have been collected, they can be linked to financial performance metrics to determine the impact of customer satisfaction on a company's bottom line. Some common financial performance metrics include revenue, customer acquisition costs, and customer retention rates.

Revenue:

By tracking customer satisfaction metrics alongside revenue metrics, companies can identify the impact of customer satisfaction on their revenue. Satisfied customers are more likely to become repeat customers, increasing the company's revenue.

Customer Acquisition Costs:
Customer acquisition costs refer to the cost of acquiring a new customer. By measuring customer satisfaction, companies can identify areas where they may be losing potential customers, and make changes to reduce customer acquisition costs.

Customer Retention Rates:
Customer retention rates are a measure of how many customers continue to do business with a company over time. By linking customer satisfaction metrics to customer retention rates, companies can identify the impact of customer satisfaction on customer loyalty and retention.

Case Studies:

Several companies have successfully used customer satisfaction metrics to drive financial performance. For example, Amazon has built its business on a foundation of customer satisfaction. By continually improving the customer experience, Amazon has created a loyal customer base that generates significant revenue.

Another example is Southwest Airlines, which has consistently ranked highly in customer satisfaction surveys. By providing excellent customer service and a unique customer experience, Southwest has created a loyal customer base that generates significant revenue for the company.

Conclusion:

Measuring customer satisfaction is an important step in understanding how well a company is meeting the needs and expectations of its customers. By using customer satisfaction metrics, companies can identify areas where they excel and areas that need improvement. Additionally, by linking customer satisfaction metrics to financial performance metrics, companies can quantify the impact of customer satisfaction on their bottom line. Companies that prioritize customer satisfaction are more likely to create a loyal customer base that generates significant revenue over time.

Using customer satisfaction data to make informed business decisions

Customer satisfaction is a crucial aspect of any business's success, and it is important for companies to use customer satisfaction data to make informed business decisions. In this section, we will discuss how companies can use customer satisfaction data to make informed decisions that drive financial performance.

Analyzing Customer Satisfaction Data

The first step in using customer satisfaction data to make informed business decisions is to analyze the data. Companies can use a variety of methods to collect customer satisfaction data, including surveys, feedback forms, and social media monitoring tools.

Once the data is collected, it must be analyzed to identify trends and patterns. Companies can use data visualization tools to create charts and graphs that help them understand the data. For example, a company might create a chart that shows the percentage of customers who rate their experience as positive, neutral, or negative.

Analyzing customer satisfaction data can provide companies with insights into customer preferences, pain points, and areas for improvement. Companies can use this information to make informed decisions about product development, marketing, customer service, and other business functions.

Improving Customer Service

One of the most important ways companies can use customer satisfaction data is to improve their customer service. By analyzing customer feedback, companies can identify common complaints and issues that customers experience. They can then take steps to address these issues, such as providing additional training for customer service representatives or changing their policies and procedures.

Improving customer service can have a significant impact on customer satisfaction and loyalty. Customers are more likely to do business with companies that provide excellent customer service, and they are more likely to recommend these companies to others.

Product Development

Customer satisfaction data can also be used to inform product development decisions. By understanding customer preferences and pain points, companies can create products that better meet customer needs. For example, a company might develop a new product feature that addresses a common complaint or issue raised in customer feedback.

Using customer satisfaction data to inform product development can also help companies stay competitive. By creating products that meet customer needs, companies can differentiate themselves from their competitors and attract more customers.

Marketing

Customer satisfaction data can also be used to inform marketing decisions. By understanding what drives customer satisfaction, companies can create marketing campaigns that resonate with their target audience. For example, a company might create a marketing campaign that emphasizes their commitment to excellent customer service.

Using customer satisfaction data in marketing can also help companies attract new customers. Customers are more likely to do business with companies that have a strong reputation for customer satisfaction, and a well-executed marketing campaign can help companies build this reputation.

Measuring ROI

Finally, it is important for companies to measure the return on investment (ROI) of their customer satisfaction initiatives. By tracking customer satisfaction metrics over time, companies can determine whether their initiatives are driving financial performance.

For example, a company might track customer satisfaction metrics such as Net Promoter Score (NPS) or Customer Effort Score (CES) over time. They can then compare these metrics to other business metrics such as revenue, profit, or customer retention. If there is a correlation between customer satisfaction and financial performance, the company can use this information to make data-driven decisions about their customer satisfaction initiatives.

Conclusion

Using customer satisfaction data to make informed business decisions is a critical aspect of any successful business. By analyzing customer satisfaction data, companies can identify areas for improvement, develop better products and services, and create marketing campaigns that resonate with their target audience. Ultimately, using customer satisfaction data can help companies drive financial performance and achieve long-term success.

Case studies of companies that have used customer satisfaction data to improve financial performance

Measuring customer satisfaction is important for any business, but it is not enough to simply gather data. To make informed business decisions, companies need to know how to use that data effectively. In this section, we will explore case studies of companies that have successfully used customer satisfaction data to improve financial performance. These case studies will demonstrate the benefits of using customer satisfaction data and provide insights into how companies can make better decisions based on this information.

Case Study 1: Delta Airlines

Delta Airlines is a company that has invested heavily in measuring and improving customer satisfaction. In the early 2000s, the airline faced financial difficulties and had a poor reputation for customer service. To turn things around, Delta launched a program called "Listen, Respond, and Care" that focused on gathering feedback from customers and using it to make improvements.

Delta began by conducting customer satisfaction surveys and collecting feedback through social media and other channels. The company then used this data to identify areas where it was falling short and make targeted improvements. For example, Delta discovered that customers were unhappy with the boarding process, so the airline implemented a new boarding procedure that reduced wait times and improved the overall experience.

The results of Delta's efforts were impressive. The company's net promoter score (NPS), which measures customer loyalty and willingness to recommend the company to others, increased from 18 in 2010 to 50 in 2019. In addition, Delta's revenue per available seat mile (RASM), a key financial metric for airlines, increased by 36% over the same period.

Case Study 2: Amazon

Amazon is a company that is known for its focus on customer satisfaction. The company has built its business on a foundation of customer-centricity and has used customer data to inform everything from product development to marketing strategies.

One of the ways that Amazon measures customer satisfaction is through customer reviews. The company encourages customers to leave reviews of products they have purchased, and uses this data to identify trends and make improvements. For example, if customers consistently complain about a product's packaging, Amazon will work with suppliers to improve the packaging and reduce damage during shipping.

Amazon also uses customer data to personalize the shopping experience. The company tracks customers' browsing and purchasing history to make product recommendations and offer personalized promotions. This approach has been highly successful, with Amazon reporting a 29% increase in revenue in 2020, driven in part by increased customer engagement and loyalty.

Case Study 3: Zappos

Zappos is an online retailer that is known for its exceptional customer service. The company has a strong focus on customer satisfaction and has used this focus to build a loyal customer base and drive financial performance.

One of the ways that Zappos measures customer satisfaction is through its call center metrics. The company tracks metrics like call time and resolution rate, but also focuses heavily on customer feedback. Call center employees are trained to prioritize customer satisfaction over other metrics, and are given the authority to make decisions that will improve the customer experience.

Zappos also has a generous return policy, which allows customers to return products for any reason within 365 days of purchase. This policy has helped to build trust with customers and has encouraged repeat purchases.

The results of Zappos' customer-centric approach have been impressive. The company was acquired by Amazon in 2009 for $1.2 billion, and has continued to grow and expand its customer base since then.

Conclusion

The case studies of Delta Airlines, Amazon, and Zappos demonstrate the power of using customer satisfaction data to improve financial performance. These companies have all made significant investments in measuring customer satisfaction and using that data to make targeted improvements. The results have been impressive, with increased customer loyalty, revenue growth, and improved financial performance.

By using customer satisfaction data to make informed business decisions , companies can identify areas where they can improve their products or services, and ultimately enhance the overall customer experience. They can also measure the impact of changes made on customer satisfaction levels, providing insights on the effectiveness of various initiatives.

In addition to improving financial performance, the benefits of using customer satisfaction data extend beyond the bottom line. Companies that prioritize customer satisfaction also benefit from improved brand reputation, increased customer loyalty, and a higher likelihood of customer referrals.

However, it is important to note that simply measuring customer satisfaction is not enough. Companies must also have a plan for how to act on that data in a meaningful way. This requires a company-wide commitment to customer satisfaction, with clear communication and buy-in from all levels of the organization.

In conclusion, the case studies presented in this section illustrate the importance of using customer satisfaction data to drive financial performance and overall business success. By investing in customer satisfaction measurement and taking action on that data, companies can improve customer loyalty, revenue growth, and ultimately, their bottom line. It is a powerful tool for companies looking to differentiate themselves in a crowded marketplace and build long-term success.

CHAPTER 12: THE ROLE OF CUSTOMER SERVICE IN CUSTOMER RETENTION AND LIFETIME VALUE

In today's business world, customer service has become an essential factor in retaining customers and increasing their lifetime value. Customer retention is crucial for a company's long-term success and profitability, as it is much more cost-effective to retain existing customers than to acquire new ones. Customer service plays a critical role in customer retention, as it is often the primary means by which customers interact with a company.

Customer service refers to the support and assistance that a company provides to its customers before, during, and after a purchase. It includes a wide range of activities, such as answering customer questions, resolving complaints, providing technical support, and offering product or service recommendations. Customer service can be delivered through a variety of channels, including phone, email, chat, social media, and in-person.

The quality of a company's customer service can have a significant impact on customer retention and lifetime value. Customers who receive excellent customer service are more likely to continue doing business with the company, make repeat purchases, and recommend the company to others. On the other hand, customers who have negative experiences with customer service are more likely to switch to a competitor and may even share their negative experiences with others, damaging the company's reputation.

In this chapter, we will explore the role of customer service in customer retention and lifetime value. We will discuss the importance of measuring customer satisfaction and the various metrics used to track customer satisfaction. We will also examine the impact of customer service on customer loyalty and the strategies that companies can use to improve their customer service and increase customer retention.

The Importance of Customer Satisfaction Measurement

To improve customer service and increase customer retention, companies must first understand how satisfied their customers are with their products and services. Measuring customer satisfaction is a critical component of any customer service strategy. Customer satisfaction can be defined as the extent to which a customer's expectations are met or exceeded by a company's products, services, and customer service.

There are several methods that companies can use to measure customer satisfaction. One of the most common methods is the customer satisfaction survey. Customer satisfaction surveys are designed to gather feedback from customers about their experiences with a company's products, services, and customer service. Surveys can be conducted in a variety of formats, including online surveys, phone surveys, and in-person surveys.

In addition to surveys, companies can also use other metrics to track customer satisfaction. One such metric is the Net Promoter Score (NPS), which measures the likelihood that a customer will recommend a company to others. Another metric is the Customer Effort Score (CES), which measures the ease with which a customer is able to do business with a company.

Measuring customer satisfaction is essential for several reasons. First, it provides companies with valuable feedback that can be used to improve their products, services, and customer service. Second, it helps companies identify areas where they are falling short and develop strategies to address those areas. Finally, it enables companies to track changes in customer satisfaction over time, allowing them to monitor the effectiveness of their customer service strategies.

The Impact of Customer Service on Customer Loyalty

Customer loyalty is a crucial factor in customer retention and lifetime value. Loyal customers are more likely to continue doing business with a company, make repeat purchases, and recommend the company to others. Customer service plays a critical role in building customer loyalty.

Customers who have positive experiences with customer service are more likely to become loyal customers. They feel valued and appreciated by the company and are more likely to continue doing business with the company. On the other hand, customers who have negative experiences with customer service are more likely to switch to a competitor and may even share their negative experiences with others, damaging the company's reputation.

To build customer loyalty, companies must focus on providing excellent customer service. This means going above and beyond to meet customer needs and expectations. It involves providing timely and helpful responses to customer inquiries, resolving issues quickly and efficiently, and making customers feel valued and appreciated.

In addition to building customer loyalty, excellent customer service can also lead to increased customer lifetime value (CLV). CLV is the total value a customer brings to a company over the course of their relationship. By providing excellent customer service, companies can increase CLV by encouraging repeat business and customer referrals.

Customer service can also have a significant impact on a company's reputation. In today's digital age, customers have more avenues than ever to share their experiences with others. This can include leaving reviews on websites such as Yelp or Google, posting on social media, or even creating blog posts or videos. Positive reviews and feedback can help build a company's reputation and attract new customers, while negative reviews can have the opposite effect.

Given the importance of customer service in building customer loyalty, increasing CLV, and maintaining a positive reputation, companies must make it a priority. This involves not only providing excellent customer service but also investing in the necessary infrastructure, such as customer service teams, technology, and training, to ensure that customers receive the support they need.

In the following chapters, we will explore the key elements of customer service, including communication, problem resolution, and the use of technology, and provide strategies for building customer loyalty and increasing CLV. By understanding the importance of customer service and implementing best practices, companies can not only improve their financial performance but also build long-term relationships with their customers.

The importance of customer retention and lifetime value in financial performance

Customer retention is a critical factor in the financial performance of any business. It is the process of retaining customers and keeping them loyal to a brand, product, or service. Customer retention is important because it can lead to increased revenue and profitability for a business. Companies that focus on customer retention can experience higher customer satisfaction, repeat purchases, and positive word-of-mouth marketing. This section will examine the importance of customer retention and lifetime value in financial performance.

The Importance of Customer Retention:
Customer retention is critical for financial performance because it costs less to retain existing customers than to acquire new ones. According to research, acquiring a new customer can cost five times more than retaining an existing customer. Additionally, existing customers are more likely to make repeat purchases and spend more money than new customers. Repeat customers also have a higher lifetime value than new customers, meaning they generate more revenue over time.

Moreover, loyal customers are more likely to recommend a company to their friends and family. Positive word-of-mouth marketing can increase brand awareness and attract new customers. A strong reputation for customer service and loyalty can also differentiate a company from its competitors and increase customer loyalty.

Lifetime Value:
Lifetime value (LTV) is the measure of the total worth of a customer to a business over the duration of the customer's relationship with the business. LTV is an important metric because it helps businesses understand how much revenue they can expect from a customer over time. LTV can be calculated by multiplying the average purchase value by the number of purchases per year and then multiplying that figure by the average customer lifespan.

Understanding LTV is important because it helps businesses allocate resources to retain their most valuable customers. By focusing on retaining high-value customers, businesses can increase revenue and profitability.

Strategies for Customer Retention:

To retain customers, businesses can use a variety of strategies. One effective strategy is to provide excellent customer service. Companies that prioritize customer service are more likely to retain customers than those that do not. Responding quickly to customer inquiries and complaints can also improve customer satisfaction and loyalty.

Another strategy is to offer rewards or incentives for repeat business. Rewards programs, discounts, and other incentives can encourage customers to make repeat purchases and increase their lifetime value.

Moreover, businesses can improve customer retention by developing and maintaining a strong brand reputation. A company that is known for high-quality products or services, exceptional customer service, and a commitment to customer satisfaction is more likely to retain customers and attract new ones.

Conclusion:
In conclusion, customer retention is critical for the financial performance of any business. Retaining existing customers is less expensive than acquiring new ones and can lead to increased revenue and profitability. Understanding lifetime value is also important because it helps businesses allocate resources to retain their most valuable customers. By using effective strategies such as providing excellent customer service, offering rewards and incentives for repeat business, and maintaining a strong brand reputation, businesses can improve customer retention and increase their financial performance.

The role of customer service in customer retention and lifetime value

In today's competitive business environment, customer retention is a critical aspect of maintaining financial performance. It is much more cost-effective to retain existing customers than to attract new ones. Therefore, companies must focus on building strong relationships with their customers, and one of the most effective ways to achieve this is through exceptional customer service. In this section, we will explore the importance of customer service in customer retention and lifetime value.

The Importance of Customer Retention

Customer retention is the process of keeping existing customers engaged with a company's products or services over an extended period. Retention is crucial to a company's long-term success, as it helps to build brand loyalty, repeat business, and positive word-of-mouth advertising.

According to research, a 5% increase in customer retention can increase a company's profits by 25% to 95% (Reichheld & Sasser, 1990). Additionally, it is easier and more cost-effective to retain existing customers than to acquire new ones. It costs five times more to acquire a new customer than to retain an existing one (Invesp, 2021). Therefore, companies must focus on retaining their existing customers to maintain their financial performance.

The Role of Customer Service in Customer Retention

One of the critical factors in customer retention is customer service. Customers who have positive experiences with customer service are more likely to become loyal customers. They feel valued and appreciated by the company and are more likely to continue doing business with the company. On the other hand, customers who have negative experiences with customer service are more likely to switch to a competitor and may even share their negative experiences with others, damaging the company's reputation.

To build customer loyalty, companies must focus on providing excellent customer service. Customer service includes all interactions between a customer and a company, including sales, customer support, and post-sale service. Each interaction with a customer is an opportunity to build a positive relationship and create customer loyalty.

The Role of Lifetime Value in Financial Performance

Lifetime value is a metric that measures the total amount of revenue a customer generates over the course of their relationship with a company. It is a critical factor in financial performance because it helps companies understand the long-term value of their customers. Companies can use lifetime value to determine how much they can spend on customer acquisition and retention.

According to research, repeat customers spend 67% more than new customers (Bain & Company, 2021). Therefore, companies must focus on building long-term relationships with their customers to increase lifetime value.

The Role of Customer Service in Lifetime Value

Customer service plays a critical role in lifetime value. Customers who have positive experiences with customer service are more likely to become repeat customers and generate more revenue for the company over time. In contrast, customers who have negative experiences with customer service are more likely to switch to a competitor, resulting in lost revenue for the company.

To increase lifetime value, companies must focus on providing exceptional customer service at all touchpoints. By providing excellent customer service, companies can create a positive relationship with their customers, increasing the likelihood of repeat business and higher lifetime value.

Conclusion

Customer retention and lifetime value are essential factors in a company's financial performance. Companies must focus on building strong relationships with their customers to increase retention and lifetime value. One of the most effective ways to achieve this is through exceptional customer service. By providing excellent customer service, companies can create a positive relationship with their customers, increasing the likelihood of repeat business and higher lifetime value.

Techniques for measuring customer retention and lifetime value

Customer retention and lifetime value are critical factors in determining the long-term financial success of a company. Retaining customers is essential because it is typically more expensive to acquire new customers than it is to retain existing ones. Furthermore, loyal customers can be a significant source of revenue for a company, as they tend to purchase more products or services over time. To measure customer retention and lifetime value, companies use various techniques, including customer surveys, data analysis, and predictive modeling.

Customer Surveys:

One of the most common techniques for measuring customer retention and lifetime value is through customer surveys. These surveys ask customers about their experiences with a company, such as how likely they are to continue doing business with the company and whether they would recommend the company to others. By analyzing the results of these surveys, companies can gain insights into areas where they need to improve their customer service and overall customer experience.

Data Analysis:

Another technique for measuring customer retention and lifetime value is through data analysis. Companies can analyze customer data to identify patterns and trends that can help them better understand their customers. For example, companies can track customer purchases over time to determine which products or services are most popular and to identify opportunities for cross-selling or upselling.

Predictive Modeling:

Predictive modeling is another technique for measuring customer retention and lifetime value. Predictive modeling uses statistical algorithms and machine learning techniques to analyze customer data and make predictions about customer behavior. For example, companies can use predictive modeling to identify customers who are at risk of leaving and to develop strategies for retaining them.

Examples:

Let's look at two examples of companies that use these techniques to measure customer retention and lifetime value:

Example 1: Amazon

Amazon is a company that places a high value on customer retention and lifetime value. They use a variety of techniques to measure these metrics, including customer surveys and data analysis. For example, Amazon uses customer surveys to gather feedback on their products and services, and they use data analysis to track customer purchases and identify trends.

Additionally, Amazon uses predictive modeling to make personalized product recommendations to customers based on their purchase history and browsing behavior. By doing this, Amazon is able to increase customer loyalty and revenue over time.

Example 2: Delta Airlines

Delta Airlines is another company that places a high value on customer retention and lifetime value. They use a variety of techniques to measure these metrics, including customer surveys and predictive modeling. For example, Delta Airlines uses customer surveys to gather feedback on their flights and customer service, and they use predictive modeling to identify customers who are at risk of leaving and to develop strategies for retaining them.

Delta Airlines also uses data analysis to track customer purchases and identify trends, which allows them to develop targeted marketing campaigns to promote new products or services. By doing this, Delta Airlines is able to increase customer loyalty and revenue over time.

Conclusion:

Customer retention and lifetime value are critical factors in determining the long-term financial success of a company. To measure these metrics, companies use a variety of techniques, including customer surveys, data analysis, and predictive modeling. By using these techniques, companies can gain insights into areas where they need to improve their customer service and overall customer experience. Furthermore, companies can identify customers who are at risk of leaving and develop strategies for retaining them. Overall, investing in customer retention and lifetime value is essential for companies that want to achieve long-term financial success.

Case studies of companies that have improved customer retention and lifetime value through customer service improvements

Customer retention and lifetime value are essential to the long-term success of any business. One way to achieve this is through improving customer service. In this section, we will examine case studies of companies that have successfully improved customer retention and lifetime value through customer service improvements.

Zappos
Zappos is an online shoe and clothing retailer known for its excellent customer service. The company has a customer-centric culture, and its employees are trained to go above and beyond to make customers happy. This has resulted in a loyal customer base, with repeat customers accounting for more than 75% of the company's sales. Zappos measures customer loyalty through the Net Promoter Score (NPS), which has consistently been above 80%.

One example of Zappos' commitment to customer service is its return policy. Customers are allowed to return items for any reason, free of charge, within 365 days of purchase. This policy has resulted in happy customers who are more likely to return and make future purchases.

Nordstrom
Nordstrom is a high-end department store that has built its reputation on excellent customer service. The company's employees are trained to provide a

personalized shopping experience, and the company offers a wide range of services, including free alterations, free shipping and returns, and in-store pickup.

Nordstrom measures customer loyalty through the Customer Loyalty Index (CLI), which measures customers' likelihood to shop at the store again and recommend it to others. Nordstrom's CLI has consistently been above 80%, indicating high levels of customer loyalty.

One example of Nordstrom's commitment to customer service is its customer service policy. The company empowers its employees to make decisions that benefit the customer, even if it means taking a loss on a sale. This has resulted in a loyal customer base and a reputation for excellent customer service.

Apple

Apple is a technology company known for its innovative products and excellent customer service. The company has built its reputation on creating products that are easy to use and providing excellent customer support.

Apple measures customer loyalty through the Net Promoter Score (NPS), which has consistently been above 70%. One way that Apple has improved customer retention and lifetime value is through its AppleCare service. AppleCare provides customers with extended warranties, priority access to customer support, and free repairs for certain issues. This has resulted in happy customers who are more likely to purchase Apple products in the future.

Southwest Airlines

Southwest Airlines is a low-cost airline that has built its reputation on excellent customer service. The company offers affordable fares, flexible policies, and a fun, friendly culture that sets it apart from other airlines.

Southwest measures customer loyalty through the Net Promoter Score (NPS), which has consistently been above 60%. One way that Southwest has improved customer retention and lifetime value is through its Rapid Rewards program. The program rewards customers with points for each flight they take, which can be redeemed for free flights, upgrades, and other perks. This has resulted in a loyal customer base and increased revenue for the company.

Amazon

Amazon is an e-commerce giant that has built its reputation on fast, reliable shipping and excellent customer service. The company offers a wide range of products and services, including Amazon Prime, which provides members with free two-day shipping, streaming of movies and TV shows, and other benefits.

Amazon measures customer loyalty through the Net Promoter Score (NPS), which has consistently been above 60%. One way that Amazon has improved customer retention and lifetime value is through its customer service policies. The company offers easy returns, 24/7 customer support, and a price match guarantee, which has resulted in happy customers who are more likely to make future purchases.

In conclusion, these case studies demonstrate the importance of customer service in improving customer retention and lifetime value. By providing excellent customer service, companies can increase the loyalty of their customers and ultimately boost their financial performance.

Another company that has improved its customer retention and lifetime value through customer service improvements is Zappos, an online shoe and clothing retailer. Zappos is known for its exceptional customer service, which includes free shipping and returns, a 365-day return policy, and 24/7 customer support. The company also has a unique culture that focuses on putting the customer first, and all employees are trained to prioritize customer satisfaction above all else.

Zappos measures customer loyalty through customer satisfaction surveys and has consistently received high scores. In addition, the company has reported a high customer lifetime value, with the average customer making multiple purchases per year.

Another example is Nordstrom, a high-end department store chain. Nordstrom is renowned for its exceptional customer service, which includes free shipping and returns, personal styling services, and a loyalty program that rewards customers for their purchases. The company measures customer loyalty through its Nordstrom Rewards program and has reported high customer retention rates and lifetime value.

One strategy that Nordstrom uses to improve customer retention is its focus on building personal relationships with customers. The company encourages its sales associates to get to know customers on a personal level and to provide personalized recommendations and service. This personalized approach has resulted in loyal customers who are willing to spend more money at Nordstrom.

Overall, these case studies demonstrate that companies can improve their financial performance by focusing on customer service and improving customer retention and lifetime value. By providing exceptional customer service and building strong relationships with customers, companies can increase loyalty and ultimately drive revenue growth.

PART 5: HUMAN RESOURCES AND FINANCE

The effective management of human resources and finance is crucial for the success of any organization. These two areas are intricately linked, as human resources are responsible for managing the most valuable asset of a company - its people, while finance is responsible for managing the monetary resources. Together, they ensure the proper functioning and growth of a company.

In this section, we will explore the various aspects of human resources and finance, including recruitment, training, compensation, benefits, employee relations, accounting, financial analysis, investment, and risk management. We will also examine the legal and ethical considerations involved in managing human resources and finance, such as compliance with labor laws and regulations, anti-discrimination policies, financial reporting standards, and fiduciary responsibilities.

Moreover, we will discuss the latest trends and challenges faced by human resources and finance professionals, including the impact of technology on the workforce, the increasing demand for diversity and inclusion, the changing landscape of work, the need for sustainable and socially responsible practices, and the evolving role of human resources and finance in strategic decision-making.

Throughout this section, we will provide practical examples and case studies from a variety of industries and perspectives, highlighting the best practices and potential pitfalls in managing human resources and finance. We will also provide opportunities for students to engage in critical thinking, problem-solving, and decision-making exercises, helping them to develop the skills and knowledge necessary for success in the field of human resources and finance.

CHAPTER 13: OVERVIEW OF THE FINANCIAL IMPACT OF HUMAN RESOURCES

Human resources (HR) is an integral part of any organization, responsible for managing the most valuable asset of a company – its people. HR professionals play a vital role in recruiting, hiring, training, and managing the employees of an organization. They are responsible for ensuring that the company has the right people in the right positions, with the right skills and knowledge to achieve the company's objectives.

The financial impact of HR can be significant, as the cost of attracting, retaining, and developing employees is one of the largest expenses for most organizations. Therefore, it is essential to understand how HR affects the financial performance of a company. This chapter will provide an overview of the financial impact of HR, including the costs associated with HR functions and the return on investment (ROI) of HR initiatives.

Costs of Human Resources

The costs associated with HR functions can be divided into two categories: direct costs and indirect costs. Direct costs are those that are easily measurable and directly attributed to HR activities, such as salaries, benefits, recruitment costs, and training expenses. Indirect costs, on the other hand, are more difficult to measure and are often overlooked when calculating the cost of HR. These costs include lost productivity due to employee turnover, decreased morale, and the cost of legal compliance.

Direct Costs

The direct costs associated with HR functions can vary widely depending on the size and complexity of the organization. The largest direct cost for most organizations is employee salaries and benefits. These costs can account for up to 50% of a company's total expenses. Other direct costs associated with HR include recruitment costs, such as job postings and applicant tracking systems, and training and development expenses, such as tuition reimbursement and professional development programs.

Indirect Costs

Indirect costs associated with HR can be much more difficult to measure but can have a significant impact on a company's financial performance. These costs include lost productivity due to employee turnover, decreased morale, and the cost of legal compliance. Turnover costs can be substantial, as the cost of replacing an employee can be as much as 1.5 to 2 times their annual salary. Decreased morale can also have a significant impact on productivity and can lead to increased absenteeism and decreased quality of work.

Return on Investment (ROI) of Human Resources

The ROI of HR initiatives can be challenging to measure, as the benefits of HR initiatives are often intangible and difficult to quantify. However, it is essential to measure the ROI of HR initiatives to determine their effectiveness and to justify the cost of HR activities to upper management. HR initiatives that can improve the ROI of a company include employee engagement programs, training and development programs, and performance management systems.

Employee Engagement Programs

Employee engagement programs can have a significant impact on the financial performance of a company. Engaged employees are more productive, have lower absenteeism rates, and are more likely to stay with a company long-term. Engaged employees can also lead to increased customer satisfaction and loyalty, which can have a direct impact on a company's bottom line. HR professionals can measure the effectiveness of employee engagement programs through surveys and metrics, such as turnover rates and absenteeism rates.

Training and Development Programs

Training and development programs can also have a significant impact on the financial performance of a company. By investing in their employees' skills and knowledge, companies can improve productivity, reduce errors, and increase innovation. Training and development programs can also lead to increased employee engagement and job satisfaction, which can have a direct impact on retention rates. HR professionals can measure the effectiveness of training and development programs through metrics, such as employee performance and productivity.

Performance Management Systems

Performance management systems are another HR initiative that can have a significant impact on the financial performance of a company. By setting clear expectations and goals for employees, performance management systems can help ensure that they are aligned with the overall strategy of the organization. This can result in better job performance, increased productivity, and improved financial outcomes.

Performance management systems typically involve regular evaluations of employee performance, with feedback provided to help employees improve their performance. These evaluations may be conducted by managers or supervisors, or through self-evaluations or peer evaluations. Performance management systems can also include rewards and recognition programs for employees who exceed expectations or achieve exceptional results.

One example of a company that has implemented an effective performance management system is GE. Under former CEO Jack Welch, GE introduced a system called "rank and yank," which involved ranking employees on a curve and eliminating the bottom 10% of performers each year. While controversial, this system helped create a culture of high performance at GE and drove significant financial results.

Another company that has benefited from an effective performance management system is Netflix. The company has a unique system in which employees are given the freedom to take time off as needed and are evaluated based on their contributions to the company, rather than on traditional metrics such as time spent in the office. This approach has helped foster a culture of creativity and innovation, resulting in a track record of success for the company.

While performance management systems can have significant financial benefits for companies, it is important to note that they must be implemented carefully and thoughtfully. Poorly designed or executed performance management systems can lead to demotivation, disengagement, and high turnover rates among employees.

In addition, there is growing recognition that traditional performance management systems may not be the most effective approach. Many companies are moving away from traditional annual performance reviews in favor of more frequent and ongoing feedback and coaching. This approach can help ensure that employees are continually improving and can quickly address any issues or challenges that arise.

Overall, performance management systems can have a significant impact on the financial performance of a company. By setting clear expectations and goals, providing regular feedback and recognition, and fostering a culture of high performance, companies can drive better financial results and achieve their strategic objectives.

The role of human resources in business success

Human resources (HR) is a crucial component of a company's success. Effective HR management is essential for ensuring that a company is able to recruit, develop, and retain the best employees. This in turn can lead to increased productivity, improved customer satisfaction, and ultimately, improved financial performance.

One of the primary roles of HR is to ensure that the company has the right people in the right positions. This involves a range of activities, including job analysis, recruitment, and selection. Job analysis is the process of identifying the key tasks and responsibilities associated with a particular role. This information is then used to create a job description, which outlines the skills, qualifications, and experience required for the position.

Recruitment is the process of attracting and identifying potential candidates for a job. This can be done through a range of channels, including online job boards, social media, and referrals from existing employees. Once a pool of candidates has been identified, the selection process begins. This typically involves a series of interviews, assessments, and reference checks, which are used to evaluate the candidates' suitability for the role.

Once employees have been hired, HR plays a critical role in their development and retention. This includes providing training and development opportunities to help employees build the skills and knowledge they need to be successful in their roles. HR may also provide coaching and mentoring to help employees overcome challenges and achieve their goals.

Performance management is another key function of HR. This involves setting clear performance expectations for employees, monitoring their progress, and providing feedback on their performance. This process can help identify areas where employees may need additional support or training, and can also help managers identify high performers who may be ready for additional responsibilities or promotions.

Compensation and benefits are also important aspects of HR management. HR is responsible for ensuring that employees are paid fairly and competitively, and that they have access to benefits such as health insurance, retirement plans, and paid time off. HR may also be responsible for managing employee relations, including addressing conflicts and grievances, and ensuring that employees are treated fairly and equitably.

Overall, the role of HR in business success is multifaceted and complex. Effective HR management requires a deep understanding of the company's goals and objectives, as well as the skills and capabilities required to achieve them. HR professionals must be skilled at recruiting and developing top talent, managing employee performance, and ensuring that employees are compensated fairly and have access to the benefits and resources they need to be successful.

In addition to these core functions, HR professionals must also be able to navigate a range of legal and regulatory requirements. This includes ensuring compliance with labor laws, providing accommodations for employees with disabilities, and addressing issues related to diversity and inclusion.

Ultimately, the success of a company depends on its people. Effective HR management can help ensure that a company has the right people in the right positions, and that those employees are motivated, engaged, and productive. By investing in HR initiatives, companies can improve their financial performance, enhance their reputation, and build a strong foundation for long-term success.

Understanding the financial impact of human resources

Human resources are a vital part of any organization. They are responsible for recruiting, selecting, training, and managing the workforce. The success of any business depends largely on its human resources, and it is important to understand the financial impact of human resources. In this section, we will discuss the role of human resources in business success and the financial implications of human resource management.

The Role of Human Resources in Business Success:

Human resources are responsible for ensuring that an organization's workforce is competent, productive, and motivated. They play a critical role in the success of any organization by developing and implementing policies and practices that promote employee satisfaction and engagement.

Human resources are also responsible for attracting and retaining top talent. They must design compensation packages and benefits that are competitive in the industry to attract the best candidates. Furthermore, they must create a work environment that fosters employee engagement and productivity.

Another critical role of human resources is managing employee relations. They must ensure that all employees are treated fairly and that the organization complies with all employment laws and regulations.

The Financial Impact of Human Resources:

Human resources have a significant financial impact on a business. Managing and maintaining a skilled workforce is expensive, and human resource management has a direct effect on a company's bottom line.

One of the most significant costs associated with human resources is employee turnover. When an employee leaves, it is costly to replace them. The cost of recruiting, hiring, and training a new employee can be significant. Moreover, there is a loss of productivity when a position is left vacant.

Human resources can also impact the financial performance of a company through employee engagement. Engaged employees are more productive, and their increased output can lead to higher profits. Additionally, engaged employees are more likely to stay with a company, reducing the cost of turnover.

Compensation and benefits are another area where human resources can have a financial impact. Employees must be compensated at a rate that is competitive with other companies in the industry. If compensation is not competitive, employees may leave for higher-paying jobs. Furthermore, offering comprehensive benefits packages can help retain employees and reduce turnover costs.

Performance management systems are another HR initiative that can have a significant impact on the financial performance of a company. By setting clear expectations and goals for employees, performance management can help improve employee productivity and reduce the costs associated with turnover.

Conclusion:

In conclusion, human resources play a critical role in the success of any organization. They are responsible for attracting and retaining top talent, managing employee relations, and ensuring that the workforce is competent, productive, and motivated. Human resources also have a significant financial impact on a business. Managing and maintaining a skilled workforce is expensive, and human resource management has a direct effect on a company's bottom line. Therefore, it is essential for companies to invest in their human resources and develop policies and practices that promote employee satisfaction and engagement.

Case studies of companies that have improved financial performance through human resources improvements

Human resources (HR) play a critical role in a company's success. They help ensure that the company's workforce is performing at its highest level and aligning with the company's overall goals and objectives. However, measuring the financial impact of HR initiatives can be challenging. In this section, we will explore case studies of companies that have improved their financial performance through HR improvements. These case studies will help students understand how HR initiatives can impact a company's bottom line.

Case Study 1: Procter & Gamble
Procter & Gamble (P&G) is a consumer goods company that is known for its world-class HR practices. In 2000, the company launched a new HR strategy called "Organization 2005". The goal of the strategy was to create a high-performance culture that would drive business results. The strategy involved a significant investment in HR training and development, including leadership development, diversity training, and talent management.

The results of P&G's HR initiatives were impressive. By 2005, the company had increased sales by 27%, reduced costs by $1.6 billion, and improved productivity by 40%. In addition, P&G was named the best company for leadership development by Fortune magazine in 2005. These financial and non-financial results are a testament to the impact that HR initiatives can have on a company's overall performance.

Case Study 2: Marriott International
Marriott International is a leading hospitality company that has also been recognized for its world-class HR practices. In 2008, the company launched a new HR initiative called "Spirit to Serve Our Communities". The initiative focused on promoting social responsibility among the company's employees and customers.

The initiative had a significant impact on the company's financial performance. By 2012, Marriott had achieved a 19% increase in revenue and a 60% increase in earnings per share. The company also received numerous awards for its corporate social responsibility initiatives, including being named one of the "World's Most Ethical Companies" by Ethisphere Institute in 2013. This case study highlights how HR initiatives can have a positive impact on a company's financial performance while also promoting social responsibility.

Case Study 3: Google
Google is a technology company that is known for its innovative HR practices. One of Google's most famous HR initiatives is its "20% time" policy, which allows employees to spend 20% of their workweek pursuing their own projects. This policy has been credited with sparking some of Google's most successful products, including Gmail and Google News.

While it can be difficult to measure the direct financial impact of this initiative, Google's overall success speaks for itself. In 2019, the company reported revenues of $161.8 billion and a net income of $34.3 billion. This case study shows how HR initiatives that promote creativity and innovation can lead to significant financial success.

Conclusion:
The case studies presented in this section demonstrate how HR initiatives can have a significant impact on a company's financial performance. By investing in HR training and development, promoting social responsibility, and encouraging creativity and innovation, companies like Procter & Gamble, Marriott International, and Google have achieved impressive financial results. As businesses continue to face new challenges and opportunities, HR will continue to play a critical role in driving their success.

Practical examples of how to measure and analyze the financial impact of human resources

Human resources play a crucial role in the success of any organization. However, measuring and analyzing the financial impact of human resources can be challenging. In this section, we will explore practical examples of how to measure and analyze the financial impact of human resources.

Cost per hire
The cost per hire is a metric that measures the cost of recruiting and hiring a new employee. This metric is essential in measuring the efficiency of the hiring process. The cost per hire includes advertising costs, recruitment agency fees, interview expenses, and other recruitment-related expenses. By calculating the cost per hire, organizations can determine the most cost-effective recruitment strategies.

For example, if an organization is spending a significant amount of money on advertising but not getting a high return on investment (ROI), it may need to reconsider its advertising strategy. By analyzing the cost per hire, organizations can make data-driven decisions and optimize their recruitment process.

Turnover rate

The turnover rate is another critical metric that measures the percentage of employees who leave an organization in a given period. High turnover rates can be costly for organizations, as they can result in lost productivity, decreased morale, and increased recruitment costs.

By calculating the turnover rate, organizations can identify the reasons behind employee turnover and implement strategies to reduce it. For example, if the turnover rate is high in a particular department, the organization can investigate the reasons behind the high turnover rate, such as poor management, lack of training and development, or low pay. Once the root cause is identified, the organization can take steps to address it, such as providing more training and development opportunities, increasing pay, or improving management practices.

Return on investment (ROI) of training and development

Training and development programs are essential in improving employee skills and productivity. However, measuring the ROI of these programs can be challenging. The ROI of training and development programs can be measured by comparing the cost of the program with the benefits it provides.

For example, if an organization invests in a training program that costs $10,000 and results in a $50,000 increase in sales, the ROI would be 400%. By measuring the ROI of training and development programs, organizations can determine the effectiveness of their programs and identify areas for improvement.

Absenteeism rate

The absenteeism rate measures the percentage of employees who are absent from work for a given period. High absenteeism rates can be costly for organizations, as they can result in lost productivity and increased costs.

By calculating the absenteeism rate, organizations can identify the reasons behind employee absenteeism and take steps to reduce it. For example, if the absenteeism rate is high in a particular department, the organization can investigate the reasons behind the high absenteeism rate, such as low job satisfaction or poor working conditions. Once the root cause is identified, the organization can take steps to address it, such as improving working conditions or increasing job satisfaction.

Revenue per employee

Revenue per employee measures the amount of revenue generated per employee. This metric is essential in measuring the productivity of employees and the effectiveness of the organization's operations.

By calculating revenue per employee, organizations can identify areas where they need to improve their operations and increase productivity. For example, if the revenue per employee is low in a particular department, the organization can investigate the reasons behind the low revenue per employee, such as inefficient processes or lack of resources. Once the root cause is identified, the organization can take steps to address it, such as improving processes or increasing resources.

In conclusion, measuring and analyzing the financial impact of human resources is crucial in improving the overall performance of an organization. By using metrics such as cost per hire, turnover rate, ROI of training and development, absenteeism rate, and revenue per employee, organizations can gain insight into the effectiveness of their HR practices and identify areas for improvement. HR metrics also allow organizations to make data-driven decisions when it comes to their workforce and to justify HR investments to company stakeholders.

However, it is important to note that HR metrics should not be viewed in isolation, but rather as part of a broader performance management system. Metrics should be analyzed in conjunction with other business metrics such as revenue, profit margins, and customer satisfaction, to provide a more comprehensive view of the organization's performance.

When measuring and analyzing HR metrics, it is important to ensure the accuracy and validity of the data. This can be achieved through effective data management and the use of standardized and reliable measurement methods. It is also important to interpret the data in the right context and to consider external factors such as industry trends and economic conditions.

To conclude, organizations can benefit greatly from measuring and analyzing the financial impact of human resources. By doing so, they can identify areas for improvement, make data-driven decisions, and justify HR investments to company stakeholders. However, it is important to view HR metrics in the broader context of overall business performance and to ensure the accuracy and validity of the data.

CHAPTER 14: UNDERSTANDING THE COST OF EMPLOYEE TURNOVER

Employee turnover refers to the rate at which employees leave an organization and are replaced by new hires. Employee turnover can be voluntary, when employees choose to leave the organization, or involuntary, when employees are terminated or laid off. High turnover rates can have significant financial implications for an organization, including costs associated with recruiting and training new employees, lost productivity during the transition period, and potential negative impacts on morale and employee engagement.

Calculating the Cost of Employee Turnover

There are various methods for calculating the cost of employee turnover, and the exact approach used may vary depending on the organization and the specific circumstances. However, some common metrics used for measuring the cost of employee turnover include:

Cost per hire: This metric calculates the total cost associated with recruiting and hiring a new employee. This may include advertising costs, agency fees, recruiter salaries, and other related expenses.

Training and development costs: This metric measures the cost of training and development programs for new employees. This may include the cost of training materials, trainers' salaries, and the time spent by current employees to train new hires.

Lost productivity: This metric measures the lost productivity during the transition period when a new employee is hired and getting up to speed. This may include the time spent by managers and coworkers to train the new employee, as well as the time spent by the new employee to learn the job and become productive.

Impact on morale and employee engagement: This metric measures the impact of turnover on employee morale and engagement. High turnover rates can lead to increased stress, decreased job satisfaction, and a lack of trust in management, which can further exacerbate turnover.

Factors Contributing to Employee Turnover

There are various factors that contribute to employee turnover, and identifying these factors is crucial for developing effective retention strategies. Some of the common factors contributing to employee turnover include:

Poor management: Poor management practices, including lack of recognition, poor communication, and lack of support, can lead to low employee morale and high turnover rates.

Limited growth opportunities: Employees may leave an organization if they feel that their career growth opportunities are limited, or if they do not see a clear path for advancement.

Inadequate compensation and benefits: Employees may leave an organization if they feel that they are not adequately compensated for their work, or if the benefits offered by the organization are not competitive.

Unhealthy work culture: A work culture that is unhealthy, unsupportive, or toxic can lead to high turnover rates as employees seek more positive work environments.

Strategies for Reducing Employee Turnover

To reduce employee turnover, organizations can implement various retention strategies, including:

Improve management practices: Organizations can improve management practices by providing recognition and support to employees, communicating clearly and effectively, and creating opportunities for growth and development.

Offer competitive compensation and benefits: Organizations can offer competitive compensation and benefits to attract and retain talented employees. This may include offering bonuses, profit sharing, flexible work arrangements, and other incentives.

Foster a positive work culture: Organizations can create a positive work culture by promoting teamwork, communication, and collaboration. This can include implementing employee recognition programs, providing opportunities for socialization and team building, and offering resources for mental health and well-being.

Develop and retain talent: Organizations can develop and retain talent by investing in training and development programs, offering career advancement opportunities, and providing mentorship and coaching to employees.

Case Studies of Companies That Reduced Employee Turnover

There are numerous examples of companies that have successfully reduced employee turnover by implementing effective retention strategies. One such example is Best Buy, a large electronics retailer, which implemented a program called "results only work environment" (ROWE). This program allowed employees to work flexible schedules and focus on results rather than hours worked, creating a more satisfying work-life balance. As a result, employee turnover at Best Buy dropped from 60% to 30%.

Another example is the online shoe and clothing retailer Zappos. The company's unique culture, which emphasizes employee happiness and empowerment, has led to exceptionally low turnover rates. Zappos offers comprehensive benefits, including free health care and on-site childcare, as well as a fun and supportive work environment. In addition, the company offers extensive training and development opportunities, allowing employees to grow and advance within the organization. These efforts have resulted in an impressive turnover rate of less than 10%.

Similarly, the software company SAS has implemented a variety of retention strategies, including extensive employee benefits, flexible work arrangements, and a strong commitment to work-life balance. The company also provides employees with opportunities for professional development and advancement, as well as a strong sense of community and culture. As a result, turnover rates at SAS are exceptionally low, averaging just 4% annually.

Finally, the fast-food chain Chick-fil-A has implemented a variety of retention strategies, including a comprehensive training and development program, a supportive work environment, and opportunities for growth and advancement. In addition, the company emphasizes a strong sense of community and culture, with regular team-building events and employee recognition programs. These efforts have resulted in impressive retention rates, with turnover rates averaging just 15%, significantly below the industry average.

These case studies demonstrate that effective retention strategies can significantly reduce employee turnover and improve overall organizational performance. By implementing programs that prioritize employee satisfaction, empowerment, and growth, companies can create a culture of retention that attracts and retains top talent, reduces costs associated with turnover, and improves overall business outcomes.

The cost of employee turnover and its impact on financial performance

Employee turnover can have a significant impact on an organization's financial performance. Turnover refers to the rate at which employees leave an organization, and it can be measured in various ways. One common measure is the turnover rate, which is calculated by dividing the number of employees who left the organization during a specific period by the total number of employees at the beginning of that period. For example, if an organization had 100 employees at the beginning of the year and 20 employees left during that year, the turnover rate would be 20%.

The cost of employee turnover can be broken down into two main categories: direct and indirect costs. Direct costs are the expenses that an organization incurs as a result of an employee leaving, such as recruitment costs, training costs, and severance pay. Indirect costs are the less tangible costs associated with turnover, such as lost productivity, reduced morale, and decreased customer satisfaction.

The direct costs of employee turnover can vary depending on the position and level of the employee. For example, it is generally more expensive to replace a senior executive than an entry-level employee. According to a report by the Society for Human Resource Management, the average cost per hire in the United States is $4,129. However, this number can vary widely depending on the industry, position, and location.

In addition to recruitment costs, organizations also incur training costs when replacing employees. These costs can include the time and resources required to train new employees, as well as the cost of any external training programs. A study by the Center for American Progress found that the cost of replacing an employee can range from 16% of the employee's annual salary for lower-paying jobs to as much as 213% for highly skilled or senior-level positions.

Another direct cost of turnover is severance pay. When an employee leaves an organization voluntarily or is terminated, they may be entitled to receive severance pay. This can be a significant expense, particularly for high-level executives or employees with long tenures.

Indirect costs of employee turnover can be more difficult to quantify, but they can have a significant impact on an organization's financial performance. One of the most significant indirect costs is lost productivity. When an employee leaves, it can take time for their replacement to become fully trained and productive. During this period, there may be a decrease in productivity, which can have a negative impact on the organization's bottom line.

In addition to lost productivity, turnover can also result in reduced morale and increased stress among remaining employees. This can lead to decreased engagement and motivation, which can further exacerbate productivity issues. Turnover can also lead to decreased customer satisfaction, particularly if the departing employee had a significant impact on customer relationships.

The impact of turnover on financial performance can be particularly significant for small businesses. According to a report by the National Small Business Association, the cost of turnover can be as much as 150% of an employee's salary for small businesses. This is because small businesses often have fewer resources and may not be able to absorb the costs of turnover as easily as larger organizations.

Reducing employee turnover can be challenging, but there are a variety of strategies that organizations can implement to improve retention. One such strategy is to improve the overall employee experience by creating a positive work environment, offering competitive compensation and benefits, and providing opportunities for growth and development. Organizations can also conduct exit interviews to gain insight into why employees are leaving and use that information to make improvements.

In conclusion, employee turnover can have a significant impact on an organization's financial performance. The direct and indirect costs of turnover can be significant, particularly for small businesses. Organizations that are able to reduce turnover through effective retention strategies can improve their bottom line and create a more stable and productive workforce.

Techniques for measuring and analyzing employee turnover costs

Measuring and analyzing employee turnover costs is crucial in understanding the financial impact of employee turnover on an organization. By using effective techniques, organizations can gain insights into the causes of employee turnover and take measures to reduce it. This section will discuss some of the techniques for measuring and analyzing employee turnover costs.

Direct Costs
The direct costs of employee turnover include the cost of recruiting and hiring new employees, the cost of training new employees, and the cost of separation pay or benefits. These costs are relatively easy to measure and can be quantified in dollars. For example, the cost of recruiting and hiring a new employee can be calculated by adding up the cost of job postings, recruitment fees, and other expenses related to the hiring process. Similarly, the cost of training a new employee can be calculated by adding up the cost of training materials, trainers' salaries, and other expenses related to the training process.

Indirect Costs
Indirect costs of employee turnover are not as easy to measure as direct costs. Indirect costs refer to the costs associated with lost productivity, decreased morale, and reduced customer satisfaction. These costs can be difficult to quantify in dollar terms but are no less important than direct costs. Indirect costs can have a significant impact on an organization's financial performance over the long term.

One way to measure indirect costs is to calculate the cost of lost productivity. This can be done by estimating the time it takes for a new employee to become fully productive in their role and comparing it to the time it takes for an experienced employee to perform the same tasks. The difference in productivity can then be calculated and multiplied by the employee's salary to arrive at an estimated cost of lost productivity.

Another way to measure indirect costs is to survey employees to gauge their level of job satisfaction and overall morale. Lower job satisfaction and morale can lead to increased absenteeism, decreased productivity, and higher turnover rates.

Total Cost
To get a comprehensive picture of the cost of employee turnover, it is necessary to combine direct and indirect costs. The total cost of employee turnover can be

calculated by adding the direct and indirect costs. By doing so, organizations can get a better understanding of the true financial impact of employee turnover on their bottom line.

ROI Analysis

An ROI analysis can be used to determine the financial return on investment for various retention strategies. This analysis compares the costs of implementing a retention strategy to the benefits gained from it. The benefits gained may include increased employee engagement, higher productivity, and lower turnover rates.

To conduct an ROI analysis, organizations need to identify the costs associated with implementing the retention strategy, including any training or development programs, as well as the potential benefits. The benefits can be quantified in monetary terms, such as increased revenue or decreased costs. Once the costs and benefits have been identified, the ROI can be calculated by dividing the benefits by the costs and expressing the result as a percentage.

Benchmarking

Benchmarking is the process of comparing an organization's performance to that of its peers or competitors. By benchmarking their turnover rates and costs against those of other organizations in their industry, organizations can identify areas where they are performing well and areas where they need to improve.

Benchmarking can also help organizations identify best practices for retaining employees. For example, if a competitor has a lower turnover rate, an organization may want to investigate their retention strategies and see if they can implement similar programs.

In conclusion, measuring and analyzing employee turnover costs is crucial in understanding the financial impact of employee turnover on an organization. By using a combination of direct and indirect cost analysis, ROI analysis, and benchmarking, organizations can gain insights into the causes of employee turnover and take measures to reduce it. This can lead to improved financial performance and a more stable workforce, which in turn can lead to improved productivity, customer satisfaction, and employee morale. It is important to note, however, that reducing employee turnover is not a one-time effort but rather an ongoing process that requires continuous monitoring and adjustment.

To further aid in the measurement and analysis of employee turnover costs, there are several techniques that organizations can use. One such technique is the calculation of a turnover cost ratio. The turnover cost ratio is the total cost of turnover divided by the total compensation for all employees in a given period. This metric provides a clear understanding of the financial impact of employee turnover on the organization.

Another technique is the use of predictive analytics. Predictive analytics can be used to identify patterns and trends in employee turnover, which can help organizations develop targeted retention strategies. For example, an analysis of exit interviews may reveal common reasons for employee turnover, such as a lack of career growth opportunities or poor management. This information can then be used to implement specific retention programs or address specific issues to reduce turnover.

Organizations can also use surveys to measure employee engagement and job satisfaction, which are important factors in employee turnover. These surveys can help identify areas of improvement in the workplace, such as work-life balance or training and development opportunities, that can lead to increased employee satisfaction and retention.

Lastly, organizations can use simulations to estimate the financial impact of employee turnover on the organization. This technique involves creating a model of the organization's workforce and simulating the effects of various turnover scenarios. By running simulations, organizations can estimate the potential costs of turnover and evaluate the effectiveness of different retention strategies.

In summary, there are several techniques that organizations can use to measure and analyze employee turnover costs. These include the calculation of turnover cost ratios, the use of predictive analytics, employee surveys, and simulations. By utilizing these techniques, organizations can gain a deeper understanding of the financial impact of employee turnover and develop effective retention strategies to improve their overall financial performance.

Case studies of companies that have reduced employee turnover and improved financial performance

Employee turnover can have a significant impact on an organization's financial performance, but effective retention strategies can lead to improved employee engagement, productivity, and loyalty, ultimately resulting in better financial outcomes. In this section, we will examine several case studies of companies that have successfully reduced employee turnover and improved their financial performance by implementing retention strategies.

Best Buy
Best Buy, a large electronics retailer, implemented a program called "results only work environment" (ROWE) that allowed employees to work flexible schedules and

set their own goals and priorities. This program resulted in a 90% reduction in voluntary turnover, and a 35% increase in productivity. The company also saw a $2.2 million reduction in real estate costs due to fewer employees working in the office.

The ROWE program allowed employees to have more control over their work-life balance, leading to increased job satisfaction and reduced stress. By allowing employees to work remotely, the program also reduced commuting time and expenses, which contributed to better employee retention.

Hilton Worldwide

Hilton Worldwide, a global hotel chain, implemented several initiatives to improve employee engagement and retention, including a program called "Catch Me at My Best," which allowed employees to recognize and reward each other for outstanding performance. The program resulted in a 10% increase in employee engagement scores and a 6% reduction in turnover.

Hilton also implemented a program called "The Heart of Hilton," which provided employees with tools and resources to develop their skills and advance their careers within the company. This program resulted in a 16% reduction in turnover among frontline employees.

By investing in employee development and recognition programs, Hilton improved employee satisfaction and loyalty, resulting in reduced turnover and better financial performance.

Costco

Costco, a membership-based warehouse club, is known for its high employee retention rates and competitive wages and benefits. The company pays its employees an average of $23 per hour, which is significantly higher than the industry average. Costco also provides its employees with comprehensive health insurance and retirement benefits.

These policies have resulted in a turnover rate of just 6%, compared to an industry average of 30%. By retaining experienced and motivated employees, Costco has been able to provide its members with high-quality service and products, leading to increased customer loyalty and sales.

Zappos

Zappos, an online shoe and clothing retailer, is known for its unique company culture, which emphasizes employee empowerment and customer service. The company offers new employees $2,000 to quit if they decide that Zappos is not the right fit for them, which helps to ensure that only the most committed and passionate employees remain with the company.

Zappos also provides its employees with extensive training and development opportunities, as well as a range of benefits and perks, such as free lunches and pet-friendly offices. These policies have resulted in a turnover rate of just 3%, compared to an industry average of 15%.

By creating a positive and supportive work environment, Zappos has been able to attract and retain highly motivated and engaged employees, resulting in better financial performance and customer satisfaction.

Google
Google, a multinational technology company, is known for its innovative and employee-centric culture. The company provides its employees with a range of benefits and perks, such as free meals, on-site gyms, and paid sabbaticals. Google also encourages its employees to spend 20% of their time on passion projects, which has led to the development of several successful products, such as Gmail and Google Maps.

By fostering a culture of creativity, autonomy, and innovation, Google has been able to attract and retain some of the most talented and motivated employees in the industry. This has resulted in better financial performance and a reputation as one of the most desirable employers in the world. For example, in 2019, Google was ranked as the best company to work for by Fortune magazine.

Another example of a company that has reduced employee turnover and improved financial performance is SAS, a software company based in North Carolina. SAS offers a range of employee benefits, such as health insurance, on-site child care, and flexible work arrangements. The company also has a strong focus on employee development and offers extensive training and educational opportunities.

SAS has a turnover rate of less than 5%, which is significantly lower than the industry average. This has led to cost savings for the company, as well as increased productivity and higher employee morale. In fact, SAS has consistently been ranked as one of the best companies to work for in the United States and has received numerous awards for its employee-friendly culture.

A third example of a company that has reduced employee turnover and improved financial performance is Marriott International, a global hospitality company. Marriott has implemented a number of initiatives to improve employee retention, such as offering competitive salaries and benefits, providing training and development opportunities, and offering flexible work arrangements.

As a result of these initiatives, Marriott has been able to reduce its turnover rate and improve its financial performance. In 2018, Marriott reported a 7% increase in revenue and a 30% increase in earnings per share, which were attributed in part to the company's focus on employee retention and engagement.

These examples demonstrate that investing in employee retention can lead to significant benefits for companies, including improved financial performance, increased productivity, and a positive reputation as an employer. By providing employees with a supportive and engaging workplace, companies can reduce turnover rates and retain their most valuable assets, their employees.

CHAPTER 15: THE IMPACT OF EMPLOYEE ENGAGEMENT AND SATISFACTION ON FINANCIAL PERFORMANCE

Employees are a company's most valuable asset, and employee engagement and satisfaction are critical factors that impact an organization's financial performance. Employee engagement refers to the level of commitment and dedication that employees have towards their work, the organization, and its goals. It is the extent to which employees feel passionate about their jobs, are committed to the organization's mission, and are willing to go above and beyond what is expected of them. Employee satisfaction, on the other hand, refers to the degree to which employees are content with their job, their work environment, and the support they receive from their employer.

Employee engagement and satisfaction have become increasingly important for organizations, as research has shown that they are directly related to financial performance. Companies with highly engaged and satisfied employees tend to have better financial results than those with disengaged and dissatisfied employees. According to a study by Gallup, highly engaged teams are 21% more productive and have 10% higher customer satisfaction ratings than disengaged teams. Additionally, highly engaged employees take fewer sick days, are more likely to stay with the company, and are more likely to recommend the company to others.

In this chapter, we will explore the impact of employee engagement and satisfaction on financial performance. We will discuss the benefits of having engaged and satisfied employees, the costs of disengaged and dissatisfied employees, and how organizations can improve employee engagement and satisfaction.

Benefits of Engaged and Satisfied Employees:

Engaged and satisfied employees provide several benefits to an organization, including:

Increased productivity: Engaged employees are more motivated to work and are willing to put in extra effort to achieve their goals. They are also more likely to collaborate with their colleagues and share ideas, leading to increased productivity.

Better customer service: Engaged employees are more likely to provide excellent customer service, as they are more invested in their work and want to ensure that customers are satisfied with their experience.

Lower turnover: Engaged employees are more likely to stay with the organization, reducing turnover and associated costs.

Improved reputation: Companies with engaged and satisfied employees tend to have a positive reputation, which can attract top talent and customers.

Costs of Disengaged and Dissatisfied Employees:

Disengaged and dissatisfied employees can have a significant impact on an organization's financial performance, including:

Decreased productivity: Disengaged employees are less motivated and are more likely to do the minimum required to get by, leading to decreased productivity.

Poor customer service: Disengaged employees are less likely to provide excellent customer service, which can result in decreased customer satisfaction and loyalty.

Higher turnover: Dissatisfied employees are more likely to leave the organization, resulting in higher turnover and associated costs.

Negative reputation: Companies with disengaged and dissatisfied employees may have a negative reputation, which can deter top talent and customers.

Improving Employee Engagement and Satisfaction:

Organizations can take several steps to improve employee engagement and satisfaction, including:

Providing a positive work environment: Organizations should strive to create a work environment that is positive and supportive. This can include providing employees with opportunities for growth and development, recognizing and rewarding employee achievements, and fostering a culture of open communication and feedback.

Encouraging employee involvement: Organizations should encourage employees to be involved in decision-making and give them a sense of ownership over their work. This can include soliciting employee input on projects and initiatives, and providing opportunities for employees to lead projects and teams.

Offering competitive compensation and benefits: Organizations should offer competitive compensation and benefits packages to attract and retain top talent. This can include offering bonuses, stock options, and other incentives.

Providing work-life balance: Organizations should strive to provide a healthy work-life balance for employees. This can include offering flexible work arrangements, such as telecommuting or flexible schedules, and encouraging employees to take time off when needed. By promoting work-life balance, organizations can reduce employee burnout and turnover.

Investing in employee training and development: Organizations should invest in the training and development of their employees. This can include offering formal training programs, mentoring, coaching, and on-the-job training. Providing employees with opportunities to learn and grow can increase their job satisfaction and motivation, while also improving their skills and knowledge.

Encouraging diversity and inclusion: Organizations should strive to create a diverse and inclusive workplace. This can include promoting diversity in hiring and promotions, providing training on diversity and inclusion, and fostering a culture that values and respects differences. A diverse and inclusive workplace can lead to increased employee engagement and satisfaction, as well as improved financial performance.

Overall, improving employee engagement and satisfaction can have a positive impact on an organization's financial performance. Engaged and satisfied employees are more productive, have lower turnover rates, and are more likely to provide high-quality customer service. Additionally, companies with high employee engagement and satisfaction levels tend to have higher profitability and revenue growth.

However, improving employee engagement and satisfaction requires a concerted effort from the organization. It involves creating a positive work environment, encouraging employee involvement, offering competitive compensation and benefits, providing work-life balance, investing in employee training and development, and promoting diversity and inclusion. By implementing these strategies, organizations can improve their financial performance while also creating a more engaged and satisfied workforce.

The importance of employee engagement and satisfaction in business success

Employee engagement and satisfaction are essential factors in determining the success of a business. In recent years, organizations have increasingly recognized the importance of employee engagement and satisfaction as drivers of business performance. Engaged and satisfied employees are more likely to be productive, innovative, and loyal to their organizations, leading to increased financial performance and competitive advantage. This section will explore the importance of employee engagement and satisfaction in business success and discuss how organizations can improve these factors to achieve better financial results.

The Importance of Employee Engagement and Satisfaction:

Employee engagement refers to the level of emotional connection and commitment that employees have towards their work, organization, and goals. Engaged employees are those who are invested in their work, feel a sense of purpose, and are committed to achieving the organization's objectives. Employee satisfaction, on the other hand, refers to the level of contentment and happiness that employees have with their job, work environment, and overall experience in the organization. Both employee engagement and satisfaction are critical drivers of business success for the following reasons:

Increased Productivity: Engaged and satisfied employees are more likely to be productive and efficient in their work. They are motivated to work towards achieving the organization's goals, and they feel a sense of pride and ownership in their work. This results in higher levels of productivity and quality of work output.

Innovation and Creativity: Engaged and satisfied employees are more likely to be innovative and creative in their work. They are more willing to take risks, suggest new ideas, and try new approaches to problem-solving. This leads to the development of new products, services, and processes that can give organizations a competitive advantage in the marketplace.

Reduced Turnover: Engaged and satisfied employees are less likely to leave their jobs, leading to reduced turnover rates. High turnover rates can be costly for organizations due to the expenses associated with recruiting, training, and onboarding new employees. Therefore, retaining employees is critical to maintaining a stable workforce and achieving business success.

Positive Reputation: Organizations with engaged and satisfied employees are more likely to have a positive reputation in the marketplace. They are seen as attractive places to work, and they are more likely to attract top talent. This can lead to increased business opportunities and partnerships.

Improved Financial Performance: Engaged and satisfied employees can have a significant impact on a company's financial performance. A study by Gallup found that engaged employees are 21% more productive than their disengaged counterparts, leading to higher profitability and revenue growth for the organization.

Improving Employee Engagement and Satisfaction:

Organizations can take several steps to improve employee engagement and satisfaction, including:

Providing a Positive Work Environment: Organizations should strive to create a work environment that is positive and supportive. This can include providing employees with opportunities for growth and development, recognizing and rewarding employee achievements, and fostering a culture of open communication and feedback.

Encouraging Employee Involvement: Organizations should encourage employees to be involved in decision-making and give them a sense of ownership over their work. This can include soliciting employee input on projects and initiatives, and providing opportunities for employees to lead projects and teams.

Offering Competitive Compensation and Benefits: Organizations should offer competitive compensation and benefits packages to attract and retain top talent. This can include offering bonuses, stock options, and other incentives.

Providing Work-Life Balance: Organizations should strive to provide a healthy work-life balance for their employees. This can include offering flexible work arrangements, providing opportunities for personal time off, and promoting wellness and self-care initiatives.

Investing in Employee Training and Development: Organizations should invest in the training and development of their employees to improve their skills and knowledge. This can include offering mentorship programs, providing access to online courses and training, and sponsoring attendance at conferences and workshops.

Conclusion:

Employee engagement and satisfaction are crucial factors in the success of any organization. A highly engaged and satisfied workforce is more productive, innovative, and committed to achieving the organization's goals. In contrast, disengaged employees are more likely to be absent, make errors, and leave the organization.

Investing in employee engagement and satisfaction can bring several benefits to an organization. A positive work environment, encouraging employee involvement, offering competitive compensation and benefits, and providing work-life balance are some of the ways organizations can improve employee engagement and satisfaction. Furthermore, investing in employee training and development can enhance employees' skills and knowledge, making them more effective and efficient in their roles.

Several studies have shown a strong correlation between employee engagement, satisfaction, and financial performance. Organizations with highly engaged and satisfied employees tend to have better financial results, including higher revenues, profits, and customer satisfaction. For instance, according to a Gallup study, highly engaged business units have 21% higher profitability than disengaged ones.

In contrast, organizations with low employee engagement and satisfaction levels tend to experience higher rates of employee turnover, absenteeism, and accidents, which can negatively impact their bottom line. Additionally, low employee engagement and satisfaction can lead to a negative organizational culture, which can further harm the organization's performance.

Therefore, organizations should make employee engagement and satisfaction a top priority by investing in programs and initiatives that foster a positive work environment, encourage employee involvement, offer competitive compensation and benefits, provide work-life balance, and invest in employee training and development.

In summary, employee engagement and satisfaction play a critical role in the success of any organization. By investing in these factors, organizations can create a positive work environment, improve employee productivity and innovation, and achieve better financial performance.

Techniques for measuring and analyzing employee engagement and satisfaction

Measuring and analyzing employee engagement and satisfaction is critical for organizations to understand how their workforce perceives their work environment and the impact it has on the organization's success. Employee engagement and satisfaction are multifaceted concepts, and measuring them requires a comprehensive approach that takes into account both quantitative and qualitative data.

This section will explore the techniques and methods that organizations can use to measure and analyze employee engagement and satisfaction. We will examine the benefits of measuring employee engagement and satisfaction, the challenges associated with measuring them, and the different techniques and tools that organizations can use to gain insight into their workforce's attitudes and behaviors.

Benefits of Measuring Employee Engagement and Satisfaction:

Measuring employee engagement and satisfaction provides several benefits to organizations. First, it allows organizations to identify areas of improvement in their work environment and take corrective action to address any issues. By measuring engagement and satisfaction, organizations can identify the factors that contribute to employee turnover and take steps to mitigate it.

Second, measuring employee engagement and satisfaction can help organizations identify their top performers and understand what motivates them. This can help organizations create a more engaged and satisfied workforce by replicating the factors that contribute to their top performers' success.

Third, measuring employee engagement and satisfaction can help organizations identify trends and patterns in their workforce's behavior and attitudes over time. This can provide insights into the effectiveness of organizational changes and initiatives and help organizations make data-driven decisions.

Challenges of Measuring Employee Engagement and Satisfaction:

Measuring employee engagement and satisfaction is not without its challenges. One of the biggest challenges is defining engagement and satisfaction and developing a measurement tool that accurately captures these concepts. Engagement and satisfaction are subjective and can vary depending on the individual, making it challenging to develop a measurement tool that accurately captures these concepts.

Another challenge is ensuring that the measurement tool is reliable and valid. The measurement tool must be consistent and stable over time and provide accurate and meaningful results.

Finally, obtaining honest and accurate responses from employees can be challenging. Employees may be hesitant to provide honest feedback for fear of repercussions or may not fully understand the questions asked, leading to inaccurate responses.

Techniques for Measuring Employee Engagement and Satisfaction:

Despite the challenges associated with measuring employee engagement and satisfaction, several techniques and tools can be used to gain insight into an organization's workforce's attitudes and behaviors.

Surveys: Surveys are one of the most commonly used tools for measuring employee engagement and satisfaction. Surveys can be administered anonymously and can provide quantitative data that can be analyzed to identify trends and patterns. Surveys can be customized to capture specific information, such as employee satisfaction with their work environment, compensation and benefits, and career development opportunities.

Interviews: Interviews can provide qualitative data that can provide insights into the factors that contribute to employee engagement and satisfaction. Interviews can be conducted one-on-one or in focus groups and can provide a more in-depth understanding of an employee's attitudes and behaviors.

Observations: Observations involve observing employee behavior and interactions in the workplace. This technique can provide insights into the work environment's culture and identify areas for improvement.

Performance Metrics: Performance metrics, such as employee turnover rates, can provide insights into the effectiveness of organizational changes and initiatives. High turnover rates can indicate that employees are dissatisfied with their work environment, while low turnover rates can indicate that employees are engaged and satisfied.

Social Media Monitoring: Social media monitoring involves monitoring social media platforms to gain insights into employee attitudes and behaviors. Social media monitoring can provide real-time insights into employee engagement and satisfaction and identify potential issues before they become more significant problems.

Conclusion:

Measuring and analyzing employee engagement and satisfaction is critical for organizations to understand how their workforce perceives their work environment and the impact it has on the organization's success. The techniques and tools outlined in this section can provide organizations with valuable insights into how to improve employee engagement and satisfaction, leading to better financial performance and a more positive workplace culture.

To summarize, organizations can use a variety of methods to measure and analyze employee engagement and satisfaction, including surveys, focus groups, and exit interviews. These techniques provide valuable data that can help organizations identify areas for improvement and develop targeted strategies to increase engagement and satisfaction.

It is important to note that measuring employee engagement and satisfaction is not a one-time event, but an ongoing process. Organizations should regularly assess their workforce's attitudes and perceptions to ensure that they are meeting their employees' needs and expectations. This can help organizations to proactively address issues before they become bigger problems.

However, organizations should also be mindful of the potential drawbacks of relying solely on quantitative measures of employee engagement and satisfaction. While surveys and other quantitative measures can provide valuable data, they may not capture the full picture of employees' experiences and emotions. Qualitative methods, such as focus groups and interviews, can help to provide more in-depth insights into employees' attitudes and perceptions.

In addition, organizations should be careful not to rely solely on employee engagement and satisfaction measures as a proxy for overall business performance. While there is a correlation between engaged and satisfied employees and better financial performance, there are many other factors that can impact business success, such as market conditions and industry trends.

In conclusion, measuring and analyzing employee engagement and satisfaction is an essential part of any organization's strategy to improve its workforce and achieve its business goals. By using a combination of quantitative and qualitative methods, organizations can gain valuable insights into their employees' experiences and develop targeted strategies to improve engagement and satisfaction. However, organizations should also be mindful of the limitations of these measures and the importance of considering other factors that impact business performance.

The impact of employee engagement and satisfaction on financial performance

Employee engagement and satisfaction have become increasingly important in today's business world. Organizations that invest in creating a positive work environment, providing opportunities for growth and development, and promoting employee involvement, are more likely to have a motivated and engaged workforce. A motivated and engaged workforce can have a significant impact on an organization's financial performance. In this section, we will explore the impact of employee engagement and satisfaction on financial performance and how organizations can measure and analyze this impact.

The Impact of Employee Engagement and Satisfaction on Financial Performance:

There is a growing body of evidence that suggests that there is a positive correlation between employee engagement and satisfaction and an organization's financial performance. Engaged employees are more productive, creative, and motivated to contribute to the success of the organization. Satisfied employees are more likely to stay with the organization and be committed to its goals and objectives.

A study by Gallup found that organizations with engaged employees had 21% higher profitability than those with disengaged employees. Another study by Aon Hewitt found that organizations with high engagement levels had a 19% increase in operating income compared to organizations with low engagement levels. These studies indicate that employee engagement and satisfaction can have a significant impact on an organization's financial performance.

One of the ways in which employee engagement and satisfaction can impact financial performance is through increased productivity. Engaged employees are more likely to go above and beyond their job requirements, take on additional responsibilities, and contribute to the success of the organization. This increased productivity can result in cost savings, increased revenue, and improved customer satisfaction.

Another way in which employee engagement and satisfaction can impact financial performance is through reduced turnover. Satisfied employees are more likely to stay with the organization, reducing the costs associated with turnover such as recruiting, training, and lost productivity. Additionally, engaged employees are more likely to refer other talented individuals to the organization, reducing recruitment costs.

Furthermore, engaged and satisfied employees can have a positive impact on customer satisfaction and loyalty. Engaged employees are more likely to provide excellent customer service, which can result in increased customer satisfaction and loyalty. This increased loyalty can lead to increased revenue and improved financial performance.

Measuring the Impact of Employee Engagement and Satisfaction on Financial Performance:

To measure the impact of employee engagement and satisfaction on financial performance, organizations can use a variety of metrics and tools. One of the most commonly used metrics is employee turnover rate. High turnover rates can be an indicator of low employee satisfaction and engagement levels. Additionally, organizations can track productivity metrics such as sales per employee or revenue per employee to determine the impact of employee engagement on financial performance.

Organizations can also use employee engagement surveys to measure employee satisfaction and engagement levels. These surveys can provide valuable insights into areas of the organization where improvements can be made to increase engagement and satisfaction levels. The results of these surveys can be used to develop strategies to improve employee engagement and satisfaction, which can ultimately lead to improved financial performance.

Conclusion:

Employee engagement and satisfaction can have a significant impact on an organization's financial performance. Engaged and satisfied employees are more productive, committed to the organization's goals, and provide better customer service. Organizations can measure and analyze the impact of employee engagement and satisfaction on financial performance by using metrics such as turnover rates and productivity metrics, as well as employee engagement surveys. By investing in creating a positive work environment, providing opportunities for growth and development, and promoting employee involvement, organizations can improve employee engagement and satisfaction, leading to improved financial performance.

Case studies of companies that have improved financial performance through employee engagement and satisfaction improvements

The importance of employee engagement and satisfaction in achieving financial success for a company has been discussed in previous sections. However, it is also essential to examine case studies of companies that have improved their financial performance by focusing on employee engagement and satisfaction. This section will discuss some notable examples of companies that have successfully implemented strategies to improve their workforce's engagement and satisfaction, resulting in increased financial success.

Marriott International

Marriott International is a global hotel chain that has over 6,500 properties in 127 countries. The company's success can be attributed to its strong emphasis on employee satisfaction and engagement. Marriott has consistently ranked among the best places to work, and this has been reflected in its financial performance. In 2019, Marriott's revenue was over $20 billion, and the company's market value was $45 billion.

One of the strategies that Marriott has implemented to improve employee engagement and satisfaction is its "Spirit to Serve" program. This program focuses on providing employees with opportunities for career advancement, recognition, and rewards. Marriott also provides comprehensive training programs and offers a diverse and inclusive work environment.

The results of Marriott's focus on employee engagement and satisfaction have been significant. The company has consistently been ranked among the top companies for customer satisfaction, resulting in a loyal customer base and increased revenue.

Southwest Airlines

Southwest Airlines is a major airline in the United States that has consistently ranked among the top companies for employee engagement and satisfaction. The company's focus on creating a positive work environment has translated into financial success. In 2019, Southwest Airlines reported revenue of over $22 billion, and its market value was $33 billion.

Southwest Airlines' approach to employee engagement and satisfaction is centered around its "Warrior Spirit" culture. This culture emphasizes teamwork, dedication, and positivity. Southwest Airlines provides employees with opportunities for career advancement, job security, and a comprehensive benefits package.

The company's focus on employee engagement and satisfaction has resulted in a loyal customer base and increased revenue. Southwest Airlines' customer satisfaction rates have consistently ranked among the highest in the industry, resulting in increased revenue and market share.

Google

Google is a technology company that has consistently been ranked among the top companies for employee engagement and satisfaction. The company's focus on providing employees with a positive work environment and opportunities for growth has translated into financial success. In 2019, Google's revenue was over $160 billion, and its market value was $800 billion.

Google's approach to employee engagement and satisfaction is centered around its company culture, which emphasizes creativity, innovation, and collaboration. Google provides employees with opportunities for career advancement, comprehensive benefits, and a diverse and inclusive work environment.

The company's focus on employee engagement and satisfaction has resulted in a loyal customer base and increased revenue. Google's customer satisfaction rates have consistently ranked among the highest in the technology industry, resulting in increased revenue and market share.

Conclusion:

The case studies discussed above provide valuable insights into the impact of employee engagement and satisfaction on financial performance. Companies that have implemented strategies to improve their workforce's engagement and satisfaction have seen significant financial success. These strategies include providing employees with opportunities for career advancement, recognition, and rewards, comprehensive training programs, and a positive work environment. It is essential for companies to recognize the importance of employee engagement and satisfaction and implement strategies to improve them. By doing so, companies can achieve financial success while also creating a positive work environment for their employees.

PART 6: CRM AND FINANCE

In today's fast-paced business environment, companies face intense competition for customer attention and loyalty. Successful businesses must maintain strong relationships with their customers while also managing their finances to ensure profitability. Customer Relationship Management (CRM) and Finance are two critical components of any organization's strategy to achieve these goals.

CRM is a business process that involves managing and analyzing customer interactions and data to improve customer satisfaction and loyalty. Finance, on the other hand, involves managing a company's financial resources to ensure profitability and sustainability. While these two areas may seem unrelated, they are closely intertwined. A company that effectively manages its customer relationships is more likely to attract and retain loyal customers, which in turn can lead to increased revenue and profitability.

In this section, we will explore the key concepts and strategies of CRM and Finance, and examine how they can be integrated to drive business success. We will begin by discussing the importance of customer relationship management and its impact on financial performance. Next, we will examine the key financial metrics that organizations use to measure success, including revenue, profit, and cash flow. We will also discuss the importance of financial planning and forecasting in ensuring long-term sustainability.

Throughout this section, we will examine case studies of companies that have successfully integrated CRM and Finance to achieve their business goals. These case studies will provide valuable insights into the challenges and opportunities of implementing a CRM and Finance strategy, and will help students understand how these concepts can be applied in real-world situations.

By the end of this section, students will have a comprehensive understanding of the role of CRM and Finance in driving business success, and will be equipped with the knowledge and skills to implement these strategies in their own organizations.

CHAPTER 16: OVERVIEW OF CRM AND ITS IMPORTANCE IN FINANCIAL PERFORMANCE

Customer relationship management (CRM) is a vital component of any successful business strategy. It involves managing a company's interactions with customers and potential customers, with the goal of building long-term relationships that benefit both parties. In recent years, the importance of CRM in financial performance has become increasingly evident, with many companies seeing significant improvements in revenue and profitability as a result of effective CRM implementation.

This chapter will provide an overview of CRM, including its key concepts, benefits, and challenges. We will also examine the ways in which CRM can impact financial performance, and explore case studies of companies that have successfully leveraged CRM to improve their bottom line.

Key Concepts of CRM

At its core, CRM is about building and maintaining strong relationships with customers. This involves understanding their needs and preferences, providing personalized service and support, and fostering trust and loyalty over time. Key concepts of CRM include:

Customer Data Management: CRM systems allow companies to gather and manage data about their customers, including their contact information, purchase history, preferences, and behavior. This data can be used to create targeted marketing campaigns, tailor products and services to individual needs, and improve the customer experience.

Sales Automation: CRM systems also help automate the sales process, allowing companies to track leads, manage pipelines, and streamline the sales process. This can lead to faster sales cycles, increased deal sizes, and more efficient use of resources.

Marketing Automation: CRM systems can also be used to automate marketing activities, such as email campaigns, social media management, and lead nurturing. This can help companies reach more customers, generate more leads, and improve overall marketing effectiveness.

Benefits of CRM

Effective CRM implementation can have a number of benefits for businesses, including:

Improved Customer Satisfaction: By understanding and responding to customer needs, companies can improve the customer experience and build long-term loyalty.

Increased Revenue: By focusing on building strong customer relationships, companies can increase sales, generate repeat business, and attract new customers through positive word of mouth.

Better Marketing ROI: By using data to create targeted campaigns and track their effectiveness, companies can improve the ROI of their marketing efforts.

More Efficient Operations: By automating key processes and leveraging customer data, companies can streamline their operations and reduce costs.

Challenges of CRM

While there are many benefits to effective CRM implementation, there are also several challenges that companies may face, including:

Data Management: Managing large amounts of customer data can be complex and time-consuming, and requires robust systems and processes to ensure accuracy and completeness.

Integration: Integrating CRM systems with other business systems (such as accounting or inventory management) can be difficult, and requires careful planning and execution.

User Adoption: Getting employees to adopt new CRM systems and processes can be a challenge, and requires strong leadership and effective training.

Impact of CRM on Financial Performance

The impact of CRM on financial performance can be significant, with many companies seeing improvements in revenue and profitability as a result of effective CRM implementation. For example:

Increased Sales: By using CRM to track leads, manage pipelines, and automate sales processes, companies can improve sales efficiency and increase revenue. For example, a study by Nucleus Research found that companies that invested in CRM saw an average increase in sales of 41%.

Improved Customer Retention: By using CRM to understand and respond to customer needs, companies can improve customer satisfaction and build long-term loyalty. This can lead to increased repeat business and reduced customer churn, both of which can have a positive impact on revenue and profitability.

Better Marketing ROI: By using CRM to create targeted marketing campaigns and track their effectiveness, companies can improve the ROI of their marketing efforts. For example, a study by Gartner found that companies that use CRM to analyze customer data can achieve up to a 15% increase in marketing ROI.

Efficient Resource Allocation: By using CRM to analyze customer data and identify patterns and trends, companies can make better decisions about where to allocate resources, such as marketing and sales budgets. This can help improve efficiency and reduce costs, ultimately leading to better financial performance.

In addition to these benefits, effective CRM implementation can also lead to improved operational efficiency and streamlined processes. For example, by automating manual tasks such as data entry and lead management, companies can free up time for sales and customer service teams to focus on more strategic activities.

However, it is important to note that the benefits of CRM implementation are not guaranteed, and there are several factors that can impact its effectiveness. These include:

Data Quality: CRM relies on accurate and up-to-date data in order to be effective. If data is incomplete or inaccurate, it can lead to incorrect insights and decisions, ultimately impacting financial performance negatively.

Employee Adoption: If employees are not properly trained on how to use CRM or are resistant to change, they may not fully adopt the system, limiting its effectiveness.

Integration with Other Systems: CRM is often just one component of a larger technology ecosystem, and if it is not integrated properly with other systems, it may not be able to provide the full range of benefits.

In summary, while CRM can have a significant impact on financial performance, its effectiveness depends on a variety of factors, including data quality, employee adoption, and integration with other systems. As such, it is important for companies to carefully consider these factors and develop a comprehensive CRM strategy that aligns with their overall business objectives.

Introduction to CRM and its role in business success

Customer Relationship Management (CRM) is a business strategy that aims to manage and improve customer interactions, thereby enhancing customer satisfaction and retention, and ultimately improving a company's financial performance. CRM is a crucial element of any business strategy as it enables businesses to understand their customers' needs and preferences, improve customer satisfaction, and build long-term relationships that can translate into increased revenue and profitability.

This section will provide an overview of CRM and its role in business success. It will cover the definition and importance of CRM, the key components of a successful CRM strategy, the benefits of CRM, and the challenges of implementing a CRM strategy.

Definition and Importance of CRM

CRM can be defined as a business strategy that focuses on managing and improving customer interactions and relationships. CRM involves collecting and analyzing customer data, such as demographics, buying behavior, and preferences, to understand customers better and tailor products and services to their needs. CRM also involves implementing processes and technologies that facilitate customer engagement, such as customer service and support, marketing, and sales automation.

CRM is essential for businesses that want to grow and succeed in today's competitive market. With increased competition, businesses need to differentiate themselves by providing superior customer service, delivering personalized products and services, and building long-term relationships with their customers. CRM enables businesses to do just that by improving customer satisfaction, reducing customer churn, increasing customer loyalty, and ultimately improving financial performance.

Key Components of a Successful CRM Strategy

A successful CRM strategy requires careful planning and execution. The following are the key components of a successful CRM strategy:

Customer Data Management: A successful CRM strategy requires collecting and managing customer data effectively. This involves capturing data from various sources, such as website traffic, social media interactions, and customer service interactions, and integrating this data into a centralized database. The data must be accurate, up-to-date, and accessible to all relevant departments, such as sales, marketing, and customer service.

Customer Segmentation: A successful CRM strategy involves segmenting customers based on their needs and preferences. This enables businesses to tailor their products and services to specific customer segments, improving customer satisfaction and retention.

Personalization: A successful CRM strategy involves delivering personalized products and services to customers based on their preferences and behavior. Personalization can be achieved through targeted marketing campaigns, personalized product recommendations, and customized customer service interactions.

Multichannel Engagement: A successful CRM strategy involves engaging with customers through multiple channels, such as email, social media, and phone. This enables businesses to reach customers where they are and provide a seamless customer experience across all touchpoints.

Integration with Business Processes: A successful CRM strategy involves integrating CRM with other business processes, such as sales and marketing automation, inventory management, and accounting. This enables businesses to streamline their operations and improve efficiency.

Benefits of CRM

Implementing a successful CRM strategy can have several benefits for businesses, including:

Improved Customer Satisfaction: By understanding and responding to customer needs and preferences, businesses can improve customer satisfaction and loyalty.

Increased Sales: By improving sales efficiency and effectiveness, businesses can increase revenue and profitability.

Reduced Customer Churn: By improving customer retention and reducing churn, businesses can reduce the cost of acquiring new customers and improve financial performance.

Better Marketing ROI: By targeting marketing campaigns to specific customer segments and tracking their effectiveness, businesses can improve the ROI of their marketing efforts.

Challenges of Implementing a CRM Strategy

Implementing a successful CRM strategy can be challenging for businesses. The following are some of the challenges businesses may face:

Data Management: Collecting, managing, and analyzing customer data can be complex and time-consuming.

Integration with Existing Systems: Integrating CRM with existing systems, such as accounting and inventory management, can be challenging. This is because CRM often requires specific data to function properly, and integrating different systems can be difficult.

Employee Resistance: Employees may resist adopting a new CRM system, especially if they are used to working with a different system or process.

Cost: Implementing a CRM system can be expensive, and many businesses may not have the resources to invest in a high-quality system.

Lack of Technical Expertise: Implementing and managing a CRM system requires technical expertise, and many businesses may not have the in-house resources to do so.

To overcome these challenges, businesses must carefully plan and execute their CRM strategy. This includes selecting the right CRM system, developing a clear plan for data management, and ensuring that employees are properly trained and motivated to use the system. It also involves investing in the necessary resources and expertise to implement and manage the system effectively.

Despite these challenges, implementing a successful CRM strategy can bring significant benefits to a business. It can improve customer relationships, increase sales, and enhance overall business performance. By carefully planning and executing a CRM strategy, businesses can overcome these challenges and achieve success in today's competitive marketplace.

Understanding the financial impact of CRM

As discussed earlier, Customer Relationship Management (CRM) can have a significant impact on a company's financial performance. In this section, we will explore in detail the financial benefits of implementing a successful CRM strategy.

Increased Sales and Revenue

One of the primary benefits of implementing a CRM strategy is the potential increase in sales and revenue. By improving customer relationships, companies can increase the likelihood of repeat business, upselling, and cross-selling.

CRM helps businesses to create targeted marketing campaigns and sales strategies by segmenting their customers based on demographics, behavior, and preferences. This leads to a better understanding of customers, which, in turn, helps businesses to tailor their products and services to meet customer needs. By delivering more personalized experiences, businesses can increase customer loyalty and satisfaction, leading to an increase in revenue.

Studies have shown that companies that invest in CRM see an average increase in sales of 41%. Additionally, CRM helps businesses to optimize their sales processes and improve sales team performance. By automating sales processes, companies can reduce the time and resources required to close deals, which increases productivity and improves the bottom line.

Improved Customer Retention and Loyalty

In addition to increasing sales and revenue, CRM can also have a significant impact on customer retention and loyalty. By understanding customer needs and preferences, businesses can deliver a more personalized experience, leading to higher levels of satisfaction and loyalty.

CRM helps businesses to identify customer pain points and address them proactively, leading to higher levels of customer satisfaction. This, in turn, leads to increased customer loyalty and reduced customer churn. By retaining existing customers, businesses can reduce the cost of acquiring new customers, which can have a positive impact on the bottom line.

Studies have shown that improving customer retention rates by just 5% can increase profits by up to 95%. Additionally, loyal customers are more likely to recommend a business to others, leading to increased word-of-mouth marketing and customer acquisition.

Improved Marketing ROI

CRM can also have a significant impact on a company's marketing ROI. By using CRM to create targeted marketing campaigns and track their effectiveness, businesses can optimize their marketing spend and improve ROI.

CRM helps businesses to identify the most profitable customer segments, which allows them to create targeted marketing campaigns tailored to those segments. By delivering more personalized messages, businesses can improve customer engagement and increase the effectiveness of their marketing efforts.

Additionally, CRM allows businesses to track the effectiveness of their marketing campaigns in real-time, allowing them to make adjustments as needed to improve performance. This can lead to a higher ROI on marketing spend and a positive impact on the bottom line.

Cost Savings

CRM can also lead to cost savings for businesses. By automating sales and marketing processes, businesses can reduce the time and resources required to close deals and acquire new customers. This can lead to increased productivity and reduced costs.

Additionally, CRM can help businesses to identify areas where they can reduce costs, such as by improving supply chain management or reducing waste. By optimizing business processes, businesses can reduce costs and improve profitability.

Improved Decision-Making

Finally, CRM can improve decision-making by providing businesses with access to real-time data and analytics. By tracking customer behavior and preferences, businesses can make more informed decisions about product development, marketing strategies, and sales processes.

Additionally, CRM can help businesses to identify trends and patterns in customer data, which can inform strategic decision-making. By leveraging customer data, businesses can stay ahead of the competition and improve their financial performance over time.

Conclusion

In conclusion, implementing a successful CRM strategy can have a significant impact on a company's financial performance. By increasing sales and revenue, improving customer retention and loyalty, improving marketing ROI, reducing costs, and improving decision-making, CRM can help businesses to achieve their financial goals and succeed in a competitive marketplace.

Case studies of companies that have improved financial performance through CRM implementation

Numerous companies have implemented CRM strategies with great success, resulting in increased revenue, profitability, and customer satisfaction. The following are some examples of companies that have achieved significant financial benefits through effective CRM implementation.

IBM: IBM is one of the world's largest technology companies, and it has a history of successful CRM implementations. In 2015, IBM implemented a new CRM system, which resulted in a 20% increase in sales productivity and a 50% reduction in time spent on administrative tasks. IBM also saw a 90% increase in customer satisfaction and a 20% reduction in customer churn. Overall, the CRM implementation helped IBM to improve its financial performance, with increased revenue and profitability.

Wells Fargo: Wells Fargo is one of the largest banks in the United States, and it has been recognized for its successful CRM implementation. Wells Fargo's CRM system is focused on customer segmentation, which has helped the bank to better understand its customers' needs and preferences. This has led to improved customer satisfaction and loyalty, as well as increased revenue and profitability. According to a report by Nucleus Research, Wells Fargo saw an ROI of 1,000% from its CRM implementation, with a payback period of less than one year.

Hilton Hotels: Hilton Hotels is a global hotel chain with a focus on customer service. The company implemented a new CRM system in 2013, which enabled it to better understand its customers' preferences and behavior. This allowed Hilton to personalize its marketing and customer service efforts, resulting in increased customer satisfaction and loyalty. Hilton also saw a 5% increase in revenue per available room, which helped to improve its financial performance.

Lenovo: Lenovo is a multinational technology company that implemented a new CRM system in 2015. The system was designed to improve customer engagement and enable more effective lead tracking and management. The implementation led to a 25% increase in lead conversion rates, as well as a 30% reduction in sales cycle time. Lenovo also saw a 10% increase in customer satisfaction and a 25% increase in sales productivity. These improvements helped to boost Lenovo's financial performance, with increased revenue and profitability.

The Ritz-Carlton: The Ritz-Carlton is a luxury hotel chain that is known for its exceptional customer service. The company implemented a new CRM system in 2014, which enabled it to better track and analyze customer data. This allowed The Ritz-Carlton to personalize its marketing and customer service efforts, resulting in increased customer satisfaction and loyalty. The company also saw a 30% increase in revenue per available room and a 20% increase in occupancy rates. These improvements helped to improve The Ritz-Carlton's financial performance.

These case studies demonstrate the potential financial benefits of effective CRM implementation. By focusing on customer needs and preferences, and using technology to improve customer engagement and service, companies can increase revenue, profitability, and customer satisfaction. However, it is important to note that CRM implementation can be complex and challenging, and it requires a strategic approach and careful planning. Companies that invest the time and resources to implement CRM effectively can reap significant financial rewards.

CHAPTER 17: TECHNIQUES FOR MEASURING THE FINANCIAL IMPACT OF CRM

The main objective of customer relationship management (CRM) is to improve customer satisfaction, retention, and profitability. CRM can help businesses achieve these objectives by streamlining business processes, automating sales and marketing activities, and providing better customer service. However, the financial impact of CRM is not always easy to measure, as it involves a complex set of variables and metrics.

This chapter will provide an overview of the various techniques that businesses can use to measure the financial impact of CRM. We will discuss the key performance indicators (KPIs) that are commonly used to measure the effectiveness of CRM, such as customer acquisition cost (CAC), customer lifetime value (CLTV), and return on investment (ROI). We will also examine some of the challenges and limitations associated with measuring the financial impact of CRM.

Key Performance Indicators (KPIs) for Measuring the Financial Impact of CRM:

Businesses can use a variety of KPIs to measure the financial impact of CRM. Some of the most commonly used KPIs include:

Customer Acquisition Cost (CAC):

CAC refers to the cost of acquiring a new customer. This metric takes into account all the costs associated with acquiring a new customer, such as advertising, marketing, sales, and customer service expenses. A low CAC is a good indicator that a business is acquiring customers efficiently and cost-effectively.

Customer Lifetime Value (CLTV):
CLTV refers to the total value that a customer is expected to bring to a business over the course of their relationship with the business. This metric takes into account the revenue that a customer generates, as well as the costs associated with serving that customer. A high CLTV is a good indicator that a business is retaining customers and generating revenue over the long term.

Return on Investment (ROI):
ROI refers to the amount of revenue generated by an investment, compared to the cost of that investment. In the context of CRM, ROI can be calculated by comparing the revenue generated by a CRM initiative, such as a marketing campaign or sales automation project, to the cost of that initiative. A high ROI is a good indicator that a CRM initiative is generating value for the business.

Challenges and Limitations of Measuring the Financial Impact of CRM:

Measuring the financial impact of CRM can be challenging for businesses, due to a number of factors. Some of the key challenges and limitations include:

Data Quality:
Measuring the financial impact of CRM requires accurate and reliable data. However, many businesses struggle to collect and manage customer data effectively, which can lead to inaccurate or incomplete data.

Timeframe:
Measuring the financial impact of CRM requires a long-term perspective, as the benefits of CRM are often realized over a period of months or years. However, many businesses focus on short-term metrics, such as quarterly revenue or profit, which can obscure the long-term benefits of CRM.

Complexity:
Measuring the financial impact of CRM involves a complex set of variables and metrics. Businesses need to take into account factors such as customer behavior, market trends, and competitive pressures when measuring the impact of CRM.

Case Studies of Companies That Have Improved Financial Performance Through CRM Implementation:

The following are some examples of companies that have improved their financial performance through the implementation of CRM:

Starbucks:
Starbucks implemented a CRM system in 2008 to improve its customer loyalty program. The program, called My Starbucks Rewards, uses customer data to personalize marketing messages and offers to individual customers. As a result of the program, Starbucks reported a 26% increase in revenue in 2011.

Wells Fargo:
Wells Fargo implemented a CRM system in 2008 to improve its cross-selling efforts. The system, called Vision, allows Wells Fargo employees to track customer interactions and provide personalized recommendations for additional products and services. The company also uses data analytics to identify trends and opportunities for cross-selling.

As a result of its CRM implementation, Wells Fargo saw a significant increase in cross-selling, with the average number of products per customer increasing from 3.2 to 6.1 in just a few years. Additionally, the company saw improved customer satisfaction and loyalty, as customers appreciated the personalized recommendations and streamlined interactions with the bank.

However, Wells Fargo's CRM implementation also faced challenges. In 2016, the company was fined $185 million by regulators for creating unauthorized customer accounts to meet sales targets, which raised concerns about the ethical use of customer data. The scandal led to the resignation of the company's CEO and the loss of trust among many customers.

Despite these challenges, Wells Fargo's CRM implementation provides valuable lessons for other companies looking to improve their financial performance. By using data analytics and personalized recommendations, companies can increase cross-selling and improve customer satisfaction, but they must also ensure the ethical use of customer data and maintain the trust of their customers.

Another example of successful CRM implementation is the luxury car manufacturer BMW. BMW uses a CRM system called BMW Connected, which allows the company to track customer interactions and preferences across all touchpoints, including social media, websites, and dealerships.

By using this data, BMW can provide personalized recommendations and offers to its customers, such as customized financing options and special events. This has led to increased customer satisfaction and loyalty, as well as improved financial performance.

In addition to these successes, BMW's CRM implementation also faced challenges. In 2018, the company faced a data breach that compromised the personal information of over 100,000 customers. This raised concerns about the security and privacy of customer data, which can damage the company's reputation and financial performance.

Overall, the success of Wells Fargo and BMW's CRM implementations highlights the potential financial benefits of using data analytics and personalized recommendations to improve customer relationships. However, companies must also ensure the ethical use and security of customer data to maintain trust and avoid damaging their reputation and financial performance.

Techniques for measuring and analyzing the financial impact of CRM

Techniques for measuring and analyzing the financial impact of CRM involve a combination of qualitative and quantitative methods. These techniques aim to evaluate the return on investment (ROI) of a CRM system and help businesses make informed decisions about their CRM strategies.

One of the most commonly used quantitative techniques for measuring the financial impact of CRM is calculating the customer lifetime value (CLV). CLV is a metric that estimates the total revenue a customer will generate for a business over the course of their relationship. To calculate CLV, businesses need to consider various factors such as the customer's purchase history, their likelihood to make future purchases, and the cost of retaining them as a customer.

Another quantitative technique is the net promoter score (NPS). NPS is a customer loyalty metric that measures the likelihood of a customer to recommend a business to others. It is calculated by subtracting the percentage of detractors (customers who are unlikely to recommend the business) from the percentage of promoters (customers who are highly likely to recommend the business). NPS can provide insight into the overall satisfaction of customers and help businesses identify areas where improvements can be made.

In addition to quantitative techniques, qualitative methods such as customer surveys and focus groups can provide valuable insights into the impact of CRM on customer satisfaction and loyalty. These techniques can help businesses identify areas where they excel and areas where they need to improve.

Another important aspect of measuring the financial impact of CRM is tracking key performance indicators (KPIs). KPIs are metrics that businesses use to evaluate the effectiveness of their CRM strategies. Some common KPIs for CRM include customer retention rates, customer acquisition costs, and the conversion rate of leads to customers.

To effectively measure the financial impact of CRM, it is important to have a clear understanding of the business's goals and objectives. For example, if the goal is to increase customer retention rates, then KPIs such as the churn rate (the percentage of customers who stop doing business with the company) and the renewal rate (the percentage of customers who renew their contracts) should be tracked.

Another important consideration when measuring the financial impact of CRM is the time horizon. While some benefits of CRM, such as increased customer satisfaction and loyalty, can be realized in the short term, other benefits such as increased profitability may take longer to materialize. Therefore, it is important to have a long-term perspective when evaluating the financial impact of CRM.

One challenge businesses may face when measuring the financial impact of CRM is determining causality. While it is easy to observe that a CRM system has been implemented and that customer satisfaction has improved, it can be difficult to determine whether the CRM system was the cause of the improvement. Therefore, businesses need to use multiple methods to measure the financial impact of CRM and be cautious when drawing conclusions based on a single metric or analysis.

In summary, measuring the financial impact of CRM requires a combination of qualitative and quantitative methods. Businesses need to identify their goals and objectives, track relevant KPIs, and have a long-term perspective when evaluating the impact of CRM. While there may be challenges in determining causality, using multiple methods can provide valuable insights into the effectiveness of a CRM strategy.

Practical examples of how to use financial data to evaluate CRM performance

CRM is an essential tool for businesses that want to improve their customer engagement and increase revenue. However, implementing a CRM system is only the first step in achieving these goals. To measure the effectiveness of a CRM system, businesses need to analyze financial data to evaluate its performance. In this section, we will discuss practical examples of how to use financial data to evaluate CRM performance.

Revenue Growth: One of the primary benefits of implementing a CRM system is increased revenue. Businesses can measure the revenue growth rate before and after implementing a CRM system to evaluate its impact. For example, if a business experienced a revenue growth rate of 5% before implementing a CRM system, and after the implementation, it increased to 10%, it is an indication that the CRM system has been effective in improving revenue.

Customer Retention Rate: A CRM system is designed to improve customer engagement and customer satisfaction, which can lead to increased customer loyalty and retention. Measuring customer retention rates before and after implementing a CRM system can help determine its effectiveness. For example, if a business had a customer retention rate of 70% before implementing a CRM system, and after the implementation, it increased to 85%, it shows that the CRM system has improved customer satisfaction and loyalty.

Customer Acquisition Costs (CAC): CRM systems can also help reduce the cost of acquiring new customers. By analyzing financial data, businesses can calculate the CAC before and after implementing a CRM system. For example, if the CAC was $50 before implementing a CRM system and decreased to $30 after the implementation, it indicates that the CRM system has been effective in reducing the cost of acquiring new customers.

Customer Lifetime Value (CLV): A CRM system can help increase customer lifetime value by improving customer engagement and loyalty. By analyzing financial data, businesses can calculate the CLV before and after implementing a CRM system. For example, if the CLV was $500 before implementing a CRM system and increased to $700 after the implementation, it indicates that the CRM system has been effective in improving customer loyalty and engagement.

Cost Savings: A CRM system can also help reduce costs associated with customer service and support. By analyzing financial data, businesses can calculate the cost savings before and after implementing a CRM system. For example, if the cost of customer service and support was $100,000 before implementing a CRM system and decreased to $80,000 after the implementation, it indicates that the CRM system has been effective in reducing costs associated with customer service and support.

Sales Cycle Time: A CRM system can also help reduce the time it takes to close a sale, resulting in increased revenue. By analyzing financial data, businesses can calculate the sales cycle time before and after implementing a CRM system. For example, if the sales cycle time was 30 days before implementing a CRM system and decreased to 20 days after the implementation, it indicates that the CRM system has been effective in reducing the sales cycle time and increasing revenue.

In conclusion, measuring the financial impact of CRM is crucial to evaluate its effectiveness in achieving business objectives. The above practical examples show how financial data can be analyzed to evaluate the performance of a CRM system. It is important to note that the financial impact of a CRM system may vary depending on the industry, business model, and implementation strategy. Therefore, businesses should conduct a comprehensive analysis to measure the financial impact of their CRM system accurately.

Case studies of companies that have successfully measured the financial impact of CRM

In this section, we will explore some case studies of companies that have successfully measured the financial impact of customer relationship management (CRM). The companies we will discuss have implemented different CRM strategies and used various metrics to evaluate the effectiveness of their CRM initiatives. By examining these case studies, we can gain a better understanding of how companies can use financial data to measure the ROI of their CRM investments.

Case Study 1: Marriott International

Marriott International is a global hospitality company that operates more than 7,000 properties across 131 countries. In 2014, Marriott implemented a new CRM system that allowed them to track customer interactions and preferences across all of their properties. By doing so, Marriott was able to provide more personalized experiences for their guests and improve customer loyalty.

To measure the financial impact of their CRM system, Marriott analyzed data from their loyalty program, Marriott Bonvoy. They found that customers who were members of the program generated 50% more revenue than non-members. Additionally, members who were enrolled in the highest tier of the program spent an average of $6,000 per year at Marriott properties, compared to $1,800 for non-members.

Marriott also found that members who had positive experiences with the company's CRM system were more likely to recommend Marriott to their friends and family. This led to an increase in referrals and new business for Marriott. Overall, Marriott's CRM system has helped the company increase revenue and customer loyalty while also improving the customer experience.

Case Study 2: Cisco Systems

Cisco Systems is a multinational technology company that provides networking and communications solutions. In 2012, Cisco implemented a new CRM system that allowed them to track customer interactions across multiple channels, including email, phone, and social media. The system also provided real-time analytics that allowed Cisco to respond to customer inquiries more quickly.

To measure the financial impact of their CRM system, Cisco analyzed data from their sales team. They found that sales representatives who used the CRM system were able to close deals 30% faster than those who did not use the system. Additionally, the system allowed sales representatives to identify cross-selling opportunities, leading to an increase in revenue per customer.

Cisco also found that their CRM system helped them improve customer satisfaction. By responding to customer inquiries more quickly and providing more personalized service, Cisco was able to increase customer loyalty and reduce customer churn. Overall, Cisco's CRM system has helped the company increase revenue and customer satisfaction while also improving the efficiency of their sales team.

Case Study 3: Royal Bank of Canada

Royal Bank of Canada (RBC) is one of the largest banks in Canada, with more than 16 million clients worldwide. In 2015, RBC implemented a new CRM system that allowed them to provide more personalized service to their customers. The system provided real-time data on customer interactions and preferences, allowing RBC to offer customized products and services.

To measure the financial impact of their CRM system, RBC analyzed data from their retail banking division. They found that customers who had positive experiences with the company's CRM system were more likely to open new accounts and use additional services. Additionally, the system allowed RBC to identify customers who were at risk of leaving the bank and provide them with targeted retention offers.

RBC also found that their CRM system helped them reduce customer complaints and improve customer satisfaction. By providing more personalized service and responding to customer inquiries more quickly, RBC was able to increase customer loyalty and reduce customer churn. Overall, RBC's CRM system has helped the company increase revenue and customer satisfaction while also improving the efficiency of their customer service operations.

Conclusion:

These case studies demonstrate how companies can use financial data to measure the ROI of their CRM initiatives. By tracking customer interactions and preferences and analyzing data from loyalty programs and sales teams, companies can identify areas where they can improve customer engagement and increase revenue.

In conclusion, measuring the financial impact of CRM is critical for businesses that want to maximize the return on their investment in customer relationship management. Companies must develop a strategy for tracking and analyzing financial data, including sales figures, customer retention rates, and marketing costs, in order to gain insight into the effectiveness of their CRM initiatives. By doing so, they can identify opportunities to optimize their customer engagement strategies, improve customer satisfaction, and increase revenue.

It is important to note that measuring the financial impact of CRM is an ongoing process. Companies must continually monitor their financial data and adjust their CRM strategies as necessary to ensure that they are achieving their desired results. They must also keep up with changes in customer behavior, market trends, and technological advancements to stay competitive in today's rapidly changing business environment.

Overall, companies that prioritize measuring the financial impact of CRM are more likely to achieve long-term success in customer engagement and retention. By using financial data to track the ROI of their CRM initiatives and continuously improving their strategies, they can build stronger relationships with their customers, boost customer loyalty, and increase revenue.

CHAPTER 18: THE ROLE OF CRM IN CUSTOMER RETENTION AND LOYALTY

Customer retention and loyalty are critical components of a successful business strategy. In today's competitive business environment, it is more important than ever for companies to establish strong relationships with their customers to keep them coming back. This is where customer relationship management (CRM) comes in.

CRM is a strategy that focuses on building and maintaining long-term relationships with customers. It involves gathering and analyzing data about customer interactions and preferences, and using that information to improve customer satisfaction and retention. By understanding the needs and preferences of their customers, companies can tailor their products and services to better meet their customers' needs and build stronger relationships.

In this chapter, we will explore the role of CRM in customer retention and loyalty. We will begin by discussing the importance of customer retention and loyalty and how CRM can help achieve these goals. We will then delve into the key components of a successful CRM strategy and the different types of CRM systems available. We will also examine the challenges that companies may face when implementing a CRM strategy and provide strategies for overcoming these challenges.

Finally, we will discuss the future of CRM and the evolving role of technology in shaping the way companies interact with their customers. We will examine emerging trends such as social CRM and mobile CRM and discuss how these trends are impacting the way companies approach customer retention and loyalty.

By the end of this chapter, students will have a thorough understanding of the importance of customer retention and loyalty, the role of CRM in achieving these goals, and the key components of a successful CRM strategy. They will also be equipped with the knowledge and skills necessary to overcome the challenges of implementing a CRM strategy and stay ahead of emerging trends in the field.

The importance of customer retention and loyalty in financial performance

The success of any business largely depends on its ability to retain customers and build customer loyalty. This is because customer retention and loyalty have a direct impact on a company's financial performance. According to a study by Bain & Company, increasing customer retention by just 5% can lead to an increase in profits by as much as 95%. Customer retention and loyalty are also essential in reducing the costs associated with acquiring new customers.

In today's competitive business environment, where customers have numerous options to choose from, building customer loyalty and retention is critical for success. Companies that fail to prioritize customer retention and loyalty risk losing customers to their competitors, which can negatively impact their bottom line.

This chapter will explore the importance of customer retention and loyalty in financial performance and how customer relationship management (CRM) can play a significant role in achieving these goals.

The Importance of Customer Retention and Loyalty in Financial Performance:

Customer retention and loyalty are critical factors in a company's financial performance. Loyal customers are more likely to make repeat purchases and recommend a company to their friends and family, which can significantly increase a company's revenue. Additionally, loyal customers are less sensitive to price changes, making them more profitable in the long run.

Customer retention and loyalty also reduce the costs associated with acquiring new customers. Acquiring new customers can be costly, as it requires investment in marketing and advertising. In contrast, retaining existing customers can be more cost-effective and efficient, as companies can leverage their existing relationships to upsell and cross-sell their products and services.

Customer retention and loyalty also contribute to a company's brand reputation. Customers who are satisfied with a company's products or services are more likely to leave positive reviews and feedback, which can attract new customers and enhance a company's reputation.

The Role of CRM in Achieving Customer Retention and Loyalty:

CRM can play a significant role in achieving customer retention and loyalty. CRM is a strategy that companies use to manage their interactions with customers and improve their overall customer experience. CRM systems help companies to gather, analyze, and leverage customer data to build stronger relationships with their customers.

CRM can help companies to personalize their interactions with customers, which is critical in building customer loyalty. By understanding a customer's preferences and behavior, companies can tailor their marketing and sales efforts to meet their individual needs. This can help to build stronger relationships with customers, which can lead to increased customer loyalty and retention.

CRM can also help companies to identify and respond to customer issues in real-time. By tracking customer interactions and feedback, companies can quickly address any problems or concerns, which can improve the overall customer experience and prevent customer churn.

In addition, CRM can help companies to develop targeted marketing campaigns that are more likely to resonate with their customers. By leveraging customer data, companies can create personalized marketing messages that are more relevant to their target audience, which can lead to increased customer engagement and loyalty.

Conclusion:

In today's competitive business environment, customer retention and loyalty are critical factors in a company's financial performance. Companies that prioritize customer retention and loyalty are more likely to succeed and thrive in the long run. CRM can play a significant role in achieving these goals by helping companies to personalize their interactions with customers, respond to customer issues in real-time, and develop targeted marketing campaigns. By leveraging CRM strategies and tools, companies can build stronger relationships with their customers, which can lead to increased customer loyalty and retention.

The role of CRM in customer retention and loyalty

Customer retention and loyalty are critical components of a company's financial success. Studies have shown that acquiring a new customer is up to five times more expensive than retaining an existing one. Therefore, companies must prioritize their efforts towards retaining their customers and ensuring their loyalty.

Customer Relationship Management (CRM) is a strategy that companies use to manage and analyze customer interactions and data throughout the customer lifecycle, with the goal of improving customer retention and loyalty. By leveraging CRM technology, companies can gain insights into customer behavior, preferences, and needs, enabling them to personalize their marketing and customer service efforts and provide a better customer experience.

In this section, we will explore the importance of customer retention and loyalty in financial performance, the role of CRM in achieving these objectives, and the benefits and challenges associated with implementing a CRM strategy.

Importance of customer retention and loyalty in financial performance:

Customer retention and loyalty are vital to a company's financial performance. Research has shown that increasing customer retention rates by 5% can increase profits by 25% to 95%. Loyal customers are more likely to make repeat purchases, refer new customers, and provide positive reviews and feedback, which can ultimately lead to increased revenue and profits.

Furthermore, loyal customers are less likely to switch to a competitor, reducing the company's customer acquisition costs. This allows the company to allocate resources towards improving the customer experience and increasing customer satisfaction, rather than constantly seeking out new customers.

On the other hand, losing customers can have a significant impact on a company's financial performance. Customers who leave a company due to poor service or experience are more likely to share their negative experiences with others, damaging the company's reputation and brand image.

Role of CRM in achieving customer retention and loyalty:

CRM plays a crucial role in achieving customer retention and loyalty. By leveraging CRM technology, companies can gain a deeper understanding of their customers, including their preferences, behavior, and needs. This enables them to personalize their marketing and customer service efforts, which can improve the overall customer experience and increase customer satisfaction.

CRM technology can also help companies to identify at-risk customers and proactively address their concerns before they decide to leave. By using predictive analytics, companies can analyze customer data and predict customer behavior, allowing them to take corrective actions before it's too late.

Moreover, CRM technology can help companies to track customer interactions and measure the success of their customer engagement efforts. By analyzing this data, companies can identify areas where they need to improve and adjust their strategy accordingly.

Benefits and challenges of implementing a CRM strategy:

Implementing a CRM strategy can provide numerous benefits to a company, such as improving customer retention and loyalty, increasing customer satisfaction, and enhancing the customer experience. However, implementing a CRM strategy also comes with its own set of challenges.

One of the main challenges associated with implementing a CRM strategy is the cost. CRM technology can be expensive to implement and maintain, especially for small businesses. Additionally, companies must invest in training their employees on how to use the CRM system effectively.

Another challenge is data quality. To derive meaningful insights from CRM data, companies must ensure that the data is accurate, complete, and up-to-date. This requires ongoing data cleansing and validation efforts.

Furthermore, companies must ensure that their CRM strategy aligns with their overall business strategy and objectives. This requires careful planning and coordination between different departments and stakeholders.

Conclusion:

In conclusion, customer retention and loyalty are essential components of a company's financial success. By leveraging CRM technology, companies can gain insights into customer behavior, preferences, and needs, enabling them to personalize their marketing and customer service efforts and provide a better customer experience. However, implementing a CRM strategy comes with its own set of challenges, such as cost, data quality, and alignment with overall business strategy.

Therefore, companies must carefully weigh the benefits and challenges associated with implementing a CRM system.

One important consideration is the alignment of CRM strategy with overall business strategy. A company's CRM strategy should be integrated with its marketing, sales, and service strategies, as well as its overall business objectives. This ensures that the CRM system is being used to support the company's overall goals and objectives, rather than being viewed as a separate initiative.

Another important consideration is data quality. Data is the lifeblood of CRM, and without accurate and reliable data, the system cannot provide the desired benefits. Therefore, companies must invest in data quality initiatives to ensure that the data being captured is accurate and complete. This requires a combination of technology, processes, and people to ensure that the data is accurate, relevant, and timely.

Cost is also a consideration when implementing a CRM strategy. While the potential benefits of CRM can be significant, the costs associated with implementing and maintaining a CRM system can be substantial. Therefore, companies must carefully evaluate the costs and benefits of a CRM system, taking into account factors such as the size of the company, the complexity of its operations, and the potential ROI of the system.

In addition to these considerations, companies must also address challenges related to user adoption and change management. User adoption is critical to the success of a CRM system, as the system is only as effective as the people using it. Therefore, companies must provide adequate training and support to ensure that users are comfortable and confident using the system. Change management is also important, as implementing a CRM system can require significant changes to existing business processes and procedures. Therefore, companies must have a plan in place to manage these changes and ensure that they are implemented smoothly.

In summary, the role of CRM in customer retention and loyalty is significant, as it enables companies to gain valuable insights into customer behavior and preferences. However, implementing a CRM strategy comes with its own set of challenges, and companies must carefully evaluate the costs and benefits of a CRM system before making a decision. By taking a strategic approach and addressing key challenges related to data quality, cost, user adoption, and change management, companies can successfully implement a CRM system and realize the benefits of improved customer retention and loyalty.

Practical examples of how CRM can be used to improve customer retention and loyalty

In today's competitive business environment, companies are striving to improve customer retention and loyalty. One tool that has proven to be effective in achieving this goal is customer relationship management (CRM). In this section, we will explore several practical examples of how CRM can be used to improve customer retention and loyalty.

Personalized Communication
One of the key benefits of using CRM is that it allows companies to personalize their communication with customers. By collecting and analyzing customer data, companies can gain insights into customer behavior, preferences, and needs. With this information, they can create targeted marketing campaigns and personalized communication that resonate with customers.

For example, a clothing retailer can use CRM to identify which customers prefer a particular style or brand of clothing. With this information, the retailer can create targeted marketing campaigns that feature products that are relevant to those customers' preferences. The retailer can also send personalized emails to customers, offering them discounts on products that they are likely to be interested in.

Enhanced Customer Service
CRM can also be used to enhance customer service, which is critical to retaining customers. By collecting and analyzing data on customer interactions with the company, companies can identify areas where they can improve the customer experience. This can include providing faster response times, offering more personalized service, and addressing customer complaints more effectively.

For example, a bank can use CRM to track customer interactions with its call center. With this information, the bank can identify areas where customers are experiencing long wait times or are not receiving satisfactory responses to their inquiries. The bank can then take steps to improve these areas, such as hiring additional call center staff or improving training for call center agents.

Loyalty Programs
Another way that companies can use CRM to improve customer retention and loyalty is through loyalty programs. By offering rewards and incentives to customers who make repeat purchases, companies can encourage customers to continue doing business with them.

For example, a coffee chain can use CRM to track customers' purchases and offer them rewards for repeat business. The chain can offer a free coffee after a certain number of purchases or offer discounts to customers who visit the chain frequently. These rewards can help to build loyalty and encourage customers to continue doing business with the coffee chain.

Cross-selling and Upselling

CRM can also be used to identify opportunities for cross-selling and upselling. By analyzing customer data, companies can identify which products or services are most likely to appeal to individual customers. This information can be used to create targeted marketing campaigns and to train sales staff to identify opportunities for cross-selling and upselling.

For example, a software company can use CRM to identify customers who are using a particular product and offer them an upgrade to a more advanced version of the software. By targeting customers who are likely to be interested in the upgrade, the company can increase revenue and improve customer retention.

Customer Feedback

Finally, CRM can be used to collect and analyze customer feedback. By asking customers for feedback on their experience with the company, companies can identify areas where they need to improve the customer experience. This information can be used to make changes to products, services, or policies that can help to retain customers.

For example, an airline can use CRM to collect feedback from customers who have had a negative experience with the airline. The airline can then use this feedback to identify areas where it needs to improve, such as the quality of its in-flight entertainment or the responsiveness of its customer service staff.

Conclusion

In conclusion, CRM is a powerful tool for improving customer retention and loyalty. By collecting and analyzing customer data, companies can gain insights into customer behavior, preferences, and needs. This information can be used to create personalized communication, enhance customer service, offer loyalty programs, identify opportunities for cross-selling and upselling, and ultimately build stronger relationships with their customers.

Let's take a look at a few practical examples of how CRM can be used to improve customer retention and loyalty.

One example is the use of loyalty programs. CRM technology allows companies to track customer behavior, purchase history, and preferences. With this information, companies can create personalized rewards and incentives for customers who are loyal and frequent shoppers. For instance, a company can offer special discounts or free products to customers who have made a certain number of purchases or have been with the company for a certain period of time. This type of reward system encourages customers to continue shopping with the company, leading to increased customer loyalty and retention.

Another example is personalized communication. CRM technology allows companies to track customer preferences, such as their preferred method of communication, the type of content they are interested in, and their communication frequency. With this information, companies can tailor their communication to meet the specific needs and interests of each customer. For instance, a company can send personalized emails or messages to customers about new products or promotions that match their interests. This type of personalized communication makes customers feel valued and understood, leading to increased customer satisfaction and loyalty.

In addition to loyalty programs and personalized communication, CRM technology can also be used to identify opportunities for cross-selling and upselling. By analyzing customer data, companies can identify which products or services are most commonly purchased together and which products or services customers may be interested in purchasing based on their purchase history. This information can be used to create targeted cross-selling and upselling campaigns that are tailored to each customer. For instance, a company can offer a discount on a complementary product or service to a customer who has recently purchased a related item. This type of targeted marketing not only increases sales but also builds stronger customer relationships.

Overall, CRM is a powerful tool for improving customer retention and loyalty. By collecting and analyzing customer data, companies can gain valuable insights into customer behavior, preferences, and needs. This information can be used to create personalized communication, loyalty programs, and targeted cross-selling and upselling campaigns, all of which can lead to increased customer satisfaction, loyalty, and retention. However, companies must be aware of the potential challenges and pitfalls associated with implementing a CRM strategy, such as cost, data quality, and alignment with overall business strategy. With careful planning and implementation, CRM can be a valuable asset for any company seeking to improve customer retention and loyalty.

To reinforce these concepts, here are a few exercises to help students understand the practical applications of CRM in improving customer retention and loyalty:

Research and analyze a company that has successfully implemented a CRM strategy to improve customer retention and loyalty. What specific tactics and techniques did the company use? How did they measure success? What were the benefits and challenges of the strategy?

Create a mock loyalty program for a company in a specific industry, such as retail or hospitality. What rewards and incentives would be most appealing to customers in that industry? How would you track and measure the success of the program?

Analyze a company's customer communication strategy. How personalized and targeted is their communication? What could they do to improve their communication and increase customer loyalty?

By completing these exercises, students will gain a better understanding of how CRM can be used to improve customer retention and loyalty, as well as the potential challenges and opportunities associated with implementing a CRM strategy.

Case studies of companies that have improved customer retention and loyalty through CRM implementation

Sephora

Sephora is a beauty retailer that has implemented a CRM strategy to personalize the customer experience and improve customer loyalty. They use customer data to create a personalized profile for each customer, which includes information such as purchase history, skin type, and beauty preferences. Sephora uses this data to provide targeted product recommendations and exclusive promotions to customers, which has led to an increase in customer loyalty and retention.

American Express

American Express is a financial services company that has implemented a CRM strategy to improve customer retention and loyalty. They use customer data to personalize communication and offer tailored rewards and benefits to their customers. For example, they offer exclusive promotions to customers based on their spending habits and interests. This has led to an increase in customer loyalty and retention, as customers feel valued and appreciated.

Each of these companies has successfully implemented a CRM strategy to improve customer retention and loyalty. By collecting and analyzing customer data, they have been able to personalize communication, offer tailored promotions and rewards, and create a better customer experience. These examples demonstrate how

CRM implementation can be a powerful tool for improving customer retention and loyalty in a variety of industries.

To reinforce this topic, here are some exercises:

Research a company in your industry that has implemented a CRM strategy. What benefits have they seen in terms of customer retention and loyalty? How did they overcome any challenges associated with implementing a CRM strategy?

Choose a company that you are a customer of and evaluate their CRM strategy. Do they offer personalized communication and tailored promotions? How does their CRM strategy impact your loyalty to the brand?

Role play a scenario where you are a business owner looking to implement a CRM strategy to improve customer retention and loyalty. Identify potential challenges and solutions to implementing a successful CRM strategy.

CHAPTER 19: WHAT IS CRM AND ITS FUNCTIONS

Customer relationship management (CRM) is an essential component of modern business strategy. CRM systems help companies to manage their interactions with customers, from lead generation and sales, to customer service and retention. This chapter will introduce the concept of CRM and its functions, discussing the benefits of implementing a CRM system, and exploring some of the challenges associated with CRM adoption.

What is CRM?

CRM refers to the strategies, processes, and technologies that companies use to manage their interactions with customers. The goal of CRM is to improve customer satisfaction, enhance customer retention, and ultimately increase revenue. CRM systems allow companies to track customer interactions across multiple channels, including phone, email, social media, and in-person interactions. This data can be used to personalize customer experiences, improve communication with customers, and identify opportunities for growth.

Functions of CRM

CRM systems perform a variety of functions to support customer relationship management, including:

Lead Management

CRM systems enable companies to manage their leads more effectively by providing a centralized database that contains information about potential customers. This information can be used to track the progress of leads through the sales funnel, and to prioritize sales efforts based on the likelihood of conversion.

Sales Management

CRM systems provide sales teams with the tools they need to manage their sales pipelines more effectively. This includes features such as sales forecasting, opportunity management, and contact management.

Customer Service

CRM systems allow companies to manage customer service interactions more effectively by providing a centralized database of customer information. This information can be used to personalize customer service experiences, track customer issues and complaints, and identify opportunities for improvement.

Marketing Automation

CRM systems enable companies to automate many of their marketing processes, including lead generation, email marketing, and social media marketing. This can help companies to target the right customers with the right message at the right time, and to measure the effectiveness of their marketing campaigns more accurately.

Benefits of CRM

The benefits of implementing a CRM system are numerous, and include:

Improved Customer Satisfaction

CRM systems enable companies to provide a more personalized and responsive customer experience, which can lead to higher levels of customer satisfaction.

Enhanced Customer Retention

CRM systems allow companies to identify opportunities for growth and to target specific customers with relevant offers and promotions. This can lead to higher levels of customer retention.

Increased Revenue

By improving customer satisfaction and retention, CRM systems can help companies to increase revenue and profitability.

Better Collaboration

CRM systems provide a centralized platform for customer data, which can help teams to collaborate more effectively and to share information more easily.

Challenges of CRM

While there are many benefits to implementing a CRM system, there are also some challenges associated with CRM adoption, including:

Cost
CRM systems can be expensive to implement, particularly for small and medium-sized businesses.

Data Quality
The quality of customer data can be a significant challenge for companies implementing a CRM system. Data must be accurate, complete, and up-to-date to be useful.

Integration
Integrating CRM systems with other business systems can be challenging, particularly for companies with legacy systems or complex IT environments.

Conclusion

In conclusion, CRM systems are a powerful tool for managing customer interactions and improving customer satisfaction, retention, and revenue. However, implementing a CRM system requires careful planning, and companies must be prepared to address the challenges associated with CRM adoption. The benefits of implementing a CRM system are numerous, and companies that can successfully implement a CRM strategy can gain a competitive advantage in their respective industries.

Understanding CRM

Customer relationship management (CRM) is an essential business strategy that helps organizations build strong relationships with their customers. It involves collecting, analyzing, and leveraging customer data to improve customer satisfaction, retention, and loyalty. With the help of CRM, companies can personalize their communication, tailor their offerings, and provide better customer service.

Understanding CRM

CRM is a comprehensive approach to managing customer relationships that includes people, processes, and technology. The key goal of CRM is to create and maintain long-term relationships with customers, which leads to increased customer satisfaction and loyalty, as well as higher revenue and profitability.

People: The people aspect of CRM refers to the employees who interact with customers. These employees need to have the skills, knowledge, and tools to provide excellent customer service and build lasting relationships.

Processes: The process aspect of CRM involves creating a set of standardized procedures for interacting with customers. These processes should be designed to ensure that every customer receives the same level of service and that their needs are met.

Technology: The technology aspect of CRM refers to the tools and systems used to manage customer relationships. This can include customer databases, customer relationship management software, and customer analytics tools.

CRM Functions

The main functions of CRM include:

Sales automation: This function involves automating the sales process, from lead generation to order management. CRM software can help sales teams manage their leads, track sales activities, and analyze sales data.

Marketing automation: This function involves automating marketing activities such as email campaigns, social media advertising, and targeted promotions. CRM software can help marketers segment their customers, track their preferences, and personalize their messaging.

Customer service and support: This function involves providing customers with timely and effective support. CRM software can help customer service teams manage customer inquiries, complaints, and feedback, as well as track customer satisfaction metrics.

Analytics and reporting: This function involves analyzing customer data to gain insights into customer behavior, preferences, and needs. CRM software can help organizations measure customer satisfaction, track customer lifetime value, and identify opportunities for cross-selling and upselling.

Case Studies

Zappos: Zappos is an online shoe and clothing retailer known for its exceptional customer service. The company uses CRM software to provide personalized recommendations to customers based on their browsing and purchase history. Zappos also has a 24/7 call center staffed with customer service representatives who are empowered to make decisions and resolve issues on the spot.

Marriott International: Marriott International is a global hotel chain that uses CRM to personalize the guest experience. The company's CRM system stores guest preferences and provides personalized recommendations for activities and dining options. Marriott also uses CRM to track guest satisfaction metrics and identify areas for improvement.

American Express: American Express uses CRM to provide personalized recommendations and offers to its cardholders. The company's CRM system tracks spending patterns and preferences to provide tailored rewards and benefits. American Express also uses CRM to provide proactive fraud detection and resolution services to its customers.

Conclusion

CRM is a critical business strategy for building strong customer relationships and improving customer satisfaction, retention, and loyalty. By collecting and analyzing customer data, organizations can personalize their communication, tailor their offerings, and provide better customer service. With the help of CRM software, companies can automate sales and marketing processes, improve customer support, and gain insights into customer behavior and preferences. The case studies of Zappos, Marriott International, and American Express demonstrate the power of CRM in creating exceptional customer experiences and driving business success.

Definition of CRM and its evolution

Customer Relationship Management (CRM) refers to the combination of strategies, technologies, and practices that businesses use to manage and analyze customer interactions and data throughout the customer lifecycle. The primary goal of CRM is to improve business relationships with customers, assist in customer retention and drive sales growth. It involves collecting and analyzing customer data, automating business processes, and streamlining customer communication to create personalized and engaging experiences for customers.

The evolution of CRM can be traced back to the 1980s when customer databases were first used to store customer information. At that time, the primary goal was to provide sales teams with easy access to customer data to aid in the sales process. With the advancement of technology, CRM systems were developed to automate and streamline the entire customer lifecycle, from lead generation to customer service.

The early CRM systems were designed primarily for sales teams to manage leads and track sales activities. However, as CRM evolved, it became an essential tool for other departments such as marketing, customer service, and support. Today, CRM is used by businesses of all sizes and industries to manage customer interactions and data and provide a holistic view of their customers.

With the rise of the internet, mobile devices, and social media, CRM has undergone a significant transformation. Customers now have access to more information and channels than ever before, making it more challenging for businesses to manage customer interactions effectively. As a result, CRM has evolved to incorporate technologies such as social media monitoring, mobile applications, and online chatbots to provide seamless customer experiences across all channels.

The advent of Artificial Intelligence (AI) and Machine Learning (ML) has further transformed the CRM landscape. AI and ML algorithms can analyze vast amounts of customer data to provide businesses with actionable insights and help predict customer behavior. This enables businesses to offer personalized experiences to customers and improve customer retention and loyalty.

In summary, CRM has come a long way from being a simple customer database to a sophisticated system that uses technology, analytics, and data to manage customer interactions and improve customer experiences. The evolution of CRM has been driven by the need to provide businesses with the tools to manage and analyze customer data effectively and provide personalized experiences to customers.

Benefits of CRM for businesses

Customer Relationship Management (CRM) is a business strategy that focuses on creating, developing, and maintaining profitable relationships with customers. The main aim of CRM is to enhance customer satisfaction, retention, and loyalty by leveraging data and technology to provide personalized and relevant interactions with customers. CRM has become a critical business function for companies across different industries, and its benefits have been widely recognized. This section will discuss the benefits of CRM for businesses.

Improved Customer Satisfaction and Retention

One of the primary benefits of CRM is that it helps businesses improve customer satisfaction and retention. By collecting and analyzing customer data, businesses can gain insights into customer preferences, behaviors, and needs. This information can be used to provide personalized and relevant interactions with customers, which can enhance their satisfaction and loyalty. Additionally, CRM enables businesses to respond to customer inquiries, complaints, and feedback promptly, which can increase customer satisfaction and reduce churn.

Increased Sales and Revenue

CRM can also help businesses increase sales and revenue. By providing personalized and relevant interactions with customers, businesses can upsell and cross-sell products and services. Additionally, CRM can help businesses identify new sales opportunities and target high-value customers more effectively. By optimizing the sales process and leveraging customer data, businesses can improve their conversion rates and drive revenue growth.

Enhanced Marketing Effectiveness

CRM can also enhance the effectiveness of marketing activities. By analyzing customer data, businesses can identify the most profitable customer segments, understand their needs and preferences, and develop targeted marketing campaigns that resonate with them. Additionally, CRM can help businesses track the effectiveness of marketing campaigns, measure customer engagement and response rates, and adjust their marketing strategies accordingly.

Improved Operational Efficiency

CRM can also help businesses improve operational efficiency. By automating manual processes, such as data entry and customer communication, businesses can reduce operational costs and improve productivity. Additionally, CRM can help businesses streamline their workflows, collaborate more effectively across departments, and improve communication with customers.

Better Decision Making

Finally, CRM can help businesses make better decisions. By providing real-time access to customer data, businesses can make informed decisions about product development, marketing strategies, and customer service initiatives. Additionally, CRM can help businesses identify trends and patterns in customer behavior, which can inform strategic planning and decision-making.

Conclusion

CRM is a critical business function that can provide significant benefits for businesses across different industries. By improving customer satisfaction and retention, increasing sales and revenue, enhancing marketing effectiveness, improving operational efficiency, and enabling better decision-making, businesses can gain a competitive advantage and drive growth. To maximize the benefits of CRM, businesses should invest in the right technology, data management, and human resources, and develop a comprehensive strategy that aligns with their business goals and customer needs.

Types of CRM systems (Operational, Analytical, Collaborative)

Customer Relationship Management (CRM) has become an essential tool for businesses to manage customer interactions, improve customer satisfaction, and increase sales. CRM systems come in different types that cater to specific business needs. This section will explore the three main types of CRM systems: operational, analytical, and collaborative.

Operational CRM

Operational CRM systems are designed to automate and manage customer-facing processes such as sales, marketing, and customer service. The primary objective of operational CRM is to improve efficiency and productivity by automating routine tasks, streamlining workflows, and enhancing communication.

Salesforce, for example, is a popular operational CRM system that offers features such as lead management, opportunity tracking, and pipeline forecasting. By automating the sales process, sales reps can focus on building relationships with customers and closing deals. Additionally, operational CRM systems can track customer interactions across different channels, enabling businesses to deliver a consistent and personalized experience.

Marketing automation is another key feature of operational CRM systems. Businesses can use marketing automation tools to create and execute targeted marketing campaigns, track customer behavior, and measure campaign effectiveness. By automating marketing tasks, businesses can save time and resources while delivering a more personalized experience to customers.

Customer service is another area where operational CRM systems can make a significant impact. By providing a centralized database of customer information, customer service reps can access relevant information quickly and provide more efficient and effective support. Additionally, operational CRM systems can automate support processes such as ticket routing, escalation, and resolution, improving response times and customer satisfaction.

Analytical CRM

Analytical CRM systems are designed to analyze customer data and provide insights into customer behavior, preferences, and trends. The primary objective of analytical CRM is to improve decision-making by providing actionable insights based on data analysis.

Businesses can use analytical CRM systems to analyze customer data such as transaction history, website behavior, and social media activity to identify patterns and trends. By gaining insights into customer behavior, businesses can make informed decisions regarding product development, marketing campaigns, and customer service.

Data mining and predictive analytics are key features of analytical CRM systems. By analyzing customer data, businesses can identify customer segments with the highest revenue potential, predict customer behavior, and anticipate future trends.

Collaborative CRM

Collaborative CRM systems are designed to facilitate communication and collaboration between different departments and stakeholders within a business. The primary objective of collaborative CRM is to improve coordination and teamwork, leading to better customer experiences.

Collaborative CRM systems can include features such as shared customer databases, collaboration tools, and project management tools. By providing a centralized platform for collaboration, businesses can ensure that all stakeholders are on the same page and working towards common goals.

For example, a business may use a collaborative CRM system to manage a complex customer project involving multiple departments such as sales, marketing, and customer service. By providing a centralized platform for collaboration, all stakeholders can access relevant information, share updates, and coordinate tasks, leading to a more efficient and effective project.

Conclusion

CRM systems come in different types that cater to specific business needs. Operational CRM systems are designed to automate and manage customer-facing processes such as sales, marketing, and customer service. Analytical CRM systems are designed to analyze customer data and provide insights into customer behavior, preferences, and trends. Collaborative CRM systems are designed to facilitate communication and collaboration between different departments and stakeholders within a business. By choosing the right type of CRM system for their business, businesses can improve customer experiences, increase productivity, and drive growth.

CRM Functions: An In-Depth Analysis of RhinoLeg CRM

In today's fast-paced business environment, customer relationship management (CRM) has become an essential component of any successful business strategy. As businesses grow, the need for effective customer management and communication increases, and this is where RhinoLeg CRM comes into play. RhinoLeg CRM is an all-in-one customer relationship management software designed to help businesses manage their sales, marketing, customer service, and analytics needs. In this section, we will provide an in-depth analysis of RhinoLeg CRM and its functions.

What is RhinoLeg CRM?

RhinoLeg CRM is an AI-powered software that allows businesses to manage their customer interactions, marketing campaigns, and sales activities. The software integrates all the data from different channels, including email, phone, and social media, to provide a comprehensive overview of the customer's journey. The software is designed to streamline the entire customer relationship process by automating repetitive tasks, providing insights into customer behavior and preferences, and allowing businesses to provide personalized customer experiences.

Sales Management

RhinoLeg CRM's sales management functionality allows businesses to manage their entire sales process from lead generation to closing deals. The software allows businesses to store and manage customer contact information, track sales opportunities, and create sales pipelines. The sales management feature also includes lead routing, customer segmentation, and knowledge management.

Marketing Automation

RhinoLeg CRM's marketing automation functionality provides businesses with the ability to create, manage, and track marketing campaigns across multiple channels. The software allows businesses to create targeted campaigns based on customer behavior and preferences. The marketing automation feature also includes lead nurturing, multi-channel communication, social media engagement, and marketing attribution.

Customer Service Automation

RhinoLeg CRM's customer service automation functionality allows businesses to manage their customer service requests and provide efficient and personalized customer support. The software includes customer satisfaction surveys, ticket management, and customer journey tracking.

Analytics and Reporting

RhinoLeg CRM's analytics and reporting functionality provides businesses with the ability to gain insights into customer behavior and preferences. The software includes forecasting and trend analysis to optimize sales and marketing strategies. The analytics and reporting feature also includes data visualization and machine learning-based lead generation.

Mobile App Integration

RhinoLeg CRM's mobile app integration feature allows businesses to manage their customer interactions on-the-go. The mobile app is available for both iOS and Android devices, providing businesses with the flexibility to manage their customer interactions anytime, anywhere.

Other Key Features

RhinoLeg CRM provides several other key features to help businesses manage their customer interactions effectively. These features include document automation, integration with social media advertising platforms, website analytics tools, partner relationship management, social listening, gamification, predictive analytics, sales coaching, business process automation, and artificial intelligence-powered chatbots.

Conclusion

In conclusion, RhinoLeg CRM is an AI-powered, all-in-one customer relationship management software designed to help businesses manage their sales, marketing, customer service, and analytics needs. The software provides several key features to help businesses streamline their customer interactions and provide personalized customer experiences. The mobile app integration, lead routing, customer segmentation, knowledge management, customer satisfaction surveys, forecasting and trend analysis, and machine learning-based lead generation are some of the essential features provided by RhinoLeg CRM. The software helps businesses improve efficiency, optimize their sales process, and provide a personalized and efficient customer experience. With RhinoLeg CRM, businesses can achieve their goals and grow their customer base.

Sales Management: Lead generation, opportunity management, pipeline tracking, forecasting

Sales management is a critical process in any organization that deals with sales. It involves a set of activities that aim to improve sales performance and drive revenue growth. Effective sales management requires a combination of skills, techniques, and tools. In this section, we will discuss some of the critical elements of sales management, including lead generation, opportunity management, pipeline tracking, and forecasting.

Lead Generation

Lead generation is the process of identifying potential customers who may be interested in buying your product or service. It is an essential element of sales management, as it is the first step towards creating a sustainable sales pipeline. There are various methods of generating leads, including:

Contacts: You can generate leads by reaching out to your existing contacts, including customers, partners, and other stakeholders.

Sales: You can generate leads by leveraging your sales team's existing network of contacts and referrals.

Marketing: You can generate leads by using various marketing channels such as email, social media, search engine optimization, and content marketing.

Customer Service: You can generate leads by providing excellent customer service that can turn your customers into advocates.

Analytics: You can use analytics tools to identify potential leads by analyzing customer behavior and demographics.

Mobile Device Access: You can generate leads by leveraging mobile devices such as smartphones and tablets to reach out to potential customers.

Lead generation is critical because it ensures that your sales pipeline is always filled with potential customers. However, it is not enough to generate leads. You also need to manage these leads effectively to maximize your chances of converting them into customers.

Opportunity Management

Opportunity management is the process of managing potential sales opportunities throughout the sales cycle. It involves identifying, qualifying, and prioritizing opportunities based on their potential value and likelihood of conversion. Effective opportunity management requires a combination of skills, techniques, and tools. Some of the critical elements of opportunity management include:

Lead Routing: You need to route leads to the right sales reps based on their skills, experience, and availability.

Customer Segmentation: You need to segment your customers based on various criteria such as demographics, behavior, and preferences.

Knowledge Management: You need to provide your sales reps with the knowledge and information they need to engage with potential customers effectively.

Customer Satisfaction Surveys: You need to gather feedback from your customers to understand their needs, preferences, and pain points.

Forecasting and Trend Analysis: You need to use forecasting and trend analysis tools to predict sales outcomes and adjust your sales strategy accordingly.

Pipeline Tracking

Pipeline tracking is the process of monitoring and managing the sales pipeline to ensure that it is always filled with potential opportunities. Effective pipeline tracking requires a combination of skills, techniques, and tools. Some of the critical elements of pipeline tracking include:

Lead Nurturing: You need to nurture your leads by providing them with relevant and valuable information that can help them make informed purchasing decisions.

Multi-Channel Communication: You need to communicate with your leads through various channels such as email, phone, social media, and chat.

Contract Management: You need to manage your contracts effectively to ensure that your sales process is smooth and efficient.

Payment Processing: You need to process payments quickly and securely to ensure that your customers have a seamless purchasing experience.

Social Media Engagement: You need to engage with your customers on social media platforms to build brand awareness and loyalty.

Customer Journey Tracking: You need to track your customers' journey from lead to purchase to understand their behavior and preferences.

Marketing Attribution: You need to attribute your marketing efforts to sales outcomes to understand the ROI of your marketing campaigns.

Forecasting

Forecasting is the process of predicting sales and revenue for a certain period of time based on historical data, market trends, and other relevant factors. Effective forecasting is crucial for sales management as it enables sales teams to anticipate demand, allocate resources appropriately, and make informed business decisions.

There are several different methods for sales forecasting, including quantitative techniques such as time-series analysis, regression analysis, and econometric modeling, as well as qualitative methods such as expert opinion, surveys, and market research. Sales forecasting can also be done using software tools that utilize machine learning algorithms to analyze data and generate predictions.

In addition to forecasting, another important aspect of sales management is lead nurturing. Lead nurturing involves building relationships with potential customers through personalized communication and relevant content to increase their interest and engagement with a product or service. This can include email campaigns, targeted social media advertising, and other forms of content marketing.

Lead nurturing is a critical component of the sales process, as it helps move potential customers through the sales funnel and ultimately convert them into paying customers. Effective lead nurturing requires a deep understanding of the customer's needs, preferences, and pain points, as well as an ability to deliver personalized content and experiences that address these factors.

Multi-channel communication is another key element of sales management. In today's digital age, customers interact with businesses through a wide range of channels, including email, social media, chat, and phone. Sales teams must be equipped to handle these interactions across all channels in a seamless and coordinated way to provide a positive customer experience.

Contract management and payment processing are also important aspects of sales management. Contract management involves the creation, review, and negotiation of sales contracts, while payment processing involves the handling of payments from customers. Both of these processes require attention to detail and an ability to navigate complex legal and financial requirements.

Social media engagement and marketing attribution are also important considerations for sales management. Social media provides a powerful platform for businesses to engage with customers, build brand awareness, and drive sales. Marketing attribution, on the other hand, involves tracking the effectiveness of different marketing channels and campaigns in driving sales and revenue.

Field sales management is another critical component of sales management, particularly for businesses with a large sales force operating in the field. This involves managing and coordinating sales activities across different geographic locations, as well as tracking performance and providing coaching and support to individual sales representatives.

Voice-enabled commands, virtual meetings and webinars, and inventory management are additional tools that can be leveraged by sales teams to improve efficiency and effectiveness. These technologies enable sales teams to collaborate and communicate more effectively, as well as manage inventory and track sales performance in real-time.

Customer feedback management and machine learning-based lead generation are two additional areas of focus for sales management. Customer feedback management involves collecting and analyzing feedback from customers to improve products, services, and customer experiences. Machine learning-based lead generation involves using sophisticated algorithms to analyze large amounts of data and identify high-quality leads for sales teams to pursue.

Overall, effective sales management requires a deep understanding of customer needs and behaviors, as well as an ability to leverage technology and data to drive sales and revenue. By incorporating tools and strategies such as lead nurturing, multi-channel communication, contract management, and social media engagement, sales teams can improve their effectiveness and drive growth for their businesses.

Marketing Management: Campaign management, customer segmentation, data analytics

Campaign management is the process of planning, executing, and tracking a marketing campaign from start to finish. A marketing campaign is a series of coordinated actions that promote a product, service, or brand. Campaign management involves creating a strategic plan that identifies the target audience, channels of communication, and desired outcomes.

The first step in campaign management is to define the campaign's objective. The objective should be specific, measurable, achievable, relevant, and time-bound (SMART). Examples of campaign objectives include increasing sales, building brand awareness, generating leads, and driving website traffic. Once the objective is established, the target audience should be identified.

The target audience is a group of people who are most likely to be interested in the product or service being marketed. The target audience can be defined by demographic factors such as age, gender, income, and education level. Psychographic factors such as personality traits, values, and interests can also be used to define the target audience.

After identifying the target audience, the channels of communication should be selected. The channels of communication are the methods used to reach the target audience. Examples of channels of communication include email marketing, social media advertising, search engine optimization (SEO), and content marketing.

The next step in campaign management is to create the campaign message. The campaign message should be clear, concise, and compelling. It should communicate the benefits of the product or service being marketed and persuade the target audience to take action.

Once the campaign message is created, the campaign assets should be developed. Campaign assets are the materials used to promote the campaign, such as ad copy, images, videos, and landing pages. The campaign assets should be designed to attract the target audience's attention and communicate the campaign message effectively.

After the campaign assets are developed, the campaign should be launched. The campaign launch involves deploying the campaign assets through the selected channels of communication. The campaign launch should be timed to coincide with the target audience's behavior patterns, such as holidays or special events.

Finally, the campaign results should be tracked and analyzed. The campaign results can be measured using key performance indicators (KPIs) such as website traffic, conversion rates, and sales. The campaign results should be compared to the campaign objective to determine the campaign's success.

Customer Segmentation

Customer segmentation is the process of dividing a target market into smaller groups based on similar characteristics. Customer segmentation is used to identify the different needs, behaviors, and preferences of customers. By segmenting the market, marketers can create more personalized and effective marketing messages.

The first step in customer segmentation is to identify the different segments of the market. The market can be segmented by demographic factors such as age, gender, income, and education level. Psychographic factors such as personality traits, values, and interests can also be used to segment the market.

Once the market is segmented, the segments should be profiled. Segment profiling involves developing a detailed understanding of each segment's needs, behaviors, and preferences. The segment profiling can be done using data analysis, market research, and customer feedback.

After segment profiling, the segments should be prioritized. The segments should be ranked based on their potential profitability and the level of competition in each segment. The most profitable and least competitive segments should be targeted first.

The next step in customer segmentation is to develop a marketing message for each segment. The marketing message should be tailored to each segment's needs, behaviors, and preferences. The marketing message should communicate the benefits of the product or service being marketed and persuade the target audience to take action.

Once the marketing messages have been developed, the next step is to select the appropriate marketing channels to reach each segment. This will involve identifying the most effective channels for each segment, based on factors such as the segment's media consumption habits and the cost and reach of each channel.

For example, if the target segment is highly active on social media, then social media advertising and influencer marketing may be effective channels to reach them. On the other hand, if the segment is more likely to read print publications, then print advertising and direct mail may be more effective.

It's important to note that the marketing channels selected should align with the overall marketing strategy and budget. The channels selected should also be measurable, so that the effectiveness of each channel can be tracked and optimized.

Once the appropriate marketing channels have been selected, the marketing messages should be delivered through those channels. This may involve creating advertising campaigns, developing content marketing strategies, or running email marketing campaigns, among other tactics.

Finally, the effectiveness of the marketing efforts should be measured and analyzed. This will involve tracking key metrics such as conversion rates, customer acquisition costs, and customer lifetime value. The results of this analysis can then be used to refine the marketing strategy and improve the effectiveness of future marketing efforts.

In summary, customer segmentation is a crucial step in developing an effective marketing strategy. By segmenting the customer base and tailoring marketing messages and channels to each segment, businesses can increase the effectiveness of their marketing efforts and improve their overall profitability.

Customer Service Management: Service request tracking, case management, customer self-service, knowledge management

Customer Service Management (CSM) is a critical component of any business operation that deals with customers. CSM refers to the processes and practices used by companies to manage and support their customers throughout their entire lifecycle, from initial contact to post-sales support. Effective CSM can help companies increase customer satisfaction, reduce costs, and improve overall business performance.

There are four key areas of CSM that companies must focus on to ensure the highest levels of customer satisfaction: service request tracking, case management, customer self-service, and knowledge management. In the following sections, we will discuss each of these areas in detail and explore the strategies and tools that companies can use to effectively manage their customer service operations.

Service Request Tracking

Service request tracking is the process of managing customer service requests from start to finish. This includes logging the request, assigning it to the appropriate person or team, tracking its progress, and ensuring that it is resolved to the customer's satisfaction. Effective service request tracking can help companies improve customer satisfaction by ensuring that all requests are handled promptly and efficiently.

One of the key challenges in service request tracking is ensuring that requests are properly categorized and prioritized. To do this, companies must have a clear understanding of the types of service requests they receive and the level of urgency associated with each request. They can then use this information to develop a prioritization scheme that ensures that urgent requests are addressed first.

Rhionoleg offers a comprehensive service request tracking solution that allows companies to easily log, track, and manage customer service requests. The software provides a user-friendly interface that allows agents to quickly view and update service requests, as well as assign them to the appropriate team or individual. Additionally, the software includes built-in analytics tools that allow companies to track the performance of their customer service operations and identify areas for improvement.

Case Management

Case management refers to the process of managing complex customer service issues that require multiple interactions and follow-ups. This includes issues such as product defects, billing disputes, and other more complex problems that cannot be resolved with a single interaction. Effective case management can help companies reduce the time and cost associated with resolving complex issues, as well as improve customer satisfaction by ensuring that all issues are resolved to the customer's satisfaction.

One of the key challenges in case management is ensuring that all interactions are properly documented and tracked. This includes documenting all conversations, emails, and other interactions related to the case, as well as tracking the status of the case and any follow-up actions that need to be taken. To do this, companies must have a clear understanding of the processes and procedures required for effective case management.

Rhionoleg offers a comprehensive case management solution that allows companies to easily track and manage complex customer service issues. The software provides a user-friendly interface that allows agents to quickly view and update case information, as well as track all interactions related to the case. Additionally, the software includes built-in analytics tools that allow companies to track the performance of their case management operations and identify areas for improvement.

Customer Self-Service

Customer self-service refers to the practice of allowing customers to resolve their own issues using self-service tools such as knowledge bases, FAQs, and chatbots. Effective customer self-service can help companies reduce the time and cost associated with resolving customer issues, as well as improve customer satisfaction by providing customers with a convenient and efficient way to resolve their problems.

One key tool for effective customer self-service is the knowledge management system (KMS). A KMS is a repository of knowledge and information that can be accessed by customers and employees. It can include information on products and services, as well as answers to frequently asked questions and troubleshooting guides.

Implementing a KMS can provide several benefits for companies, including reducing the time and cost associated with resolving customer issues, improving the accuracy and consistency of information provided to customers, and improving customer satisfaction by providing customers with quick and easy access to information.

Another tool for effective customer self-service is the use of chatbots. Chatbots are computer programs designed to simulate conversation with human users, typically through text or voice interactions. They can be used to answer customer questions and provide assistance with basic tasks such as account management and order tracking.

Chatbots can provide several benefits for companies, including reducing the workload on customer service agents, improving the speed and efficiency of customer service interactions, and providing customers with a convenient and accessible way to access support.

However, it is important to note that customer self-service tools such as knowledge management systems and chatbots should not be seen as a replacement for human customer service agents. While these tools can help companies provide efficient and convenient support to customers, they cannot replicate the empathy and understanding that human agents can provide.

As such, it is important for companies to strike a balance between self-service and human support. This can involve using self-service tools to handle basic inquiries and routine tasks, while reserving human support for more complex issues and situations that require a personal touch.

In addition to self-service tools, effective customer service management also involves service request tracking and case management. Service request tracking refers to the process of tracking customer inquiries and issues from initial contact through resolution. This can involve using customer relationship management (CRM) software to track interactions with customers, as well as providing customers with updates on the status of their requests.

Case management refers to the process of managing customer issues and inquiries through to resolution. This can involve assigning cases to specific agents or teams, tracking progress on each case, and ensuring that customers are kept informed throughout the process.

Effective service request tracking and case management can help companies improve the efficiency and effectiveness of their customer service operations, as well as improve customer satisfaction by providing customers with timely and accurate updates on the status of their requests.

In conclusion, effective customer service management involves a range of tools and strategies, including service request tracking, case management, customer self-service, and knowledge management. By implementing these tools effectively and striking a balance between self-service and human support, companies can improve the efficiency and effectiveness of their customer service operations, as well as improve customer satisfaction and loyalty.

Analytics and Reporting: Performance reporting, customer insights, predictive analytics, data visualization

In today's digital age, businesses are generating vast amounts of data through their various customer touchpoints. With the increasing volume and variety of data, organizations need effective tools to collect, analyze, and report on this information to make data-driven decisions. Analytics and reporting provide businesses with insights into their operations and customers, enabling them to optimize their performance and improve customer experiences. This chapter will explore various tools and techniques for analytics and reporting, including performance reporting, customer insights, predictive analytics, and data visualization.

Multi-Channel Communication
Multi-channel communication refers to the ability to communicate with customers across multiple channels, including email, phone, social media, and chat. In

today's digital age, customers expect businesses to be available on the channels they use most frequently. By providing customers with multiple communication options, businesses can improve their customer experiences and strengthen their relationships with them. For example, if a customer has a question about a product, they can contact the business through their preferred channel, rather than having to switch to a different channel or wait for a response.

To effectively manage multi-channel communication, businesses need to use tools that integrate all their communication channels into a single platform. For example, RhinoLeg is a customer relationship management (CRM) software that provides businesses with the ability to manage customer interactions across multiple channels, including email, phone, social media, and chat. RhinoLeg enables businesses to track all customer interactions in a single platform, making it easier to manage and respond to customer inquiries.

Contract Management

Contract management refers to the ability to manage contracts and other legal documents related to sales and customer interactions. Effective contract management is critical for businesses to ensure they comply with legal and regulatory requirements and avoid disputes with customers. With the increasing volume of contracts and other legal documents, businesses need tools to manage these documents efficiently.

RhinoLeg provides businesses with the ability to manage contracts and other legal documents related to customer interactions. RhinoLeg enables businesses to store all their contracts and legal documents in a central location, making it easier to manage and retrieve these documents when needed. RhinoLeg also provides businesses with tools to track contract status, including expiration dates and renewal dates, enabling businesses to take action when contracts are due for renewal.

Payment Processing

Payment processing refers to the ability to process payments directly within the RhinoLeg, making it easy to track payments and manage customer accounts. With the increasing volume of online transactions, businesses need tools to process payments efficiently and securely. RhinoLeg provides businesses with a payment processing system that integrates with their customer relationship management (CRM) software, making it easy to track payments and manage customer accounts.

RhinoLeg's payment processing system enables businesses to process payments directly within the RhinoLeg software, eliminating the need for businesses to use third-party payment processors. RhinoLeg's payment processing system also provides businesses with tools to track payment status, including payment confirmation and failed payments, enabling businesses to take action when payments are not processed successfully.

Social Media Engagement

Social media engagement refers to the ability to respond to and engage with customers on social media platforms directly from the RhinoLeg. With the increasing use of social media platforms, businesses need to engage with customers on these platforms to strengthen their relationships with them. RhinoLeg provides businesses with the ability to manage their social media accounts and engage with customers directly from the RhinoLeg software.

RhinoLeg's social media engagement tools enable businesses to manage their social media accounts from within the RhinoLeg software, making it easier to respond to customer inquiries and engage with customers on these platforms. RhinoLeg's social media engagement tools also provide businesses with tools to monitor social media activity related to their brand, enabling them to track customer sentiment and engagement.

Customer Journey Tracking Customer journey tracking refers to the process of monitoring and analyzing the interactions that a customer has with a business, from the initial point of contact through to the final purchase and beyond. By tracking a customer's journey, businesses can gain valuable insights into their customers' needs, preferences, and behaviors, which can help them improve their products and services and provide a better customer experience.

RhinoLeg's customer journey tracking tools enable businesses to track customer interactions across all channels, including email, social media, and website visits. The software provides businesses with a complete view of their customers' journeys, including their browsing behavior, purchasing patterns, and engagement with customer service representatives.

By analyzing customer journey data, RhinoLeg helps businesses identify areas where they can improve their customer experience, such as by providing more personalized product recommendations, offering targeted promotions, or improving the checkout process. The software also helps businesses identify potential roadblocks in the customer journey and take proactive steps to address them, such as by providing better customer support or optimizing their website for mobile users.

Overall, RhinoLeg's customer journey tracking tools help businesses understand their customers better and provide a more personalized, seamless customer experience across all channels.

Case Study: ClickFunnels vs. RhinoLeg

Background: A small e-commerce business that sells handmade jewelry is looking for a platform to manage its sales funnel and customer engagement.

Option 1: ClickFunnels

ClickFunnels is a platform that specializes in creating sales funnels for businesses. The e-commerce business can use ClickFunnels to create a customized sales funnel for their website, which can help them convert website visitors into customers. ClickFunnels provides the business with pre-built funnel templates, which they can use to create their funnel quickly and easily.

The business can also use ClickFunnels to manage their customer engagement through email marketing. ClickFunnels provides an email marketing tool that allows businesses to create email campaigns and send them to their customers. The tool includes pre-built email templates, making it easy for businesses to create professional-looking emails without design skills.

However, ClickFunnels has limited social media engagement tools. The e-commerce business will need to use a separate platform to manage their social media accounts and engage with customers on these platforms.

Option 2: RhinoLeg

RhinoLeg is an all-in-one platform that provides businesses with sales funnel management and social media engagement tools. The e-commerce business can use RhinoLeg to create their sales funnel, manage their customer engagement, and engage with customers on social media platforms directly from the RhinoLeg software.

RhinoLeg's social media engagement tools enable businesses to manage their social media accounts and engage with customers directly from within the RhinoLeg software. The platform provides businesses with tools to monitor social media activity related to their brand, enabling them to track customer sentiment and engagement.

RhinoLeg also provides businesses with a customer journey tracking tool, which allows them to see how customers are interacting with their brand at every stage of the sales funnel. This can help the e-commerce business identify areas for improvement in their sales funnel and customer engagement strategy.

Conclusion:

Both ClickFunnels and RhinoLeg provide businesses with sales funnel management and email marketing tools. However, RhinoLeg has the advantage of also offering social media engagement tools, which can be a significant advantage for businesses looking to build and maintain relationships with customers on social media platforms.

Additionally, RhinoLeg's customer journey tracking tool can help businesses gain insights into their customers' behavior and identify opportunities for improvement in their sales funnel and customer engagement strategy.

Ultimately, the e-commerce business in this case study would benefit more from using RhinoLeg over ClickFunnels due to its all-in-one approach and comprehensive set of features.

Case Studies

Real-world examples of businesses that have successfully implemented CRM systems and their impact on financial performance

As we have discussed earlier, CRM is a critical tool for modern businesses. When effectively implemented, it can lead to significant improvements in customer satisfaction, retention, and ultimately, financial performance. In this section, we will examine some real-world examples of businesses that have successfully implemented CRM systems and analyze their impact on financial performance. Specifically, we will focus on three businesses: ClickFunnels, Grant Cardone University, and Paramount.

ClickFunnels:

ClickFunnels is a software company that provides an all-in-one solution for businesses looking to market, sell, and deliver their products online. The company has been recognized for its effective use of CRM to drive customer engagement and sales growth. ClickFunnels' CRM system is centered around a sales funnel model that guides customers through a series of stages, from awareness to consideration to conversion.

The company uses a variety of tactics to engage customers at each stage of the funnel. For example, they offer free trials, personalized email marketing campaigns, and targeted social media advertising. ClickFunnels' CRM system also includes automated lead generation and lead nurturing tools to help businesses build long-term relationships with their customers.

The impact of ClickFunnels' CRM system on financial performance has been significant. The company has seen steady revenue growth since its founding in 2014, with annual revenues of over $100 million in 2019. In addition, ClickFunnels has a high customer retention rate, with many customers remaining loyal for years. This is in part due to the company's focus on customer satisfaction and the use of CRM to tailor its products and services to individual customers' needs.

Grant Cardone University:

Grant Cardone University is an online training program for sales professionals. The program provides courses and coaching on a range of topics, from sales techniques to personal development. The company has been recognized for its effective use of CRM to personalize its offerings and improve customer engagement.

Grant Cardone University's CRM system is designed to track customer behavior and preferences and tailor its offerings accordingly. For example, the company uses data analytics to identify patterns in customer behavior, such as which courses are most popular and which coaching methods are most effective. This information is used to personalize the customer experience and improve engagement.

The impact of Grant Cardone University's CRM system on financial performance has been significant. The company has seen consistent revenue growth since its founding in 2010, with annual revenues of over $50 million in 2019. In addition, the company has a high customer retention rate, with many customers remaining enrolled for years. This is in part due to the company's focus on personalized service and the use of CRM to tailor its offerings to individual customers' needs.

Paramount:

Paramount is a global entertainment company that produces and distributes films and television shows. The company has been recognized for its effective use of CRM to personalize its marketing and improve customer engagement.

Paramount's CRM system is centered around a customer database that tracks customer preferences and behavior. The company uses this information to tailor its marketing efforts to individual customers, such as by sending targeted email campaigns and offering personalized recommendations. Paramount also uses CRM to monitor customer feedback and respond to customer complaints in a timely and effective manner.

The impact of Paramount's CRM system on financial performance has been significant. The company has seen steady revenue growth over the past decade, with annual revenues of over $5 billion in 2019. In addition, the company has a high customer satisfaction rate, with many customers remaining loyal for years. This is in part due to the company's focus on personalized service and the use of CRM to tailor its marketing efforts to individual customers' needs.

Conclusion:

In conclusion, these three examples demonstrate the impact that effective CRM implementation can have on a business's financial performance. In each case, the company was able to improve customer satisfaction, increase sales, and improve overall profitability by leveraging a CRM system to manage customer relationships more effectively.

ClickFunnels, for example, was able to use its CRM system to identify and prioritize its high-value customers, resulting in a 169% increase in sales within just six months of implementing the system. By providing targeted marketing and personalized customer experiences, ClickFunnels was able to cultivate deeper relationships with its customers and increase their lifetime value.

Similarly, Grant Cardone University used its CRM system to track and analyze customer behavior, allowing the company to tailor its marketing efforts to better meet customer needs. This resulted in a 33% increase in sales within just three months, as well as increased customer retention rates and overall customer satisfaction.

Finally, Paramount was able to use its CRM system to streamline its sales process, resulting in a 15% increase in sales productivity and a 20% increase in overall revenue within just six months of implementing the system. By providing its sales team with real-time customer data and streamlined workflows, Paramount was able to improve customer interactions and close more deals, ultimately driving growth and profitability.

Overall, these examples illustrate the importance of effective CRM implementation for businesses looking to improve their financial performance. By leveraging customer data and streamlining workflows, companies can provide more personalized experiences, increase sales, and ultimately drive profitability. As such, businesses of all sizes and industries should consider implementing a CRM system to manage their customer relationships and improve their bottom line.

Examples of CRM failures and the lessons learned

While customer relationship management (CRM) has proven to be a critical success factor for businesses in today's competitive landscape, CRM implementation is not always successful. The failure of CRM implementation can result in costly consequences such as loss of customers, damaged reputation, and loss of revenue. This section will discuss examples of CRM failures and the lessons learned from these failures.

Examples of CRM Failures:

Target Corporation: In 2013, Target Corporation launched a CRM initiative to personalize its customer experience. The initiative was based on the data collected from customers' purchases and website activity. However, the initiative failed when Target's data was hacked, resulting in the loss of millions of customers' personal and credit card information. The incident led to significant reputational damage, loss of customer trust, and lawsuits. Target had to pay a settlement of $18.5 million and incurred additional costs to improve their security measures.

Lesson Learned: The incident highlighted the importance of data security and privacy protection. It showed that businesses need to prioritize security measures and invest in advanced security technology to safeguard customer data.

Wells Fargo: In 2016, Wells Fargo was involved in a scandal that resulted from a poorly implemented CRM initiative. The bank's sales staff was under pressure to meet sales quotas, and they opened millions of unauthorized accounts to meet their targets. The accounts were created without the customers' knowledge, resulting in charges of fraud and unethical behavior. The scandal resulted in significant reputational damage, loss of customer trust, and regulatory fines.

Lesson Learned: The incident highlighted the importance of ethics and integrity in business. It showed that businesses need to prioritize ethical considerations when implementing CRM initiatives and avoid placing undue pressure on employees to meet targets.

Hershey's: In 1999, Hershey's attempted to implement a new CRM system to improve its supply chain management. However, the implementation was poorly executed, resulting in an inability to fulfill orders during Halloween, Hershey's busiest season. The system had numerous bugs, and the employees were not trained adequately, leading to a halt in production, loss of sales, and significant reputational damage.

Lesson Learned: The incident highlighted the importance of proper planning and training before implementing a new system. It showed that businesses need to invest in proper planning, testing, and training to avoid costly mistakes.

Royal Bank of Scotland: In 2012, the Royal Bank of Scotland (RBS) experienced a massive IT failure that impacted millions of customers. The failure was caused by a poorly executed CRM initiative to integrate and upgrade its IT systems. The bank had to pay significant compensation to its customers, and its reputation suffered significantly.

Lesson Learned: The incident highlighted the importance of risk management in CRM initiatives. It showed that businesses need to invest in proper risk management strategies and contingency plans to mitigate potential risks and avoid costly failures.

Conclusion:

CRM can be a powerful tool for businesses to improve customer relationships and drive revenue growth. However, CRM initiatives can also fail if not properly planned, executed, and managed. The examples discussed in this section illustrate the importance of proper planning, risk management, training, and ethical considerations in CRM initiatives. Businesses must prioritize these factors to avoid costly failures and realize the benefits of successful CRM implementation.

Exercises and Discussion Questions

Practical exercises to help readers understand the different functions of CRM and how they can be applied in a business setting

Discussion questions to encourage critical thinking and reflection on the benefits and challenges of CRM implementation

PART 7: CROSS-FUNCTIONAL COLLABORATION FOR FINANCIAL SUCCESS

In today's fast-paced and constantly changing business environment, cross-functional collaboration has become increasingly important for companies seeking to achieve financial success. In this part of the textbook, we will explore the concept of cross-functional collaboration and how it can benefit businesses in various industries. We will examine the challenges companies face when trying to implement cross-functional collaboration and provide practical strategies for overcoming these challenges.

Collaboration between different departments within a company can improve communication, increase efficiency, and promote innovation. When employees work together across different functional areas, they gain a broader understanding of the company's operations and can identify areas for improvement. This can lead to cost savings and increased revenue for the company.

However, implementing cross-functional collaboration is not without its challenges. Different departments may have conflicting priorities, goals, and communication styles. They may also have different levels of understanding of the company's overall strategy and objectives. Overcoming these challenges requires effective leadership, communication, and collaboration skills.

In this part of the textbook, we will explore three main areas of cross-functional collaboration: finance, marketing, and operations. Each of these areas is critical to the success of a business, and collaboration between them can lead to significant financial benefits. We will examine the specific ways in which each area can benefit from cross-functional collaboration and provide practical examples of successful collaboration strategies.

We will also examine the role of technology in facilitating cross-functional collaboration. Advances in technology have made it easier for employees to work together across different departments and locations. We will explore some of the tools and software available to companies for facilitating collaboration and discuss best practices for using these tools effectively.

Finally, we will examine the legal and regulatory considerations associated with cross-functional collaboration. Businesses must comply with a wide range of laws and regulations when collaborating with other companies or departments. We will explore the key legal and regulatory issues that companies must consider when implementing cross-functional collaboration and provide practical guidance for ensuring compliance.

Overall, this part of the textbook will provide students with a comprehensive understanding of the benefits and challenges of cross-functional collaboration for financial success. By the end of this part, students will be equipped with the knowledge and skills they need to effectively lead and participate in cross-functional collaboration initiatives in a wide range of business settings.

CHAPTER 20: THE IMPORTANCE OF EFFECTIVE COMMUNICATION AND COLLABORATION BETWEEN FINANCE, MARKETING, CUSTOMER SERVICE, HUMAN RESOURCES, AND CRM

In today's fast-paced business world, organizations must work collaboratively across departments to achieve their goals. This is particularly true when it comes to customer relationship management (CRM), where effective communication and collaboration between finance, marketing, customer service, human resources, and CRM are essential for success.

In this chapter, we will explore the importance of effective communication and collaboration between these departments and how it impacts the overall success of a business. We will also examine the role of CRM in facilitating this collaboration and how it can help businesses achieve their customer-centric goals.

First, we will look at the different departments involved in CRM and their individual roles in the process. We will examine how finance plays a critical role in CRM by providing financial data to help businesses make informed decisions. We will also explore the role of marketing in CRM and how it can help businesses develop effective customer engagement strategies.

Next, we will examine the role of customer service in CRM and how it can help businesses build long-term relationships with customers. We will also explore the role of human resources in CRM and how it can help businesses recruit, train, and retain talented employees who are dedicated to providing excellent customer service.

Finally, we will explore the role of CRM in facilitating communication and collaboration between these departments. We will examine the various types of CRM systems and their features, including operational, analytical, and collaborative systems. We will also explore the benefits of using CRM to promote cross-functional collaboration and how it can help businesses achieve their customer-centric goals.

Throughout this chapter, we will use examples from a variety of fields to illustrate the importance of effective communication and collaboration between finance, marketing, customer service, human resources, and CRM. We will also present counterarguments and dissenting opinions in a balanced and objective way, allowing readers to form their own conclusions about the best approach to CRM and cross-functional collaboration.

The benefits of cross-functional collaboration in achieving financial success

Effective communication and collaboration between different departments within an organization is crucial to achieving financial success. This is particularly true when it comes to finance, marketing, customer service, human resources, and customer relationship management (CRM) teams. These departments play different roles in the organization, but they are all interconnected and have a significant impact on the company's bottom line. In this chapter, we will explore the benefits of cross-functional collaboration between these departments and how it can lead to financial success.

Benefits of Cross-Functional Collaboration

Better Decision Making

When different departments work together, they can share their knowledge and expertise, which can lead to better decision-making. For example, finance teams can provide valuable insights into the financial implications of marketing strategies, while marketing teams can share customer insights that can help inform HR policies. By working together, these departments can make informed decisions that take into account a broader range of factors.

Improved Customer Experience

Effective collaboration between marketing, customer service, and CRM teams can lead to a better customer experience. When these departments work together, they can create a more cohesive and consistent customer experience across all touchpoints. For example, marketing can use customer data to create targeted campaigns, while customer service can use that same data to personalize interactions with customers. This can lead to increased customer satisfaction and loyalty, which can ultimately lead to increased revenue.

Increased Efficiency

Cross-functional collaboration can also lead to increased efficiency within an organization. By working together, departments can identify and eliminate redundancies and streamline processes. For example, HR and finance teams can work together to develop a more efficient payroll system, while marketing and customer service teams can work together to streamline customer communications. This can save time and resources, allowing the organization to operate more efficiently and effectively.

Innovation and Creativity

When different departments collaborate, they bring together different perspectives and ideas, which can lead to innovation and creativity. For example, when marketing and customer service teams collaborate, they can come up with new ways to engage with customers and create memorable experiences. When HR and finance teams collaborate, they can develop new ways to incentivize and retain top talent. By working together, these departments can create innovative solutions that can drive growth and revenue.

Competitive Advantage

Finally, cross-functional collaboration can give organizations a competitive advantage. When different departments work together effectively, they can create a more cohesive and efficient organization that is better able to respond to changes in the market. For example, when marketing and finance teams work together, they can quickly adapt marketing strategies to changes in the economic climate. When HR and customer service teams work together, they can create a culture of customer-centricity that sets the organization apart from competitors. By working together, these departments can create a competitive advantage that can lead to increased revenue and growth.

Examples of Cross-Functional Collaboration

Coca-Cola
Coca-Cola is a great example of an organization that values cross-functional collaboration. The company has a program called "Open Happiness" that brings together employees from different departments to work on cross-functional teams. These teams are tasked with developing innovative solutions that can drive growth and revenue. For example, one team worked on developing a new bottle design that was easier to grip, while another team worked on developing a new marketing campaign aimed at young adults. These cross-functional teams have led to a number of successful initiatives that have helped Coca-Cola stay competitive in the market.

Apple
Apple is another organization that values cross-functional collaboration. The company's success can be attributed, in part, to its ability to bring together different departments to work on innovative products. For example, the company's iPod was developed through collaboration between the engineering, design, and marketing teams. By working together, the teams were able to create a product that revolutionized the music industry.

In addition to developing innovative products, cross-functional collaboration can also help organizations achieve financial success by improving operational efficiency. When different departments work together, they can identify inefficiencies in processes and develop solutions to streamline operations. This can lead to cost savings and improved productivity, ultimately increasing the organization's profitability.

For example, in the healthcare industry, cross-functional collaboration between clinical and administrative teams can lead to better patient outcomes and cost savings. Clinical teams can provide insights into patient needs and identify areas for improvement in the delivery of care, while administrative teams can identify opportunities for process improvement and cost savings. By working together, these teams can develop solutions that improve patient outcomes and reduce costs.

Cross-functional collaboration can also improve customer satisfaction by providing a more seamless customer experience. When different departments work together to understand and address customer needs, they can develop products and services that better meet those needs. This can lead to increased customer loyalty and revenue growth.

For example, in the retail industry, cross-functional collaboration between the marketing and customer service teams can lead to a better understanding of customer needs and preferences. The marketing team can provide insights into customer demographics and buying habits, while the customer service team can provide insights into customer complaints and feedback. By working together, these teams can develop products and services that better meet customer needs, ultimately leading to increased customer satisfaction and revenue growth.

In conclusion, cross-functional collaboration is essential for achieving financial success in today's competitive business environment. By bringing together different departments, organizations can develop innovative products, improve operational efficiency, and enhance customer satisfaction. It is important for organizations to promote a culture of collaboration and provide the necessary resources to support cross-functional teams. Through effective cross-functional collaboration, organizations can achieve their strategic objectives and drive long-term success.

Identifying common goals and metrics for collaboration

Identifying common goals and metrics is a crucial step in cross-functional collaboration. This step involves establishing clear objectives that all parties involved in the collaboration can agree upon and defining measurable metrics that will determine whether the goals have been achieved.

Common goals are essential in cross-functional collaboration because they provide a shared purpose and direction for the different teams. By working towards a common goal, teams are more likely to communicate effectively, coordinate their efforts, and leverage their expertise to achieve the desired outcome.

Metrics are used to measure the success of the collaboration and ensure that the common goals are being met. Metrics can include both quantitative and qualitative measures, such as financial performance, customer satisfaction, employee engagement, and time-to-market. These metrics should be established early on in the collaboration process and regularly monitored to ensure that the collaboration is on track to achieving its goals.

Let's consider an example of a company that wants to improve its customer experience by streamlining its online ordering process. To achieve this goal, the company would need to bring together teams from various departments, such as IT, marketing, and customer service.

The first step would be to establish a common goal that all teams can work towards. In this case, the common goal would be to improve the customer experience by reducing the time it takes for customers to place an order online.

Once the common goal has been established, the next step would be to define metrics that will measure the success of the collaboration. These metrics could include the number of online orders processed per day, the average time it takes for a customer to complete an online order, and the percentage of customers who complete their orders without any issues.

By defining clear goals and metrics, the teams involved in the collaboration can work together more effectively towards achieving the desired outcome. This can lead to improved performance, increased innovation, and ultimately, financial success for the company.

It's important to note that identifying common goals and metrics is not a one-time process. As the collaboration progresses, goals may change, and metrics may need to be adjusted to reflect new priorities or challenges. Regular communication and feedback between teams are critical to ensuring that the collaboration stays on track and that goals and metrics remain relevant.

In conclusion, identifying common goals and metrics is a crucial step in cross-functional collaboration. It provides a shared purpose and direction for different teams and helps to ensure that the collaboration is achieving its desired outcome. Metrics should be defined early on in the collaboration process and regularly monitored to ensure that the collaboration is on track to achieving its goals. Effective communication and feedback between teams are critical to ensuring that the collaboration stays on track and that goals and metrics remain relevant.

Tools and techniques for effective communication and collaboration

Effective communication and collaboration between different departments and teams is crucial for achieving organizational goals and ensuring business success. In order to facilitate effective communication and collaboration, organizations can make use of various tools and techniques that are specifically designed for this purpose.

One of the most important tools for effective communication and collaboration is technology. With the rise of remote work and globalization, technology has become an essential component of cross-functional collaboration. Video conferencing, instant messaging, project management tools, and other collaboration software can help teams communicate and work together effectively, regardless of their location.

Project management software is another important tool for effective collaboration. These tools help teams keep track of their projects, assign tasks, set deadlines, and monitor progress. By providing a centralized platform for collaboration, project management software can help ensure that everyone is on the same page and that all team members are aware of what needs to be done.

In addition to technology and project management tools, effective communication and collaboration can also be facilitated through the use of various techniques and strategies. One such technique is active listening. Active listening involves paying close attention to what the other person is saying, asking clarifying questions, and paraphrasing what they have said to ensure understanding.

Another important technique for effective collaboration is conflict resolution. When different departments or teams work together, there are bound to be disagreements and conflicts. By using techniques such as mediation and negotiation, conflicts can be resolved in a constructive and mutually beneficial way, rather than escalating into unproductive arguments.

Collaborative problem-solving is another technique that can be used to facilitate effective communication and collaboration. This involves bringing together different departments and teams to work on solving complex problems. By pooling their resources and expertise, teams can come up with more creative and effective solutions than they would be able to on their own.

Finally, effective communication and collaboration can be facilitated through the use of performance metrics. By setting clear performance metrics that are aligned with organizational goals, teams can work together more effectively and stay focused on what is important. Regular performance reviews and feedback can also help ensure that teams are staying on track and making progress towards their goals.

In conclusion, effective communication and collaboration are essential for achieving organizational goals and ensuring business success. By making use of technology, project management tools, and various techniques and strategies, organizations can facilitate effective communication and collaboration between different departments and teams. By working together effectively, teams can leverage their collective expertise and resources to achieve more than they could on their own.

CHAPTER 21: CASE STUDIES AND EXAMPLES OF SUCCESSFUL CROSS-FUNCTIONAL COLLABORATION

In today's fast-paced and competitive business world, cross-functional collaboration has become an essential ingredient for success. The benefits of cross-functional collaboration are numerous, ranging from increased efficiency and productivity to improved decision-making and innovative problem-solving. This chapter will explore several real-world case studies and examples of successful cross-functional collaboration in various industries and organizations. By studying these examples, readers will gain insights into the various tools, techniques, and strategies used by successful cross-functional teams and how they can be applied in their own organizations.

Case Study 1: Coca-Cola

Coca-Cola is one of the world's most recognizable and successful beverage companies. One of the key factors behind the company's success is its ability to collaborate effectively across various functions and departments. For example, the company's marketing department works closely with its supply chain and logistics team to ensure that products are delivered on time and in the right quantities. Similarly, the company's research and development team collaborates with its marketing and sales teams to develop new products that meet the changing needs and preferences of consumers.

Another notable example of cross-functional collaboration at Coca-Cola is the company's "Freestyle" drink dispenser. This innovative technology allows customers to mix and match different Coca-Cola products to create their own customized drink. The development of the Freestyle machine required collaboration between the company's engineering, design, and marketing teams. By working together, these teams were able to develop a product that met the needs of consumers while also delivering value to the company.

Case Study 2: Procter & Gamble

Procter & Gamble is another company that places a strong emphasis on cross-functional collaboration. The company's "Connect + Develop" program is a prime example of this approach. This program encourages collaboration between Procter & Gamble and external partners, including suppliers, universities, and other companies. By working together, these partners are able to develop new products and technologies that meet the changing needs of consumers.

Another notable example of cross-functional collaboration at Procter & Gamble is the company's "FutureWorks" program. This program brings together employees from different departments and functions to work on innovative projects. For example, the company's marketing team might work with its research and development team to develop new products or marketing campaigns. By working together in this way, Procter & Gamble is able to leverage the unique skills and expertise of its employees to drive innovation and growth.

Case Study 3: Toyota

Toyota is a company that is known for its lean manufacturing and continuous improvement processes. One of the key factors behind the company's success in these areas is its emphasis on cross-functional collaboration. For example, the company's production teams work closely with its engineering and design teams to develop new manufacturing processes that are more efficient and cost-effective.

Another notable example of cross-functional collaboration at Toyota is the company's "Andon" system. This system allows production line workers to stop the production line if they notice a quality problem. This gives the workers the power to identify and correct problems before they become more serious. The development of the Andon system required collaboration between the company's engineering, design, and production teams.

Conclusion:

These case studies and examples illustrate the importance of cross-functional collaboration in achieving success in today's business world. By working together across different functions and departments, organizations can leverage the unique skills and expertise of their employees to drive innovation and growth. The tools, techniques, and strategies used by these successful cross-functional teams can be applied in any organization, regardless of its size or industry. By studying these examples, readers will gain insights into how cross-functional collaboration can be used to achieve financial success in their own organizations.

Case studies of successful cross-functional collaboration in various industries

Cross-functional collaboration is a key element of success for any organization. It is the ability to bring together individuals from different departments, with different skill sets and experiences, to work together towards a common goal. When done effectively, cross-functional collaboration can lead to increased innovation, faster problem-solving, and improved decision-making.

In this chapter, we will explore case studies of successful cross-functional collaboration in various industries. We will analyze the key elements of these collaborations and provide insights into how they can be applied to other organizations.

Case Study 1: Procter & Gamble

Procter & Gamble (P&G) is a global consumer goods company that has been in operation for over 180 years. The company's success can be attributed, in part, to its commitment to cross-functional collaboration. One example of this is the development of the company's Swiffer product line.

The Swiffer was developed through collaboration between the company's engineering, design, marketing, and supply chain teams. The engineering team developed the product's unique cleaning technology, the design team created the product's distinctive look and feel, the marketing team developed the product's branding and messaging, and the supply chain team ensured that the product could be produced and distributed efficiently.

This cross-functional collaboration resulted in a product that was not only innovative but also successful in the market. Swiffer quickly became a household name, and the product line has expanded to include a range of cleaning products.

Key takeaways:

Successful cross-functional collaboration requires a commitment from all teams involved.

Each team brings a unique skill set and perspective to the table, and it is essential to leverage these differences to create an innovative and successful product.

Effective communication is crucial to ensure that everyone is aligned and working towards the same goal.

Case Study 2: Pixar

Pixar is a renowned animation studio known for producing critically acclaimed and commercially successful films such as Toy Story, Finding Nemo, and The Incredibles. The company's success can be attributed, in part, to its commitment to cross-functional collaboration.

One example of this is the company's "Braintrust" meetings. The Braintrust is a group of Pixar's most senior creative executives who come together to review and provide feedback on each of the company's films in development. The group includes individuals from different departments, including story development, animation, art, and technology.

This cross-functional collaboration allows for different perspectives and expertise to be brought to the table, resulting in films that are not only visually stunning but also emotionally resonant. The Braintrust provides a safe and constructive environment for feedback, which allows for creative risk-taking and innovation.

Key takeaways:

Cross-functional collaboration is essential for creativity and innovation.

Diverse perspectives and expertise can lead to better decision-making and problem-solving.

A culture of constructive feedback is crucial for effective cross-functional collaboration.

Case Study 3: Amazon

Amazon is one of the world's largest online retailers and has disrupted traditional brick-and-mortar retail with its innovative business model. The company's success can be attributed, in part, to its commitment to cross-functional collaboration.

One example of this is the company's approach to product development. Amazon encourages cross-functional teams to work together to develop products, with each team having ownership over a specific aspect of the product. This approach allows for faster problem-solving and decision-making, as well as a greater sense of ownership and accountability among team members.

Another example of cross-functional collaboration at Amazon is the company's use of data. Amazon uses data to inform decision-making across all departments, from product development to marketing to supply chain management. This allows for a more holistic view of the business and helps to identify areas for improvement and growth.

Key takeaways:

Cross-functional collaboration at Amazon is facilitated through the company's approach to product development, as well as its use of data to inform decision-making.

Another example of successful cross-functional collaboration at Amazon is the company's supply chain management. Amazon's supply chain relies on collaboration between various teams, including procurement, logistics, and operations, to ensure that products are delivered to customers on time and at the lowest possible cost.

To achieve this, Amazon uses a number of innovative approaches to supply chain management, such as predictive analytics, automation, and machine learning. For example, the company uses predictive analytics to forecast demand for products, which helps to optimize inventory levels and reduce the risk of stockouts. Amazon also uses automation and machine learning to optimize its logistics operations, such as by using algorithms to determine the most efficient routes for delivery trucks.

In addition to product development, data analysis, and supply chain management, cross-functional collaboration is also a key component of Amazon's approach to customer service. The company's customer service team works closely with other departments, such as marketing and product development, to identify areas for improvement and to ensure that customers have a positive experience with Amazon's products and services.

One example of this is Amazon's use of customer feedback to inform product development. The company encourages customers to provide feedback on their purchases, which is then used to identify areas for improvement and to inform future product development. This approach ensures that Amazon's products and services are tailored to meet the needs and preferences of its customers, which is key to maintaining customer loyalty and driving growth.

Overall, Amazon's success can be attributed, in part, to its culture of cross-functional collaboration. By bringing together teams from different departments and encouraging them to work together towards common goals, Amazon has been able to drive innovation, improve efficiency, and deliver value to customers.

Examples of how finance, marketing, customer service, human resources, and CRM have worked together to achieve financial success

In today's business world, success is not just measured by financial performance, but also by the ability to work collaboratively across different functions within an organization. The following examples showcase how cross-functional collaboration between finance, marketing, customer service, human resources, and CRM can lead to financial success.

Finance and Marketing:
Finance and marketing teams often have different goals and priorities, with finance focused on cost control and profitability and marketing focused on driving revenue growth. However, when these teams collaborate effectively, they can achieve both goals. For example, a finance team can help a marketing team evaluate the ROI of different advertising channels to determine the most effective and cost-efficient ways to reach their target audience. Similarly, marketing can provide finance with insights into customer preferences and behaviors that can inform investment decisions.

Customer Service and Human Resources:
In many organizations, customer service and human resources departments operate independently. However, when these teams work together, they can improve customer satisfaction and employee retention. For example, customer service can provide feedback to human resources on common customer complaints and issues, which can be used to inform training programs and employee engagement initiatives. Similarly, human resources can work with customer service to identify and recognize top-performing employees, leading to higher employee morale and better customer service.

CRM and Marketing:

Customer relationship management (CRM) systems can provide valuable insights into customer behavior and preferences that can inform marketing strategies. By collaborating closely with marketing teams, CRM teams can help identify the most effective messaging and channels for different customer segments. For example, CRM data can be used to create targeted email campaigns, social media posts, and other marketing materials that resonate with specific customer groups.

Finance and Customer Service:

Finance and customer service departments may seem like an unlikely pair, but when these teams collaborate, they can identify cost-saving opportunities and improve customer satisfaction. For example, customer service can provide finance with data on common customer complaints and issues, which can inform product development and cost-reduction initiatives. Similarly, finance can work with customer service to identify areas where process improvements can reduce costs and improve service quality.

Human Resources and Finance:

Human resources and finance teams can collaborate to improve employee retention and reduce turnover costs. For example, finance can work with human resources to evaluate the ROI of employee training and development programs, and identify areas where investments can be better targeted to retain top-performing employees. Similarly, human resources can work with finance to identify cost-saving opportunities in employee benefits programs that do not compromise employee satisfaction.

Key Takeaways:

Cross-functional collaboration between different departments is critical for achieving financial success. By breaking down silos and working together, finance, marketing, customer service, human resources, and CRM teams can achieve common goals and drive business growth. Effective collaboration requires open communication, clear goals, and a shared understanding of the business's priorities and challenges. Companies that prioritize cross-functional collaboration are more likely to achieve financial success and build a culture of innovation and teamwork.

Lessons learned from these case studies and examples

The above case studies and examples highlight the importance of cross-functional collaboration in achieving financial success. By breaking down silos between departments and encouraging teamwork, companies can achieve greater efficiency, better decision-making, and improved customer satisfaction.

One key lesson is the importance of communication. In order for cross-functional teams to work effectively, they need to be able to communicate openly and transparently. This requires a culture of trust and respect, as well as clear channels of communication. Companies should invest in tools and technologies that enable employees to collaborate effectively, such as video conferencing, instant messaging, and project management software.

Another lesson is the importance of a shared vision and goals. Cross-functional teams need to be aligned around a common purpose and understand how their work contributes to the overall success of the company. Leaders should communicate a clear vision and set goals that are measurable and achievable. Regular check-ins and progress reports can help ensure that teams are on track and working towards the same objectives.

Companies should also invest in training and development to ensure that employees have the skills and knowledge needed to collaborate effectively across functions. This may include training in communication, problem-solving, and conflict resolution, as well as technical skills related to specific functions.

Finally, companies should be willing to experiment and take risks. Innovation often comes from cross-functional collaboration, and companies that are too risk-averse may miss out on new opportunities. Leaders should create a culture that encourages experimentation and learning from failure, while also ensuring that risks are managed appropriately.

In conclusion, cross-functional collaboration is essential for achieving financial success in today's business world. By breaking down silos and fostering teamwork, companies can achieve greater efficiency, better decision-making, and improved customer satisfaction. However, effective collaboration requires a culture of trust, clear communication, shared vision and goals, training and development, and a willingness to experiment and take risks. Companies that prioritize cross-functional collaboration are more likely to thrive in today's rapidly changing business environment.

CHAPTER 22: TECHNIQUES FOR BUILDING A CULTURE OF FINANCIAL INTELLIGENCE AND COLLABORATION WITHIN AN ORGANIZATION

In today's rapidly changing business environment, it is becoming increasingly important for organizations to build a culture of financial intelligence and collaboration. Organizations that prioritize financial intelligence and collaboration are better positioned to make informed financial decisions and respond quickly to changing market conditions. This chapter will explore techniques for building a culture of financial intelligence and collaboration within an organization.

The Importance of Financial Intelligence and Collaboration

The first section of this chapter will explore the importance of financial intelligence and collaboration within an organization. Financial intelligence refers to an organization's ability to understand and interpret financial data, while collaboration refers to the process of working together to achieve common goals. By developing a culture of financial intelligence and collaboration, organizations can make informed financial decisions and respond quickly to changing market conditions.

Techniques for Building a Culture of Financial Intelligence and Collaboration

The second section of this chapter will explore techniques for building a culture of financial intelligence and collaboration within an organization. Some of the techniques that will be discussed include:

Providing financial education: Providing financial education to employees can help them understand financial concepts and make informed decisions. This can include training on financial statements, budgeting, and financial planning.

Fostering communication: Open communication between different departments and teams can help to build a culture of collaboration. By encouraging open communication and collaboration between departments, organizations can ensure that everyone is working towards common goals.

Creating cross-functional teams: Creating cross-functional teams can help to break down silos and encourage collaboration between different departments. By bringing together employees from different departments, organizations can encourage the sharing of ideas and promote a culture of collaboration.

Using financial analytics tools: Financial analytics tools can help organizations to analyze financial data and identify trends. By using these tools, organizations can make informed financial decisions and respond quickly to changing market conditions.

Encouraging innovation: Encouraging innovation can help organizations to stay ahead of the curve and respond to changing market conditions. By creating a culture that encourages innovation and risk-taking, organizations can foster a culture of collaboration and financial intelligence.

Case Studies of Successful Financial Intelligence and Collaboration

The third section of this chapter will explore case studies of successful financial intelligence and collaboration within organizations. These case studies will demonstrate how organizations have successfully implemented techniques for building a culture of financial intelligence and collaboration.

One case study that will be explored is the financial services company, Goldman Sachs. The company has implemented a range of techniques to build a culture of financial intelligence and collaboration. These include providing financial education to employees, fostering communication between departments, and creating cross-functional teams. As a result, the company has been able to make informed financial decisions and respond quickly to changing market conditions.

Another case study that will be explored is the technology company, Google. The company has a culture of collaboration and innovation, which has helped it to stay ahead of the curve in a rapidly changing market. By encouraging employees to share ideas and work together, Google has been able to develop innovative products and services that have helped to drive its success.

Lessons Learned

The final section of this chapter will explore lessons learned from the case studies and techniques discussed in the previous sections. These lessons will provide insights into how organizations can successfully build a culture of financial intelligence and collaboration.

Some of the key lessons that will be discussed include the importance of providing financial education to employees, the value of cross-functional teams, and the need for open communication and collaboration between departments. Additionally, the case studies will demonstrate the benefits of fostering a culture of innovation and risk-taking, and the importance of using financial analytics tools to make informed financial decisions.

Conclusion

In conclusion, building a culture of financial intelligence and collaboration is essential for organizations that want to succeed in today's fast-paced and competitive business environment. By developing a financial literacy program for employees, promoting cross-functional teams, and encouraging open communication and collaboration between departments, organizations can achieve better financial performance and reduce the risk of financial losses.

Moreover, it is crucial to create a culture of innovation and risk-taking, where employees are encouraged to come up with new ideas and take calculated risks. Organizations can also benefit from using financial analytics tools to make informed decisions about investments, cost-cutting measures, and other financial decisions.

Through the case studies and examples provided in this chapter, students will gain a deeper understanding of how these techniques have been successfully applied in real-world situations. By learning from the experiences of successful companies and leaders, students will be better equipped to build a culture of financial intelligence and collaboration within their own organizations.

Overall, the techniques discussed in this chapter are critical for any organization seeking to improve its financial performance, mitigate risk, and achieve long-term success. By embracing financial intelligence and collaboration, organizations can stay ahead of the curve and position themselves for continued growth and profitability in the years to come.

Strategies for fostering a culture of financial intelligence and collaboration

Building a culture of financial intelligence and collaboration requires a multifaceted approach that involves education, cross-functional teams, open communication, and a willingness to take calculated risks. In this section, we will discuss some of the key strategies that organizations can use to foster this type of culture.

Providing Financial Education to Employees
One of the most important strategies for building a culture of financial intelligence is providing financial education to employees at all levels of the organization. This education can take many forms, such as workshops, training sessions, or online courses. The goal is to help employees understand the basics of financial management, including budgeting, cash flow management, and financial analysis. This knowledge can then be applied to their specific roles within the organization, helping them make more informed financial decisions and understand how their actions impact the overall financial health of the company.

For example, a marketing manager who understands the financial implications of a new product launch can make better decisions about pricing and promotion, while an HR manager who understands the cost of employee benefits can make more informed decisions about compensation and benefits packages.

Creating Cross-Functional Teams

Another important strategy for building a culture of financial intelligence and collaboration is creating cross-functional teams that include representatives from different departments. These teams can work together to identify financial opportunities and risks, develop budgets and forecasts, and make informed decisions about resource allocation.

By involving employees from different departments in financial decision-making, organizations can break down silos and promote collaboration. For example, a cross-functional team that includes representatives from finance, marketing, and operations can work together to develop a product launch strategy that takes into account both financial and operational considerations.

Encouraging Open Communication and Collaboration
Open communication and collaboration are essential for building a culture of financial intelligence. Organizations should encourage employees to share information, ideas, and feedback across departments, and should create an environment where open dialogue is valued.

One way to promote open communication is through regular meetings and updates that bring together employees from different departments. For example, a monthly meeting that includes representatives from finance, marketing, and operations can provide an opportunity for these departments to share updates and discuss financial implications.

Fostering a Culture of Innovation and Risk-Taking
Organizations that foster a culture of innovation and risk-taking are more likely to be successful in building a culture of financial intelligence. This means encouraging employees to think creatively and take calculated risks, while also providing them with the tools and resources they need to make informed decisions.

One way to foster a culture of innovation is to encourage employees to come up with new ideas and initiatives, and to provide them with the support they need to bring these ideas to fruition. This might include providing funding for pilot projects, offering training and development opportunities, or creating a culture where failure is seen as a learning opportunity.

Using Financial Analytics Tools
Finally, organizations can use financial analytics tools to make more informed financial decisions and monitor their financial performance. These tools can help organizations identify trends, track key metrics, and make data-driven decisions.

For example, a financial analytics tool might be used to track customer acquisition costs, monitor sales trends, or analyze the effectiveness of marketing campaigns. By using these tools, organizations can make more informed decisions about resource allocation and identify areas where they can improve their financial performance.

Conclusion

Fostering a culture of financial intelligence and collaboration is essential for organizations that want to succeed in today's business environment. By providing financial education to employees, creating cross-functional teams, encouraging open communication and collaboration, fostering a culture of innovation and risk-taking, and using financial analytics tools, organizations can build a culture that promotes informed financial decision-making and collaboration across departments. These strategies require a long-term commitment and a willingness to invest in the development of employees, but they can yield significant benefits in terms of improved financial performance, better risk management, and increased employee satisfaction.

Here are some specific strategies that organizations can use to build a culture of financial intelligence and collaboration:

Provide Financial Education: One of the most effective ways to build financial intelligence among employees is to provide financial education and training. This can include workshops, online courses, and other resources that teach employees the basics of finance and accounting, as well as more advanced topics like financial analysis and budgeting. By giving employees the tools they need to understand financial information and make informed decisions, organizations can foster a culture of financial intelligence and collaboration.

Create Cross-functional Teams: Another key strategy for building a culture of collaboration is to create cross-functional teams that bring together employees from different departments to work on common goals. These teams can include representatives from finance, marketing, human resources, and other departments, and can be tasked with projects like developing new products, improving customer service, or reducing costs. By working together on these projects, employees can learn from one another and gain a better understanding of how their department fits into the broader financial picture of the organization.

Encourage Open Communication and Collaboration: In addition to creating cross-functional teams, organizations need to encourage open communication and collaboration between departments. This can involve regular meetings between finance and other departments to discuss financial goals and strategies, as well as open channels of communication like internal social media platforms or company-wide newsletters. By fostering a culture of open communication, organizations can ensure that everyone has access to the information they need to make informed decisions and contribute to the financial success of the organization.

Foster a Culture of Innovation and Risk-taking: Organizations that want to succeed in today's business environment need to be willing to take risks and try new things. By fostering a culture of innovation and risk-taking, organizations can encourage employees to come up with new ideas and solutions to financial challenges. This can involve giving employees the freedom to experiment and try new things, as well as recognizing and rewarding employees for their innovative ideas and contributions.

Use Financial Analytics Tools: Finally, organizations need to invest in financial analytics tools that can help them make informed financial decisions. These tools can include software that tracks financial performance and identifies trends, as well as predictive analytics tools that can help organizations forecast future financial outcomes. By using these tools, organizations can make data-driven decisions that are based on objective financial information, rather than subjective opinions or assumptions.

In summary, building a culture of financial intelligence and collaboration requires a commitment to providing financial education to employees, creating cross-functional teams, encouraging open communication and collaboration, fostering a culture of innovation and risk-taking, and investing in financial analytics tools. By implementing these strategies, organizations can build a culture that promotes informed financial decision-making and collaboration across departments, ultimately leading to improved financial performance and increased employee satisfaction.

Techniques for training and educating employees on financial concepts and their importance

In today's fast-paced and competitive business environment, it is becoming increasingly important for employees at all levels to have a basic understanding of financial concepts and how they relate to the company's overall success. This is especially true for individuals who work in departments that directly impact the company's financial performance, such as finance, accounting, and operations. In order to foster a culture of financial intelligence and collaboration within an organization, it is essential to provide employees with the necessary training and education on financial concepts and their importance.

Techniques for Training and Educating Employees on Financial Concepts

Develop a Financial Education Program

Developing a comprehensive financial education program is a critical first step in educating employees on financial concepts. This program should be designed to provide employees with a basic understanding of financial statements, budgeting, forecasting, and other essential financial concepts. The program should be tailored to meet the specific needs of the organization and should be delivered in a way that is engaging and easy to understand.

One effective way to deliver financial education is through interactive workshops and training sessions. These sessions should be led by experienced financial professionals and should include real-world examples and case studies to help employees understand how financial concepts relate to their job responsibilities.

Provide Access to Online Training Resources

In addition to interactive workshops and training sessions, providing employees with access to online training resources is another effective way to educate employees on financial concepts. There are a wide range of online training resources available, ranging from self-paced courses to webinars and online workshops.

These resources can be especially useful for employees who work remotely or have busy schedules, as they can access the training on their own time. Many online training resources also offer certification programs, which can help employees demonstrate their proficiency in financial concepts.

Provide On-the-Job Training Opportunities

Another effective way to educate employees on financial concepts is by providing on-the-job training opportunities. This can include job shadowing, cross-functional training, and mentoring programs. By providing employees with hands-on experience in financial decision-making processes, they can gain a deeper understanding of how financial concepts impact the organization's success.

Job shadowing and cross-functional training can be especially effective in helping employees gain a broader perspective on the organization's financial operations. Mentoring programs can also be beneficial, as they provide employees with one-on-one guidance and support from experienced financial professionals.

Incorporate Financial Education into Performance Reviews

Incorporating financial education into performance reviews is another effective way to ensure that employees are receiving the necessary training and education on financial concepts. This can be done by including financial performance metrics as part of the performance review process, and by providing feedback and coaching on areas where employees need improvement.

By incorporating financial education into performance reviews, organizations can create a culture where financial literacy is seen as an essential skill for all employees, not just those in finance and accounting roles.

Encourage Continuous Learning

Finally, it is important to encourage employees to engage in continuous learning and professional development opportunities. This can include attending industry conferences, participating in networking events, and pursuing advanced degrees or certifications.

Encouraging continuous learning can help employees stay up-to-date on the latest financial trends and best practices, and can help them develop new skills and knowledge that can be applied to their job responsibilities.

Conclusion

In conclusion, providing employees with the necessary training and education on financial concepts is essential for building a culture of financial intelligence and collaboration within an organization. By developing a comprehensive financial education program, providing access to online training resources, providing on-the-job training opportunities, incorporating financial education into performance reviews, and encouraging continuous learning, organizations can ensure that employees at all levels have the necessary knowledge and skills to make informed financial decisions and contribute to the company's overall success.

Best practices for building cross-functional teams and promoting collaboration within an organization

Organizations today face complex challenges that require collaboration between different departments and functions. Building cross-functional teams is one of the most effective ways to promote collaboration and ensure that different perspectives and expertise are brought to bear on organizational problems. In this section, we will explore the best practices for building cross-functional teams and promoting collaboration within an organization.

Define the problem

Before building a cross-functional team, it is important to define the problem that the team will be working on. This ensures that the team is focused and aligned on the problem at hand. The problem should be defined clearly and concisely and should be communicated to all team members.

Identify the right team members

Once the problem has been defined, the next step is to identify the right team members. The team should be composed of individuals from different departments and functions who have the necessary expertise to solve the problem at hand. It is also important to consider the personality traits and work styles of team members to ensure that they will work well together.

Establish clear goals and objectives

Clear goals and objectives are essential for ensuring that the team is aligned and working towards a common goal. The goals and objectives should be specific, measurable, achievable, relevant, and time-bound (SMART). They should also be communicated clearly to all team members.

Provide adequate resources

Cross-functional teams require adequate resources to be successful. This includes financial resources, time, and support from senior leadership. It is important to ensure that the team has access to the resources they need to carry out their work effectively.

Encourage open communication

Open communication is essential for cross-functional teams to be successful. Team members should feel comfortable sharing their ideas and opinions and should be encouraged to do so. This ensures that all perspectives are considered and that the team can make informed decisions.

Foster a culture of collaboration

Fostering a culture of collaboration is essential for cross-functional teams to be successful. This includes encouraging teamwork, recognizing and rewarding collaboration, and promoting a sense of shared purpose.

Provide training and development opportunities

Training and development opportunities are important for building the skills and knowledge necessary for effective collaboration. This includes training on communication, problem-solving, and conflict resolution.

Evaluate and adapt

Finally, it is important to regularly evaluate the performance of cross-functional teams and adapt as necessary. This ensures that the team is continuously improving and that lessons learned are applied to future projects.

Examples

One example of a company that has successfully built cross-functional teams and promoted collaboration is Procter & Gamble (P&G). P&G established a corporate-wide program called "Connect and Develop" that encourages collaboration between different departments and functions to drive innovation. This program has led to significant cost savings and revenue growth for the company.

Another example is the healthcare company Johnson & Johnson (J&J). J&J has a strong culture of collaboration and cross-functional teams, which has been instrumental in the company's success. J&J has established cross-functional teams for a variety of purposes, including new product development and supply chain management.

Exercises

Identify a problem in your organization that could benefit from a cross-functional team approach. Define the problem clearly and concisely.

Identify the right team members for your cross-functional team. What expertise is needed? What personality traits and work styles should you consider?

Establish clear goals and objectives for your cross-functional team. Make sure they are specific, measurable, achievable, relevant, and time-bound.

Identify the resources that your cross-functional team will need to be successful. What financial resources, time, and support from senior leadership will be required?

Develop a plan for fostering open communication and collaboration within the cross-functional team. How will team members communicate with each other? How will conflicts be resolved? What tools and technologies will be used to facilitate communication and collaboration?

Create a process for decision-making within the cross-functional team. Will decisions be made by consensus or by a designated leader? How will disagreements be resolved? Who will be responsible for making final decisions?

Design a feedback mechanism to assess the performance of the cross-functional team. How will progress be measured? What metrics will be used? Who will be responsible for providing feedback to team members?

Evaluate the success of your cross-functional team. Did it achieve its goals? Were team members able to work collaboratively and effectively across departments? What improvements could be made for future cross-functional teams?

Conclusion

Building cross-functional teams and promoting collaboration within an organization is critical for achieving success in today's business environment. By identifying the right team members, establishing clear goals and objectives, providing necessary resources, fostering open communication and collaboration, creating a process for decision-making, and designing a feedback mechanism, organizations can build cross-functional teams that are able to work effectively across departments and achieve their goals. These best practices require a long-term commitment and a willingness to invest in the development of employees, but the benefits of effective collaboration can be substantial, including increased innovation, improved decision-making, and better overall performance.

Lessons learned from these case studies and examples

The case studies and examples we have discussed in this section demonstrate the importance of building cross-functional teams and promoting collaboration within an organization. They also highlight the challenges that organizations may face in this process and the strategies they can use to overcome them. In this final section, we will summarize the key lessons learned from these case studies and examples.

Lesson 1: Clear goals and objectives are critical for success

One of the most important lessons learned from these case studies and examples is that clear goals and objectives are critical for success. Without clear goals and objectives, cross-functional teams can easily become unfocused and inefficient. The goals and objectives should be specific, measurable, achievable, relevant, and time-bound. When everyone on the team is clear on what they are trying to achieve and how their contribution fits into the larger picture, they are more likely to work together effectively.

Lesson 2: Communication and collaboration are essential

Effective communication and collaboration are essential for building successful cross-functional teams. Teams should be encouraged to share information openly and work together to solve problems. Regular team meetings, progress reports, and open-door policies can help to facilitate communication and collaboration. It's also important to encourage team members to be open to new ideas and perspectives.

Lesson 3: Diversity is a strength

The case studies and examples we have discussed demonstrate the strength of diversity in cross-functional teams. When teams are made up of individuals with different backgrounds, experiences, and perspectives, they are more likely to generate innovative ideas and solutions. Diversity also helps to prevent groupthink and ensure that all aspects of the problem are considered.

Lesson 4: Leadership support is crucial

Leadership support is crucial for the success of cross-functional teams. Senior leaders should provide the necessary resources and support to help the team achieve its goals. This includes financial resources, time, and the necessary tools and technologies. Leaders should also be visible and actively engaged in the team's work, providing guidance and feedback as needed.

Lesson 5: Building trust takes time

Finally, building trust among team members takes time. Trust is essential for effective communication and collaboration, and it can only be built through consistent effort over time. Team members should be encouraged to get to know each other on a personal level and to build relationships based on mutual respect and trust.

Exercises:

Identify a cross-functional team that you have been a part of or have observed. What were the goals and objectives of the team? Were they clear and specific? How did communication and collaboration contribute to the success or failure of the team?

Identify a company that has been successful in building cross-functional teams. What strategies did they use to build trust among team members and encourage communication and collaboration?

Identify a company that has struggled to build cross-functional teams. What were the challenges they faced? What strategies could they have used to overcome these challenges?

Identify a situation in which diversity was a strength in a cross-functional team. How did the team members' diverse backgrounds and experiences contribute to the success of the team?

Identify a situation in which leadership support was crucial for the success of a cross-functional team. How did senior leaders provide the necessary resources and support to help the team achieve its goals?

PART 8: CONCLUSION

In this book, we have explored a variety of topics related to business and finance, ranging from financial statements and analysis to risk management and strategic planning. Throughout our discussions, we have emphasized the importance of a holistic and integrated approach to managing a business, one that takes into account the various functional areas and stakeholders involved.

We began by examining the basics of financial statements and analysis, including the balance sheet, income statement, and cash flow statement. We discussed the various ratios and metrics used to assess a company's financial performance, and how to use this information to make informed decisions.

Next, we turned to the topic of financial management, including budgeting, forecasting, and capital budgeting. We explored the different sources of financing available to businesses, as well as the various risks associated with different types of financing.

We then delved into the topic of risk management, including the identification and assessment of risks, as well as strategies for mitigating and transferring risks. We discussed the importance of developing a comprehensive risk management plan, and how to implement this plan effectively.

In Part 5, we focused on strategic planning, including the development of a vision and mission statement, the identification of core values and strategic goals, and the creation of a strategic plan. We discussed the importance of aligning the strategic plan with the overall mission and values of the organization, as well as the need for ongoing monitoring and evaluation.

In Part 6, we explored the topic of leadership and management, including the various leadership styles and their respective strengths and weaknesses. We discussed the importance of developing strong communication skills, building effective teams, and fostering a positive organizational culture.

Part 7 focused on specific industries and business contexts, including entrepreneurship, corporate finance, and international business. We explored the unique challenges and opportunities faced by businesses in these contexts, and how to adapt and thrive in these environments.

Finally, in this section, we have examined several case studies and examples of best practices in business and finance. We have seen how businesses can leverage technology and innovation to drive growth, and how a cross-functional team approach can lead to better decision-making and collaboration.

Overall, this book has provided a comprehensive overview of the key concepts and practices involved in managing a successful business. We hope that the insights and strategies presented in this book will help you to navigate the complex and ever-changing world of business and finance, and to achieve your goals and aspirations.

CHAPTER 23: RECAP OF KEY CONCEPTS

Throughout this textbook, we have explored a wide range of topics related to business strategy, finance, accounting, marketing, operations, and organizational behavior. In this final chapter, we will summarize some of the key concepts and themes that have emerged in our discussions.

Business Strategy

In the section on business strategy, we discussed the importance of aligning the organization's vision, mission, and values with its strategy. We also examined different approaches to strategy development, including SWOT analysis, Porter's Five Forces, and the Balanced Scorecard. Additionally, we explored the role of innovation, creativity, and risk-taking in strategic decision-making.

Finance and Accounting

The finance and accounting section of the textbook provided an overview of financial statements, ratio analysis, budgeting, and capital budgeting. We also examined various methods of financing, such as debt financing, equity financing, and leasing. In addition, we discussed the importance of financial planning and forecasting for effective financial management.

Marketing

In the marketing section of the textbook, we discussed the key elements of the marketing mix: product, price, promotion, and place. We also examined the role of market research, segmentation, targeting, and positioning in developing effective marketing strategies. Additionally, we explored the impact of digital marketing and social media on modern marketing practices.

Operations

The operations section of the textbook focused on the various aspects of managing the production and delivery of goods and services. We discussed topics such as process design, capacity planning, inventory management, and quality control. Additionally, we explored the importance of lean management, Six Sigma, and total quality management in improving operational efficiency and effectiveness.

Organizational Behavior

The final section of the textbook focused on the study of organizational behavior, which examines how individuals, groups, and organizations interact and influence one another. We discussed topics such as motivation, leadership, communication, teamwork, and diversity. Additionally, we explored the importance of ethical behavior, corporate social responsibility, and sustainability in shaping organizational culture and behavior.

Conclusion

In conclusion, this textbook has provided a comprehensive overview of the key concepts and practices in business. By examining a wide range of topics across different functional areas, we have provided students with a holistic understanding of how businesses operate and succeed in today's complex and dynamic environment. We hope that the knowledge and skills gained from this textbook will empower students to make informed decisions and contribute to the success of organizations in the future.

Summary of the key concepts and topics covered in the book

Throughout this book, we have explored a wide range of concepts and topics related to the world of business, finance, and entrepreneurship. From financial analysis and accounting to legal considerations and regulatory compliance, we have covered a broad array of issues that are critical to success in today's business landscape. In this section, we will provide a summary of the key concepts and topics covered in the book.

Financial Analysis and Accounting

One of the key themes running throughout this book is the importance of financial analysis and accounting in the world of business. We have explored topics such as financial statement analysis, budgeting, cash flow management, and financial modeling. We have also discussed various accounting principles, including the principles of accrual accounting, the matching principle, and the revenue recognition principle.

Legal Considerations

Another major theme of this book has been the importance of understanding the legal considerations involved in business. We have examined topics such as contract law, intellectual property law, and employment law. We have also discussed the role of compliance officers and in-house legal departments in ensuring that businesses operate within the boundaries of the law.

Regulatory Compliance

Closely related to legal considerations are the issues of regulatory compliance. We have explored topics such as the role of the Securities and Exchange Commission (SEC), the Sarbanes-Oxley Act, and the Foreign Corrupt Practices Act. We have also discussed the importance of ethics and corporate social responsibility in ensuring that businesses act in an ethical and responsible manner.

Entrepreneurship

Throughout this book, we have explored the world of entrepreneurship, from the process of starting a business to the challenges of growing and scaling a business. We have discussed topics such as venture capital financing, the role of the entrepreneur, and the importance of market research and customer validation.

Corporate Finance

We have also delved into the world of corporate finance, exploring topics such as capital structure, dividend policy, and financial planning and analysis. We have discussed the role of investment bankers and financial analysts in advising companies on these issues.

Conclusion

In conclusion, this book has covered a broad array of concepts and topics that are critical to success in today's business landscape. From financial analysis and accounting to legal considerations and regulatory compliance, entrepreneurs, executives, lawyers, and financial analysts must understand these concepts to succeed in their roles. By providing a thorough overview of these topics, we hope that this book has provided a valuable resource for students seeking to enter these fields and for professionals seeking to advance their careers.

Importance of understanding the intersection of finance with marketing, customer service, human resources, and CRM for financial success

The field of finance has traditionally been seen as a separate entity from other aspects of business, such as marketing, customer service, human resources, and customer relationship management (CRM). However, it is becoming increasingly clear that understanding the intersection of finance with these areas is crucial for financial success.

Marketing and Finance:
Marketing and finance are two sides of the same coin. Marketing provides the crucial insights into customer needs and preferences that drive financial success, while finance provides the resources to invest in marketing and measure its effectiveness. Financial analysis and forecasting are essential tools for marketing strategy development, and understanding financial metrics is critical for marketers to make informed decisions about advertising, promotion, and pricing.

Customer Service and Finance:
Customer service plays a vital role in customer retention, and customer retention is essential for financial success. Companies that provide excellent customer service have higher customer retention rates, which translates into higher revenue and profitability. Finance plays a critical role in customer service by providing the resources necessary to invest in customer service training, technology, and infrastructure. Financial analysis can also help companies identify the most profitable customers and tailor their customer service efforts accordingly.

Human Resources and Finance:
Human resources are a crucial factor in financial success. A company's success depends on its ability to attract, retain, and develop talented employees. Finance plays a crucial role in human resource management by providing the resources necessary to invest in recruitment, training, and development. Financial analysis can also help companies identify the most cost-effective ways to manage their workforce and optimize their human resource investment.

CRM and Finance:

Customer relationship management (CRM) is the process of managing customer interactions and relationships to maximize customer loyalty and profitability. Finance plays a critical role in CRM by providing the resources necessary to invest in CRM technology and infrastructure. Financial analysis can also help companies identify the most profitable customer segments and tailor their CRM efforts accordingly.

In conclusion, understanding the intersection of finance with marketing, customer service, human resources, and CRM is essential for financial success. Financial analysis and forecasting are essential tools for developing strategies in these areas, and finance provides the resources necessary to invest in these areas. By understanding the importance of finance in these areas, businesses can maximize their financial success and achieve long-term sustainability.

CHAPTER 24: THE IMPORTANCE OF FINANCIAL INTELLIGENCE FOR NON-FINANCIAL PROFESSIONALS

In today's business environment, it is essential for non-financial professionals to have financial intelligence to be successful in their careers. Financial intelligence is the ability to understand financial information, analyze it, and use it to make informed business decisions. The importance of financial intelligence cannot be overstated, as financial data impacts every aspect of a business. From marketing to customer service, human resources to CRM, financial data is integral to decision-making in each of these areas. Therefore, in this chapter, we will discuss the importance of financial intelligence for non-financial professionals, its impact on various departments, and ways to improve financial intelligence.

Importance of Financial Intelligence

The ability to understand and analyze financial data is a vital skill for non-financial professionals. Financial intelligence helps non-financial professionals understand how their decisions impact the financial health of the company. By having this knowledge, non-financial professionals can make informed decisions that benefit the company's bottom line.

One of the critical aspects of financial intelligence is understanding financial statements. Financial statements provide a wealth of information about a company's financial health, including its profitability, liquidity, and solvency. Non-financial professionals who can read and interpret financial statements can better understand the financial health of their company and make informed decisions.

Another important aspect of financial intelligence is understanding financial metrics. Financial metrics are quantitative measurements that assess a company's financial performance. Examples of financial metrics include earnings per share, return on investment, and profit margins. Non-financial professionals who understand financial metrics can better understand how their department contributes to the company's financial success.

Impact on Marketing

Financial intelligence is essential for marketing professionals because marketing decisions can have a significant impact on a company's financial performance. For example, marketing decisions such as pricing strategies, advertising expenditures, and product development costs can impact a company's profitability. Marketing professionals who understand financial intelligence can make informed decisions about pricing, advertising, and product development that benefit the company's bottom line.

Impact on Customer Service

Financial intelligence is also critical for customer service professionals because their decisions impact a company's revenue. Customer service decisions such as refund policies, pricing negotiations, and product warranties can impact a company's revenue. Customer service professionals who understand financial intelligence can make informed decisions about refund policies, pricing negotiations, and product warranties that benefit the company's bottom line.

Impact on Human Resources

Financial intelligence is also essential for human resources professionals because their decisions impact a company's financial health. Human resources decisions such as employee benefits, compensation packages, and hiring decisions can impact a company's profitability. Human resources professionals who understand financial intelligence can make informed decisions about employee benefits, compensation packages, and hiring decisions that benefit the company's bottom line.

Impact on CRM

Financial intelligence is also important for CRM professionals because their decisions impact a company's revenue. CRM decisions such as customer acquisition costs, customer retention rates, and customer lifetime value can impact a company's revenue. CRM professionals who understand financial intelligence can make informed decisions about customer acquisition costs, customer retention rates, and customer lifetime value that benefit the company's bottom line.

Ways to Improve Financial Intelligence

There are several ways non-financial professionals can improve their financial intelligence. First, non-financial professionals can take courses in finance, accounting, and economics to gain a better understanding of financial concepts. Second, non-financial professionals can attend seminars and workshops to learn about financial analysis and financial reporting. Third, non-financial professionals can work closely with financial professionals to gain a better understanding of financial data and financial reporting. Fourth, non-financial professionals can read financial reports and financial news to stay up-to-date on financial trends and developments.

Conclusion

In conclusion, financial intelligence is a vital skill for non-financial professionals in today's business environment. Non-financial professionals who understand financial concepts, financial statements, and financial metrics can make better-informed decisions that can help drive the success of their organization. By being able to understand and interpret financial information, non-financial professionals can effectively communicate with their colleagues, work more efficiently, and contribute more to the bottom line.

In this chapter, we have discussed the key concepts of financial intelligence for non-financial professionals. We have explored financial statements, financial metrics, budgeting, and forecasting, among other topics. We have also provided examples of how financial intelligence can be applied in real-world situations.

It is important to note that financial intelligence is not just about knowing the numbers. It also involves the ability to use financial information to make sound decisions and to communicate effectively with colleagues who have different backgrounds and skill sets. Non-financial professionals who develop financial intelligence skills can help bridge the gap between finance and other areas of the organization.

As the business environment becomes increasingly complex and interconnected, the importance of financial intelligence for non-financial professionals will only continue to grow. By developing financial intelligence skills, non-financial professionals can enhance their value to their organizations and position themselves for future career success.

In conclusion, financial intelligence is an essential skill for non-financial professionals, and it is worth investing the time and effort to develop these skills. By doing so, non-financial professionals can become more effective and valuable contributors to their organizations, and they can also enhance their own career prospects.

The importance of financial intelligence for all professionals, regardless of their role

In today's fast-paced business environment, financial intelligence has become an essential skill for all professionals, regardless of their roles. Financial intelligence refers to the ability to understand financial concepts and effectively use financial data to make informed decisions. It is crucial for professionals to have a basic understanding of finance, including financial statements, metrics, and analysis, to excel in their careers.

This section aims to explore the importance of financial intelligence for all professionals and provide practical tips on how to enhance financial acumen. It will examine why financial intelligence is necessary, the benefits of financial intelligence, and the potential consequences of lacking financial literacy.

Importance of Financial Intelligence:

In today's business environment, financial intelligence is essential for all professionals, regardless of their roles. Many non-financial professionals assume that financial intelligence is only necessary for those in finance-related positions, but this is not the case. Understanding financial statements, metrics, and analysis is essential for professionals to make informed decisions, manage budgets, and effectively communicate with stakeholders.

Financial intelligence is necessary for professionals in all industries, from healthcare to technology. In healthcare, understanding financial data is critical for healthcare providers to make informed decisions and improve patient care. In technology, financial intelligence is essential for project managers to estimate budgets, manage costs, and assess profitability. Regardless of the industry, financial intelligence is necessary to make informed decisions and effectively communicate with stakeholders.

Benefits of Financial Intelligence:

There are several benefits to having financial intelligence as a professional. First, financial intelligence allows professionals to make informed decisions based on financial data. With financial intelligence, professionals can analyze financial data, identify trends, and make predictions about the future.

Second, financial intelligence enables professionals to manage budgets and control costs effectively. Budgeting is a critical aspect of financial management, and professionals who understand financial data can develop realistic budgets and monitor their progress effectively. Effective budget management can help organizations achieve their financial goals, improve profitability, and increase shareholder value.

Third, financial intelligence can help professionals communicate effectively with stakeholders. Financial data is a universal language that all stakeholders can understand. Professionals who can effectively communicate financial data to stakeholders can build trust and credibility and improve their professional reputation.

Consequences of Lacking Financial Intelligence:

Lacking financial intelligence can have several negative consequences for professionals. First, it can lead to poor decision-making. Professionals who lack financial intelligence may make decisions based on incomplete or inaccurate financial data, which can lead to negative consequences for the organization.

Second, lacking financial intelligence can result in financial mismanagement. Without a basic understanding of financial concepts, professionals may mismanage budgets, overspend, or fail to allocate resources effectively. This can lead to financial losses for the organization and affect its long-term viability.

Third, lacking financial intelligence can damage professional reputation. Professionals who cannot effectively communicate financial data may be seen as less credible and trustworthy by stakeholders. This can negatively impact their careers and opportunities for advancement.

Practical Tips for Enhancing Financial Intelligence:

There are several practical tips that professionals can use to enhance their financial intelligence. First, they can take courses or attend workshops on financial management. This can provide them with a solid foundation in financial concepts and metrics.

Second, professionals can seek mentorship from financial experts. Mentors can provide valuable guidance and advice on financial management and analysis.

Third, professionals can read financial publications, such as The Wall Street Journal or Forbes, to stay up-to-date on financial trends and analysis.

Fourth, professionals can attend financial meetings or conferences to network with financial experts and learn about best practices in financial management.

Conclusion:

Financial intelligence is essential for all professionals in today's business environment. It enables professionals to make informed decisions, manage budgets effectively, and communicate with stakeholders. Lacking financial intelligence can lead to poor decision-making, financial mismanagement, and damage to professional reputation. By taking courses, seeking mentorship, reading financial literature, and actively engaging in financial discussions, professionals can develop financial intelligence and enhance their career prospects.

Financial intelligence is not just the responsibility of financial professionals. All professionals, regardless of their role, can benefit from developing financial intelligence. For instance, marketing professionals can use financial intelligence to understand the costs and benefits of different marketing campaigns and strategies. Customer service professionals can use financial intelligence to identify ways to reduce costs while maintaining high-quality service. Human resources professionals can use financial intelligence to develop and manage budgets for employee training and development programs. Additionally, financial intelligence is particularly important for entrepreneurs and small business owners who are often responsible for managing their own finances and making critical financial decisions.

In today's rapidly changing business environment, financial intelligence is more important than ever. Technological advances, global competition, and shifting market trends are just a few of the factors that require professionals to have a deep understanding of financial concepts and metrics. Without financial intelligence, professionals risk falling behind their peers and missing out on career opportunities.

In order to develop financial intelligence, professionals must be proactive in seeking out opportunities to learn and practice financial skills. This can involve taking courses in finance, seeking mentorship from financial professionals, reading financial literature, and actively engaging in financial discussions with colleagues and stakeholders.

Furthermore, it is important for organizations to recognize the importance of financial intelligence and invest in developing the financial skills of their employees. This can include providing training programs, mentorship opportunities, and access to financial resources and tools.

In conclusion, financial intelligence is a critical skill for all professionals. By developing financial intelligence, professionals can make informed decisions, manage budgets effectively, and communicate with stakeholders. Organizations must recognize the importance of financial intelligence and invest in developing the financial skills of their employees. In today's rapidly changing business environment, financial intelligence is more important than ever and can provide a competitive advantage for professionals and organizations alike.

Benefits of having a basic understanding of financial concepts and their impact on business decisions

In today's business environment, it is essential for professionals to have a basic understanding of financial concepts and their impact on business decisions. Financial concepts provide a framework for understanding the financial health of an organization and can help professionals make informed decisions that lead to financial success. In this section, we will discuss the benefits of having a basic understanding of financial concepts and how they can impact business decisions.

Benefits of Understanding Financial Concepts

Improved Decision Making
One of the primary benefits of understanding financial concepts is improved decision-making. Financial statements such as income statements, balance sheets, and cash flow statements provide valuable information about an organization's financial health. By understanding these financial statements, professionals can make informed decisions about investments, expenses, and revenue. For example, if a company has a high debt-to-equity ratio, it may be more risky to invest in the company. By understanding this financial concept, professionals can make better investment decisions.

Effective Budgeting

Another benefit of understanding financial concepts is effective budgeting. Budgeting is a critical process in any organization, and financial concepts such as revenue, expenses, and cash flow are essential components of the budgeting process. By understanding these financial concepts, professionals can create realistic budgets that align with the organization's financial goals. Effective budgeting can help organizations control expenses, maximize revenue, and ultimately lead to financial success.

Effective Communication with Stakeholders

Effective communication is critical to the success of any organization, and financial concepts play a significant role in effective communication with stakeholders. Stakeholders such as investors, lenders, and board members rely on financial information to make informed decisions about the organization. By understanding financial concepts and being able to communicate financial information effectively, professionals can build trust with stakeholders and ensure that they have the information they need to make informed decisions.

Competitive Advantage

Having a basic understanding of financial concepts can also provide a competitive advantage in the business world. In many industries, businesses are competing against one another for customers and market share. By understanding financial concepts, professionals can make strategic decisions that lead to financial success and help their organization stand out in a competitive marketplace. For example, if a company has a lower cost of goods sold than its competitors, it may be able to offer lower prices to customers and gain a competitive advantage.

Increased Career Opportunities

Finally, having a basic understanding of financial concepts can lead to increased career opportunities. Many employers value financial skills and look for candidates who have a basic understanding of financial concepts. By having these skills, professionals can stand out in the job market and be better positioned for career advancement.

Examples of Financial Concepts and Their Impact on Business Decisions

Revenue

Revenue is a critical financial concept that impacts many business decisions. Revenue is the income generated by an organization through the sale of goods or services. By understanding revenue, professionals can make informed decisions about pricing, marketing, and sales strategies. For example, if a company wants to increase its revenue, it may need to consider lowering prices, increasing marketing efforts, or expanding its product line.

Expenses

Expenses are another critical financial concept that impacts business decisions. Expenses are the costs associated with running an organization, such as salaries, rent, and supplies. By understanding expenses, professionals can make informed decisions about cost-cutting measures, such as reducing staff or renegotiating vendor contracts. Effective cost management can help organizations maximize profits and lead to financial success.

Cash Flow

Cash flow is the amount of cash that flows in and out of an organization over a specific period. Understanding cash flow is critical to effective budgeting and financial management. By understanding cash flow, professionals can make informed decisions about investments, expenses, and revenue. For example, if a company has a negative cash flow, it may need to consider reducing expenses or increasing revenue to improve its financial situation. On the other hand, a positive cash flow can allow a company to invest in growth opportunities or pay off debt.

In addition to budgeting and financial management, understanding cash flow is essential for evaluating the financial health of a company. It can provide insight into a company's ability to meet its financial obligations, such as paying off debt or meeting payroll. Cash flow analysis is also critical for making investment decisions. For example, investors often use cash flow analysis to evaluate the potential return on investment and assess the financial risks of investing in a particular company.

Another critical financial concept is risk management. Risk management is the process of identifying, assessing, and managing risks that can affect an organization's financial performance. By understanding risk management, professionals can make informed decisions about managing financial risks and protecting their organization's financial health. For example, risk management may involve assessing the financial risks of investing in a particular market, identifying potential legal or regulatory risks, or developing strategies for managing financial risks such as fluctuations in currency exchange rates.

Overall, having a basic understanding of financial concepts and their impact on business decisions is essential for all professionals, regardless of their role. It enables professionals to make informed decisions, communicate effectively with stakeholders, and manage budgets effectively. By developing financial intelligence, professionals can enhance their career prospects, build their reputation, and contribute to the financial health of their organization.

CHAPTER 25: FINAL THOUGHTS AND RECOMMENDATIONS FOR FURTHER LEARNING

As we conclude this textbook on financial intelligence for non-financial professionals, it is important to reflect on the key takeaways and recommendations for further learning. Throughout this textbook, we have explored various financial concepts and their impact on business decisions. We have also discussed the benefits of having a basic understanding of financial concepts and the importance of financial intelligence for all professionals, regardless of their role.

In this final chapter, we will provide some final thoughts and recommendations for further learning to help non-financial professionals continue to develop their financial intelligence. We will also address some common challenges that non-financial professionals face when it comes to financial intelligence and provide some strategies for overcoming these challenges.

Final Thoughts:

As we have discussed throughout this textbook, financial intelligence is a critical skill for all professionals. It enables professionals to make informed decisions, manage budgets effectively, and communicate with stakeholders. Lacking financial intelligence can lead to poor decision-making, financial mismanagement, and damage to professional reputation.

To develop financial intelligence, it is essential to continue learning and practicing financial concepts. Professionals can take courses, seek mentorship, read financial publications, and engage in financial conversations with colleagues to improve their financial intelligence.

One key recommendation for further learning is to develop a deeper understanding of financial statements. Financial statements provide critical information about an organization's financial health and are essential for decision-making. By understanding financial statements, professionals can make informed decisions about investments, expenses, and revenue.

Another important recommendation for further learning is to stay informed about changes in financial regulations and industry standards. Financial regulations are constantly evolving, and it is essential to stay up-to-date to ensure compliance and avoid financial penalties.

Challenges and Strategies:

Despite the benefits of financial intelligence, many non-financial professionals struggle to develop this skill. Some common challenges include a lack of time, resources, and motivation. However, there are strategies that professionals can use to overcome these challenges.

One strategy is to start small and build gradually. Professionals can begin by learning basic financial concepts and gradually increase their knowledge and skills over time. This approach can help to avoid overwhelm and increase motivation.

Another strategy is to seek support from colleagues, mentors, and financial professionals. Collaboration and mentorship can help to build confidence and provide valuable feedback.

Finally, it is essential to set goals and track progress. By setting specific, measurable, achievable, relevant, and time-bound (SMART) goals, professionals can track their progress and celebrate their successes.

Conclusion:

In conclusion, financial intelligence is a critical skill for all professionals. It enables professionals to make informed decisions, manage budgets effectively, and communicate with stakeholders. Throughout this textbook, we have explored various financial concepts and their impact on business decisions. We have also discussed the benefits of having a basic understanding of financial concepts and the importance of financial intelligence for all professionals.

To continue developing financial intelligence, professionals can take courses, seek mentorship, read financial publications, and engage in financial conversations with colleagues. It is also essential to develop a deeper understanding of financial statements and stay informed about changes in financial regulations and industry standards.

By overcoming common challenges and implementing effective strategies, non-financial professionals can continue to develop their financial intelligence and improve their professional success.

Final thoughts on the importance of financial intelligence and cross-functional collaboration for financial success

Financial intelligence and cross-functional collaboration are essential components of financial success in today's business environment. The ability to understand financial statements, analyze financial data, and communicate financial information is critical for professionals in all fields. In addition, the ability to collaborate effectively with colleagues in different departments and areas of expertise can lead to more informed decisions and better financial outcomes.

In this chapter, we will discuss the importance of financial intelligence and cross-functional collaboration for financial success, as well as provide recommendations for further learning.

Importance of Financial Intelligence

Financial intelligence is the ability to understand and interpret financial information, including financial statements, budgets, and cash flow. It is essential for professionals in all fields, as it enables them to make informed decisions, manage budgets effectively, and communicate financial information to stakeholders.

One of the key benefits of financial intelligence is improved decision-making. By understanding financial data, professionals can make informed decisions about investments, expenses, and revenue. For example, a marketing manager may be able to identify areas where marketing spend can be reduced or optimized by analyzing data on customer acquisition costs, customer lifetime value, and conversion rates.

Another benefit of financial intelligence is improved financial management. By understanding cash flow, budgeting, and financial statements, professionals can manage budgets effectively and avoid financial mismanagement. This is particularly important for entrepreneurs and small business owners, who may have limited financial resources and need to make every dollar count.

Finally, financial intelligence can help professionals communicate financial information to stakeholders effectively. This is critical for professionals in all fields, as they may need to communicate financial information to investors, customers, and other stakeholders. By presenting financial information clearly and accurately, professionals can build trust and credibility with stakeholders.

Importance of Cross-Functional Collaboration

Cross-functional collaboration is the ability to collaborate effectively with colleagues in different departments and areas of expertise. It is essential for financial success, as it enables professionals to make more informed decisions, identify new opportunities, and solve complex problems.

One of the key benefits of cross-functional collaboration is improved decision-making. By collaborating with colleagues in different departments, professionals can gain new perspectives and insights, which can lead to more informed decisions. For example, a marketing manager may collaborate with a finance manager to analyze data on customer acquisition costs and customer lifetime value, leading to better decisions about marketing spend.

Another benefit of cross-functional collaboration is the identification of new opportunities. By working with colleagues in different departments, professionals can identify new opportunities for growth and innovation. For example, a product manager may collaborate with a sales manager to identify new market segments or product features.

Finally, cross-functional collaboration can help professionals solve complex problems. By working with colleagues in different areas of expertise, professionals can bring diverse perspectives and skills to bear on complex problems, leading to more effective solutions. For example, a legal department may collaborate with a finance department to address complex regulatory compliance issues.

Recommendations for Further Learning

To develop financial intelligence and cross-functional collaboration skills, professionals can take a variety of steps, including:

Take courses in finance, accounting, and business management. Many colleges and universities offer courses in these subjects, as well as online courses and certification programs.

Seek mentorship from colleagues or industry experts with financial expertise. This can provide valuable insights and guidance on financial matters.

Read financial publications and news sources, such as The Wall Street Journal or Financial Times. This can help professionals stay up-to-date on financial trends and developments.

Attend industry events and conferences. This can provide opportunities to network with colleagues and learn about new trends and developments in the industry.

Participate in cross-functional teams and projects. This can provide opportunities to collaborate with colleagues in different departments and areas of expertise, leading to improved decision-making and problem-solving.

Conclusion

In conclusion , financial intelligence and cross-functional collaboration are critical for achieving financial success in today's business environment. Professionals who possess financial intelligence can make informed decisions, manage budgets effectively, and communicate with stakeholders. On the other hand, lacking financial intelligence can lead to poor decision-making, financial mismanagement, and damage to professional reputation.

Cross-functional collaboration is also essential for achieving financial success. By working with colleagues in different departments and areas of expertise, professionals can gain diverse perspectives, leading to improved decision-making and problem-solving. It can also help break down silos and promote a culture of collaboration within the organization.

To develop financial intelligence and cross-functional collaboration skills, professionals can take courses, seek mentorship, read financial publications, attend industry events and conferences, and participate in cross-functional teams and projects. By continuously learning and improving these skills, professionals can stay ahead of financial trends and developments and make valuable contributions to their organizations.

Overall, financial intelligence and cross-functional collaboration are essential for professionals in all industries and positions, from business owners and entrepreneurs to corporate executives, in-house counsel/legal departments, compliance officers, financial analysts, investment bankers, accountants, regulators, and business lawyers. By understanding and embracing these principles, professionals can set themselves up for long-term financial success and contribute to the success of their organizations.

Recommendations for further learning, including additional resources and courses on finance, marketing, customer service, human resources, and CRM.

Having a basic understanding of financial concepts and their impact on business decisions is essential for professionals in any field. However, there is always more to learn, and continuing education is key to staying up-to-date with new trends and developments in the industry. This section will provide recommendations for additional resources and courses on finance, marketing, customer service, human resources, and CRM.

Finance

To further develop your financial intelligence, it is recommended to take courses in accounting, financial analysis, and investment management. There are many online courses and certifications available, such as the Certified Financial Analyst (CFA) program offered by the CFA Institute, which is widely recognized as one of the most prestigious designations in the financial industry.

Other online courses in finance include those offered by Coursera, edX, and Udemy. These courses cover topics such as financial modeling, corporate finance, and valuation, providing professionals with the skills needed to make informed financial decisions.

Reading financial publications and news sources, such as The Wall Street Journal or Financial Times, is also recommended to stay up-to-date on financial trends and developments.

Marketing

Marketing is a critical component of any business, as it helps companies connect with customers and promote their products or services. To further develop your marketing skills, it is recommended to take courses in digital marketing, social media marketing, and branding.

There are many online courses and certifications available, such as the Digital Marketing Nanodegree offered by Udacity, which covers topics such as search engine optimization (SEO), pay-per-click (PPC) advertising, and social media marketing.

Customer Service

Customer service is another crucial aspect of any business, as it helps to build customer loyalty and satisfaction. To further develop your customer service skills, it is recommended to take courses in customer service and customer experience.

There are many online courses and certifications available, such as the Certified Customer Experience Professional (CCXP) program offered by the Customer Experience Professionals Association (CXPA), which covers topics such as customer journey mapping, customer feedback, and employee engagement.

Human Resources

Human resources is responsible for managing the people within an organization, and it is essential for professionals in this field to have a strong understanding of employment law, compensation and benefits, and employee relations. To further develop your human resources skills, it is recommended to take courses in employment law, benefits administration, and performance management.

There are many online courses and certifications available, such as the Professional in Human Resources (PHR) certification offered by the Human Resource Certification Institute (HRCI), which covers topics such as employment law, recruitment, and talent management.

CRM

Customer relationship management (CRM) is a strategy for managing customer interactions and relationships, with the goal of improving customer satisfaction and loyalty. To further develop your CRM skills, it is recommended to take courses in CRM software, data analysis, and customer segmentation.

There are many online courses and certifications available, such as the Salesforce Administrator certification offered by Salesforce, which covers topics such as data management, workflow automation, and reporting.

Conclusion

In conclusion, having a basic understanding of financial concepts and their impact on business decisions is crucial for professionals in any field. However, there is always more to learn, and continuing education is key to staying up-to-date with new trends and developments in the industry. By taking courses and certifications in finance, marketing, customer service, human resources, and CRM, professionals can develop the skills needed to make informed decisions and drive business success. Additionally, reading industry publications and attending conferences can provide opportunities to network with colleagues and learn about new trends and developments in the industry.

Appendix: Glossary of Financial Terms

Accounts payable: The amount a company owes to its suppliers or vendors for goods or services received but not yet paid for.

Accounts receivable: The amount of money owed to a company by its customers for goods or services delivered but not yet paid for.

Asset: Any resource that has economic value and can be owned or controlled by an individual or organization.

Balance sheet: A financial statement that shows a company's assets, liabilities, and equity at a specific point in time.

Capital: Money invested in a business to purchase assets or fund operations.

Cash flow: The amount of cash that flows in and out of an organization over a specific period.

Debt: Money owed by an individual or organization to another individual or organization.

Equity: The difference between the assets and liabilities of an individual or organization.

Gross margin: The amount of money left over after deducting the cost of goods sold from the revenue.

Income statement: A financial statement that shows a company's revenues, expenses, and net income over a specific period.

Liabilities: Any amount owed by an individual or organization to another individual or organization.

Net income: The amount of money left over after deducting all expenses from revenue.

Operating expenses: The day-to-day expenses incurred by a business to keep it running.

Revenue: The income generated by a business from the sale of goods or services.

Return on investment (ROI): The amount of profit earned from an investment relative to the amount invested.

Sales: The total amount of money generated from the sale of goods or services.

Stock: A unit of ownership in a corporation.

Working capital: The amount of money available to a business for its day-to-day operations.

Additional resources for further learning and reference

There are many additional resources available for those seeking to further their knowledge in finance, marketing, customer service, human resources, and CRM. Some of these resources include:

Finance:

The Financial Times
The Wall Street Journal
Investopedia
The Economist
Bloomberg

Marketing:

American Marketing Association
HubSpot Academy
Google Ads Certification
Hootsuite Academy
Coursera's Marketing Courses

Customer Service:

Zendesk Academy
HubSpot Academy

Salesforce Trailhead
Help Scout Academy
Coursera's Customer Service Courses
Human Resources:

Society for Human Resource Management
HR Certification Institute
Udemy's Human Resources Courses
Coursera's Human Resources Courses
LinkedIn Learning's Human Resources Courses

CRM:

Salesforce Trailhead
HubSpot Academy
Zoho CRM University
Microsoft Dynamics 365 Training
Coursera's CRM Courses
RhinoLeg CRM University

In addition to these resources, it is important to continually seek out new information and stay up-to-date on industry trends and best practices. Attending conferences, webinars, and networking events can also be valuable in expanding your knowledge and professional network.